# Moses and the Gods of Egypt

# Moses and the Gods of Egypt

## Studies in Exodus

Second Edition

John J. Davis

BAKER BOOK HOUSE
Grand Rapids, Michigan 49506

Library of Congress Catalog Card Number: 77-175278
ISBN: 0-8010-2957-0

Copublished by Baker Book House and BMH Books
Second edition issued January, 1986

*Second printing, August 1986*

PRINTED IN THE UNITED STATES OF AMERICA

To

Dr. S. Herbert Bess,

scholar, teacher, and friend,

in appreciation

for his patient guidance

in the study of the Old Testament

# Contents

# Preface

Egypt with its ornate temples and tombs has long been the subject of study on the part of Bible students and rightly so. The birth of Israel as a nation took place in this land and her Pharaohs played an important role in Hebrew history before and after the great exodus.

The Book of Exodus is an interesting historical profile of a nation and its leaders. Theologically it stands at the heart of the Old Testament economy. The constant reference to the events recorded in this book by other biblical writers attests to its tremendous importance.

The purpose of this volume is to take a fresh look at the text of Exodus in the light of recent archaeological and historical studies. Special consideration is given to the first twelve chapters of the book in the light of Egyptian religious and political customs. Where appropriate, reference is made to the Hebrew text. Since space did not permit extended biblical quotations, the reader is encouraged to have a Bible at hand when reading this volume. The documentation and bibliography are designed to aid the serious Bible student in studying certain problems in greater depth. It is the author's desire that this volume will not only be intellectually informative, but spiritually stimulating, thus leading the reader to greater Christian growth and maturity.

# Acknowledgments

The author wishes to express special appreciation to the following individuals who made valuable contributions to the preparation and production of this volume.

Mrs. Irene Anderson, Mrs. Virginia Hinkel, Mrs. Ella Male, and Mrs. Frankie Putney who typed the manuscripts.

Dr. John C. Whitcomb who read the entire manuscript and made many helpful suggestions regarding the content and style of this book.

Rev. Mark Malles who read the final manuscript and made useful suggestions regarding style and format.

Prof. Robert Ramey who prepared the drawings of the tabernacle.

Dr. James Battenfield who made valuable suggestions relating to the Hebrew text.

# Transliteration

Whenever possible, Hebrew and Greek words have been transliterated according to the following form:

| *Greek* | *Consonants* | *Vocalization* |
|---|---|---|
| α — a | א — ’ | ָ — ā |
| ᾳ — a | ב — b, ḇ | ַ — a |
| ε — e | ג — g, g̱ | ֶ — e |
| η — ē | ד — d, ḏ | ֵ — ē |
| ο — o | ה — h | ֵי — ê |
| ω — ō | ו — w | ִ — i |
| ζ — z | ז — z | ִי — î |
|  | ח — ḥ | ָ — ǒ |
| θ — th | ט — ṭ | וֹ — o |
| ξ — x | י — y | וּ — û |
| υ — u | כ — k, ḵ | ֻ — u |
| φ — ph | ל — l | ְ — ( )e |
| χ — ch | מ — m |  |
| ψ — ps | נ — n |  |
| ‘ — h | ס — s |  |
|  | ע — ‘ |  |
|  | פ — p, p̱ |  |
|  | צ — ṣ |  |
|  | ק — q |  |
|  | ר — r |  |
|  | שׂ — ś |  |
|  | שׁ — š |  |
|  | ת — t, ṯ |  |

# List of Illustrations

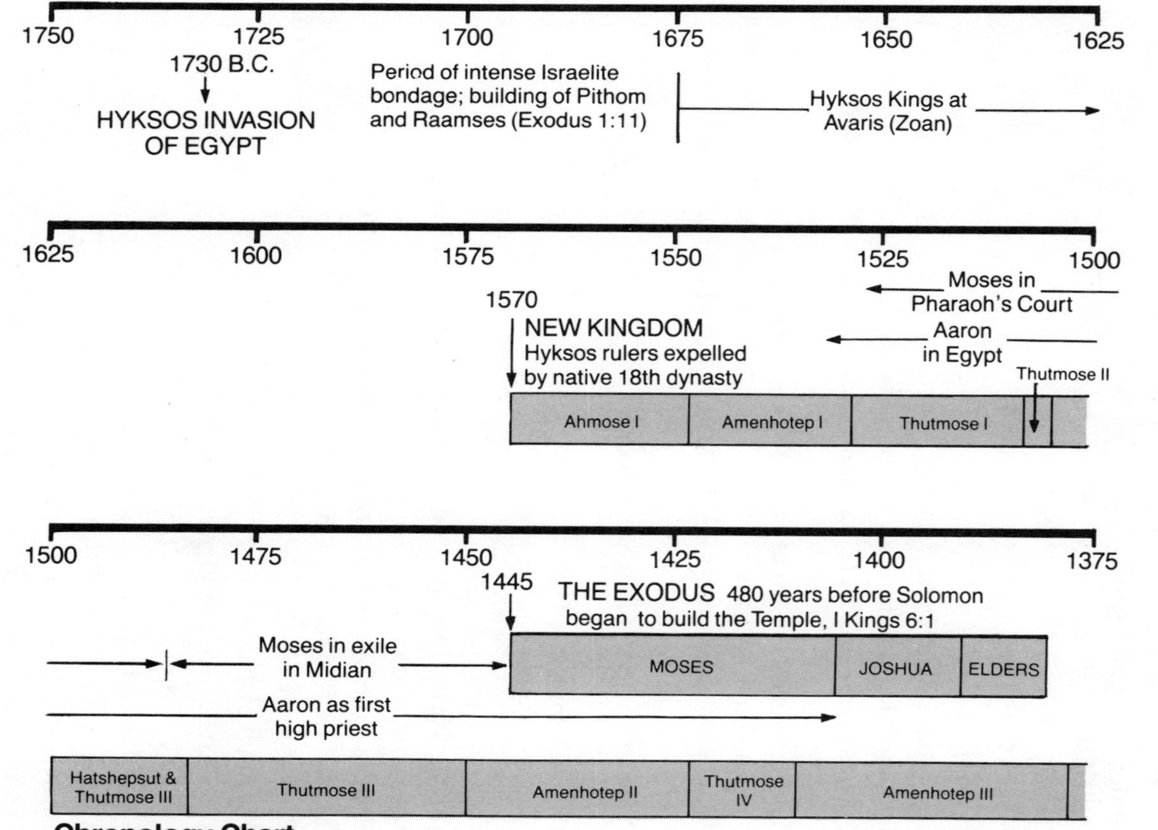


**Chronology Chart**

## Chapter 1

# *Introduction*

Egypt to the average person usually means mummies and massive pyramids, hieroglyphic inscriptions and strange-looking human forms on great monuments. The wide distribution of Egyptian materials and ornate reports of these discoveries have brought Egyptian culture to the attention of everyone in the civilized world. To the casual observer the land of the Nile generates a sense of magic and mystery, but to the ancient Israelite, the situation was quite different. For him Egypt meant slavery and humiliation, and at the same time great victory and the birth of his nation.

The Book of Exodus is a necessary sequel to the patriarchal history of Genesis. Man's origin, fall into sin and judgment by means of a universal flood mark the early presentation of human experience. Highlighting the patriarchal narratives are the election of Abraham, and special promises of a land and a people; such highlights make the Book of Genesis foundational to all subsequent biblical history. Interestingly, the final chapter of Genesis ends on a sad note with Joseph, a great leader and statesman, in a coffin in Egypt (Gen. 50:26). Such an ending leaves many questions unanswered and problems unsolved. To a certain degree the Book of Exodus begins on that very same sad note. Figuratively speaking, the Hebrews were in a coffin in Egypt. The tragedy of human suffering and slavery make the great exodus from Egypt a memorable event and one which is referred to many times in sacred Scripture.

The Book of Exodus communicates the exciting story of Israel's deliverance from slavery and the beginning of her national identity. It was also at that time that the bones of Joseph were removed to find their ultimate resting place in the Promised Land (cf. Exod. 13:19; Gen. 50:25; Heb. 11:22). In the light of the theological and historical ideas contained in this book, it becomes immediately apparent that Exodus is strategically important to both Old Testament history and a proper understanding of Hebrew customs and institutions. It stands as a vital link between the age of the patriarchs and the remaining books of the Law. How God fulfilled His promise to Abraham by multiplying his descendants into a great nation (cf. Gen. 12:2) and redeeming them from bondage (Gen. 15:13-14) is, of course, also a key feature of Exodus.

This book is not only a thrilling account of the revelation of God's person and power, but also of His covenant faithfulness. The theological and historical importance of the book is made evident by the constant reference to the exodus and related events by both Old and New Testament writers (e.g., I Kings 8:16, 21; Psalm 105:26-38; Acts 7:34-36).

## I. Historical Setting

### A. *The Date of the Exodus*

#### 1. A Survey of the Problem

The date of the exodus and its relationship to Egyptian history has long been a matter of conjecture and controversy. This is largely due to the fact that the Exodus material offers little data regarding either personal names or dates. For example, the ruler(s) in Egypt is referred to variously as "a new king" (1:8), "Pharaoh" (1:11, 19, 22; 2:15), "Egyptians" (1:13) and "King of Egypt" (1:15; 2:23).

Certain events are described which imply a period of time, but the amount of time involved is not specifically designated. To illustrate, notice that in 1:7 it is said of the children of Israel that they were ". . . fruitful, and increased abundantly, and multiplied, and (became) exceedingly mighty; and the land was filled with them." This verse implies a considerable period of time, but the exact number of years is not provided.[1] The expressions used in 2:23 are perhaps most typical of the ambiguity which exists with regard to specific chronological data. Concerning the time of the death of the king of Egypt it merely states, "Now it came about in the course of those many days that the King of Egypt died" (NASB).[2]

---

[1] In this regard compare also 1:12.

[2] Heb. *wayᵉhî ḇayyāmîn hārabbîm hāhēm*. According to Acts 7:30 this would have been some time after a 40-year period.

Adding to this problem is the fact that there is no clear extra-biblical evidence relating directly to the fact of the exodus. In an effort to explain this silence, Wright makes the following observation:

> The exodus from Egyptian slavery was the dominant and dominating event in Israelite history and faith. . . . The mighty acts of God in Egypt and in the wilderness were a sign, a wonder, giving evidence of a Power greater than all the powers of this world. . . . Yet the events which were so important to Israel were so unimportant to the Egyptians that no record of them was preserved outside the Bible.[3]

More likely, however, is the explanation of Charles F. Aling: "The peoples of the ancient Near East kept historical records to impress their gods and also potential enemies, and therefore rarely, if ever, mentioned defeats or catastrophies. Records of disasters would not enhance the reputation of the Egyptians in the eyes of their gods, nor make the enemies more afraid of their military might.[4] The Egyptians frequently took a very idealistic view of their history, and since Pharaoh was inseparably connected with the course of events as they occurred in Egypt, it was very rare indeed that failures relating to him were ever recorded. Pharaoh was regarded by the Egyptians as "lord of the world" and a god.[5] This concept of their king would decidedly affect their historiography. To understand fully the silence of Egyptian documents regarding the enslavement and exodus of the Hebrews it is important to understand the Egyptian's view of his state and king. Frankfort has well summarized that viewpoint.

> The Egyptian state was not a man-made alternative to other forms of political organization. It was god-given, established when the world was created; and it continued to form part of the universal order. In the person of pharaoh, a superhuman

---

[3]G. Ernest Wright, *Biblical Archaeology* (Philadelphia: Westminster Press, 1957), p. 53.

[4]Charles F. Aling, *Egypt and Bible History* (Grand Rapids: Baker Book House, 1981), p. 103. Also note his discussion on pp. 78-79.

[5]George Steindorff and Keith C. Seele, *When Egypt Ruled the East* (2nd ed.; Chicago: The University of Chicago Press, 1957), p. 82.

> being had taken charge of the affairs of man. And this great blessing, which insured the well-being of the nation, was not due to a fortunate accident, but had been foreseen in the divine plan. The monarchy then was as old as the world, for the creator himself had assumed kingly office on the day of creation. Pharaoh was his descendant and his successor.[6]

In the light of the above observations and the fact that all history is to some extent selective and controlled by the interests of the historiographer, we should not expect specific reference to the release of Israel following a series of catastrophic events in the land of Egypt. Indeed, such a record would be most surprising and unique.

The debate over the precise date of the exodus continues with as much energy as was expended a century ago. Emerging from this academic foray are four principal proposals. To some, it would appear that this issue does not merit such substantial engagement and research, but upon careful observation of the importance of the exodus and its chronological impact on earlier biblical history, the matter turns out to be quite crucial. H. H. Rowley has well stated that "much more than chronology is really involved, since the view that we take of Israel's religious development is materially affected by the solution we adopt."[7]

## 2. Very Early Dates

During the past decade, three proposals have appeared which would place the Israelite exodus from Egypt a little before 2000 B.C. and between 1470 and 1477 B.C.

Based on settlement patterns in the northeast region of the Sinai Peninsula, Emmanuel Anati has proposed that Israel wandered in the Wilderness shortly before 2000 B.C.[8] His conclusions are based on the fact that between the Middle Bronze and the Persian periods there was little occupation in the northern Sinai.

---

[6]Henri Frankfort, *Ancient Egyptian Religion* (New York: Harper & Brothers, 1948), p. 30.

[7]H. H. Rowley, *From Joseph to Joshua* (London: Oxford University Press, 1950), p. 2.

[8]Emmanuel Anati, "Has Mt. Sinai Been Found?" *Biblical Archaeology Review*, XI, No. 4 (1985), pp. 42-57

Most of his arguments for this date are based on the ceramic evidence, cult objects in the region and topography. Anati identifies the biblical Mount Sinai with Har Karkom or Mount Saffron, northwest of the Gulf of Aqaba.

While Anati solves some exodus problems to his own satisfaction, he creates enormous difficulties for others who take all biblical chronology seriously.[9]

According to Anati's occupational chart,[10] there was some Late Bronze Age occupation in the region as well as rock art, but this appears to be minimized. Furthermore, Anati fails to show on biblical and archaeological grounds why a southern route cannot be accepted.

The second very early date comes from Hans Goedicke, who is known for his excavations at Tell er-Rataba in Egypt. Goedicke maintains that the Israelites left Egypt in 1477 B.C. and crossed Lake Menzaleh where the Egyptian army was drowned by a tidal-like wave transmitted by a volcanic eruption in the Mediterranean Sea. Following his early chronology, the pharaoh of the exodus would then be identified as Queen Hatshepsut.[11] Goedicke also maintains that the Israelites took a northeasterly route toward Canaan.

This proposal has been largely rejected because his date of the exodus is established more on extrabiblical geologic information than on the biblical text. Where the Bible is employed, the citations are conveniently selective.[12] Also suspect is his identification of the patriarchs with the Hyksos and his claim that Queen Hatshepsut used Hebrew slaves.[13]

It would appear that Goedicke's case for the very early date

---

9See on this point the discussion of William H. Stiebling, Jr., in "Should the Exodus and the Israelite Settlement be Redated?" *Biblical Archaeology Review*, XI, No. 4 (1985), pp. 58-59.

10*Op. cit.*, p. 46.

11Hershel Shanks, "The Exodus and the Crossing of the Red Sea, According to Hans Goedicke," *Biblical Archaeology Review*, VII, No. 5 (1981), p. 42.

12*Ibid.*, p. 48. Note Eliezer D. Oren's criticism of this technique in "How Not to Create a History of the Exodus — A Critique of Professor Goedicke's Theories," *Biblical Archaeology Review* VII, No. 6 (1981), pp. 47-48.

13*Ibid.*, pp. 48-50.

of the exodus rests largely on an inscription by Hatshepsut and an assumed date for the great volcanic eruption on the island of Thera, just off the coast of the southern tip of Greece. Reference to the Hatshepsut inscription will only stand as a parallel to the exodus if his chronology is accepted. There is nothing in the inscription itself that would demand a direct correlation between the exodus of Israel and the reign of Queen Hatshepsut.

Furthermore, Professor Goedicke's reliance on natural catastrophies is quite subjective and lacks the geological evidences necessary to support them. In this respect his explanation of biblical events is much like that of Immanuel Velikovsky.[14] While such explanations are fashionable and quickly capture the imagination of the casual reader, they rarely pass the test of biblical scrutiny. Inevitably most of these proposals either hedge on, or totally ignore specific biblical information.

A third and far more responsible proposal for a very early date of the exodus comes from the pen of John J. Bimson.[15] Bimson argues that the exodus occurred at the end of the Middle Bronze Age (or about 1470 according to his revised chronology for the end of the Middle Bronze Age, which he dates to approximately 1450 B.C.) According to his revised chronology, therefore, the events of the conquest under Joshua would also fall into the catagory of Middle Bronze Age history.[16]

Bimson's contribution to the overall study of the exodus and its problems is substantial and worthy of consideration. Especially useful is his critique of the commonly held last date of the exodus.[17] Several concerns need to be raised, however, with this proposal. First, Bimson handles I Kings 6:1 in a rather cavalier manner, in which he assumes that the verse provides only a rough guide to the time of the Exodus, not a precise indication."[18] He goes on to suggest that the actual period represented

---

[14]Immanuel Velikovsky, *World in Collision* (New York: Doubleday & Co., 1950), pp. 48-53, 58-76.

[15]John J. Bimson, *"Redating the Exodus and Conquest," Journal for the Study of the Old Testament,* Supplement Series 5 (Sheffield: 1978).

[16]*Ibid.,* pp. 229-237.

[17]*Ibid.,* pp. 35-79.

[18]*Ibid.,* p. 102.

by 480 years was probably longer.[19] This is a curious approach since elsewhere his handling of biblical material is quite literal.

Another questionable aspect to Bimson's proposal is his attributing of the mass destructions at the end of the Middle Bronze Age to the Hebrews rather than to the presence of 18th-Dynasty Egyptian forces. For example, he suggests that the city of Megiddo suffered its early-fifteenth-century destruction not by the activities of Thutmose III, but by the Hebrews. His contention is that while Egyptian forces surrounded Megiddo for a seven-month period during the first campaign of Thutmose III, it was not destroyed by them.[20] Aling appropriately criticizes this view by observing that "such a view regarding Megiddo seems unrealistic. The logical conclusion of a seven-month seige ending with massive booty for Egypt would be the destruction of the city involved."[21]

Bimson's case for associating Hebrew activity with Middle Bronge Age II destruction levels also raises a serious problem with regard to the information supplied by Joshua 11:13. According to the language of that verse, after the destruction of Jericho and Ai by fire, Hazor was the only remaining city to be so destroyed. Bimson's contention is that Joshua 11:13 is not a statement of general Israelite policy, but only applied to northern towns "whose rulers had formed a coalition against Joshua."[22] His insistence that burning was a common feature of Israelite military policy arises more out of his conclusions concerning the date of the conquest than the battle descriptions of Scripture itself.

---

[19]*Ibid.*

[20]*Ibid.*, p. 154.

[21]Charles F. Aling, *op. cit.*, p. 86.

[22]John J. Bimson, *op. cit.*, p. 277. For further evaluation of Bimson's proposals see the following reviews of his book: A. F. Rainey, *Israel Exploration Journal,* XXX, Nos. 3-4 (1980), pp. 249-251; Joseph A. Callaway, *Biblical Archaeologist,* 44 (1981), pp. 252-253; J. Maxwell Miller, *Journal of Biblical Literature,* 99, No. 1 (1980), pp. 133-135; J. Alberto Soggin, *Vetus Testamentum,* XXXI, No. 1 (1981), pp. 98-99; William H. Shea, *The Catholic Biblical-Quarterly,* 42 (1980), pp. 88-90; Thomas L. Thompson, *Journal of the American Oriental Society,* 100 (1980), pp. 66-67 and J. M. de Tarragon, *Revue Biblique,* 87 (1980), pp. 137-138.

3. The Late Date

The most widely accepted date for the exodus places it in Nineteenth-Dynasty Egypt, or approximately 1280 B.C. It might also be observed that many scholars adopting this view suggest that while the main Hebrew exodus took place in the early thirteenth century B.C., there was an earlier departure of the Joseph tribes to Canaan about 1400 B.C. – associated with Habiru movements.[23] Such a proposal, however, can only be maintained when clear biblical statements to the contrary are dismissed. The uniform testimony of scripture is that all of Jacob's sons entered Egypt (Gen. 46:8-27; Exod. 1:1-5) and that all tribes were represented in the exodus (Exod. 24:4; Num. 1, 2, 10:14ff). Kitchen categorically states, "There is not a scrap of clear, explicit evidence for more than one exodus or for some tribes never going into Egypt."[24]

There are five basic arguments employed to support the late date of the exodus. These arguments follow with brief evaluation:

First, Exodus 1:11 is assumed to link the oppression of the Israelites with the building of the store-cities of Pithom and Ra'amses. This is proported to be an indication of a date for the end of oppression and for the exodus. Jack Finegan states the argument as follows:

> The basis of the theory now to be considered is the statement in Exodus 1:11 that the Israelites "built for pharoah store-cities, Pithom and Ra'amses." Ra'amses can hardly be other than Per-Ramses, the "house of Ramses (II)," which has been identified with Tanis-Qantir. . . . Since Tanis and Avaris of the Hyksos . . . was abandoned and allowed to fall into ruins after their expulsion (c. 1570 B.C.) and was only reestablished by Seti I (c. 1302-c. 1290), it is not likely that any large construction activities were being conducted in this vicinity in the years

---

[23]William F. Albright, "Historical and Mythical Elements in the Joseph Story," *Journal of Biblical Literature,* 37 (1918), pp. 138ff. Note that Albright later abandoned this concept. See "The Israelite Conquest of Canaan in the Light of Archaeology," *Bulletin of the American Schools of Oriental Research,* 74 (1939), p. 23.

[24]K. A. Kitchen, *Ancient Orient and Old Testament* (Chicago: Inter-Varsity Press, 1966), p. 71.

> before 1446 B.C. . . . Unless we are to regard Exodus 1:11 as an erroneous or anachronistic statement, we must conclude that Ramses II was the pharaoh under whom the oppression of the Israelites reached its climax.[25]

At first glance this argument appears to be impressive, but upon closer examination there are several difficulties. In the first place, this view does not take into consideration other Scriptures which deal with the general chronology of the period. For example, it is clear that the beginning of the enslavement of Israel and the building of Pithom and Ra'amses took place before the birth of Moses. His birth apparently occurred in the latter part of the oppression period as implied by Exodus 2. We know that Moses was eighty years old at the time of the exodus (Exod. 7:7); this simply means that the construction work described in chapter one would have occurred eighty years prior to the date of the exodus. If the late date of the exodus is correct (about 1280 B.C.), Moses would have been born about 1360 B.C., or in the later stages of the Eighteenth Dynasty. It is therefore obvious that Ramses II could not have been the Pharaoh who ordered the Israelites to build the store-cities of Exodus 1:11.

At issue for all who assume an earlier date for the exodus is how this name would appear prior to the Nineteenth Dynasty. Two suggestions have been made to resolve the problem. John Rea proposed that the city of Ra'amses was not named after Ramses II, but was given its title by the Hyksos sometime in the seventeenth century B.C. Rea argued that there were significant parallels between the Nineteenth Dynasty, of which Ramses II was a member, and the Hyksos invaders.[26]

Aling, on the other hand, acknowledges that the name Ramses is known from an inscription as far back as the Twelfth Dynasty, but asks the question, ". . . do these early examples of the

---

[25] *Light from the Ancient Past* (2nd ed., Princeton: Princeton University Press, 1959), pp. 136-137. Compare also G. E. Wright, *op. cit.*, p. 60.

[26] For the details on this argument see John Rea, "The Time of the Oppression and the Exodus," *Grace Journal*, II, No. 1 (1961), p. 10. For a similar argument, see Wilber Fields, *Exploring Exodus* (Joplin, Missouri: College Press, 1976), p. 26.

proper name Ramses have any bearing on the biblical city?"[27] He suggests that, based on what we know about the naming of Egyptian cities in general, it is very doubtful that scattered examples of Ramses as a personal name are really relevant to the question of the biblical city Ra'amses.[28]

The only alternative explanation for the appearance of this name is that the term *Ra'amses* is an anachronism, or as Unger has suggested, the name "was a modernization of an obsolete place named by some later scribe,"[29] a suggestion which Aling finds preferable.[30]

One of the difficulties which one faces in dealing with the origin of this term is not only its appearance in the exodus narratives (Exod. 1:11; 12:37), but also in earlier passages (Gen. 47:11; compare Num. 33:3). R. Laird Harris makes the following observation regarding this problem:

> Jacob's settlement in Egypt would be before King Rameses on anybody's chronology, and at that time he says he put them in the land of Rameses. Possibly the famous King Rameses chose his name from the land Rameses. Or there could have been another King Rameses. It is possible that Genesis 47:11 is an anachronism. It may be that some later scribe, finding a name that nobody knew anymore and being very much concerned to have a Bible name that even the high-school student could understand, inserted this new form of the name. This city of Ra'amses was earlier known as Tanis and, before that, Arvis. It is not impossible that the name of Rameses was a name brought up to date in Genesis 47:11.[31]

Until recently the consensus of opinion was that the biblical city of Ra'amses was to be associated with the delta city of Tanis, which sprawls over one thousand acres and contains an abundance of Nineteenth Dynasty monuments from the reign of

---

[27]Charles F. Aling, "The Biblical City of Ramses," *Journal of the Evangelical Society,* XXV, No. 2 (1982), p. 133.

[28]*Ibid.,* pp. 133-137.

[29]Merrill F. Unger, *Archaeology and the Old Testament* (Grand Rapids: Zondervan Publishing Co., 1954), p. 149.

[30]Charles F. Aling, "The Biblical City of Ramses," p. 137.

[31]"Problem Periods in Old Testament History," *The Seminary Review,* XVI, No. 1 (1969), p. 11.

Ramses II. However, there is a growing agreement based on substantial archaeological data that the site of Ra'amses (Avaris) should be associated with Khatana-Qantir (located south of Tanis).[32]

The second major argument employed in support of the late date is based on the description of Edomite resistance to Israelite movement through its territory (Num. 20:20, 21). It is assumed, on the basis of Nelson Glueck's explorations in southern Transjordan, that such resistance could not have been possible in the fifteenth century B.C.

> There was at about ± 1900 B.C., such a thoroughgoing destruction visited upon all the great fortresses and settlements of the land, within the limits we have examined, that the particular civilization they represented never again recovered. The blow it received was so crushing as to be utterly destructive. Its cities were never rebuilt, and much of Transjordan became the camping ground of tent dwellers, who used for containers perishable skins and not enduring pottery. Permanent villages and fortresses were no longer to rise upon the face of the earth in this region till the beginning of the Iron Age.[33]

Because of the apparent lack of sedentary occupation in this region, Glueck concluded that it was impossible to " . . . escape the conclusion that the particular exodus of the Israelites through southern Transjordan could not have taken place before the 13th century."[34] Since these statements were published most scholars have adopted them without any substantial critical reassessment.

Two things might be considered here relative to this problem. In the first place, it is not entirely clear that at this time in Israel's history the center of Edomite power was limited to south-

---

[32]For a discussion of the evidence for this identification see: E. P. Uphill, "Pithom and Raamses: Their Location and Significance," *Journal of Near Eastern Studies,* XXVII, No. 4 (1968), pp. 291-316 and XXVIII, No. 1 (1969), pp. 15-39; John Van Seters, *The Hyksos* (New Haven: Yale University Press, 1966), pp. 132-151; Charles F. Aling, "The Biblical City of Ramses," pp. 135-136 and *Egypt and Bible History,* pp. 68-69.

[33]*The Other Side of the Jordan* (New Haven: American Schools of Oriental Research, 1940), p. 114.

[34]*Ibid.,* p. 146.

ern Transjordan or the area east of Arabah. That their influence was centered in this area from the time of King Saul onward (I Sam. 14:47) is not disputed. During most of the second millennium B.C., however, it appears that the Edomites occupied a great deal of territory west of the Arabah, for the "land of Seir" (Gen. 32:3) where Esau lived was located to the south and east of Beer-Sheba (Gen. 26:23; 28:10).

If this is true, the occupational gap cited by Nelson Glueck is not of particularly grave consequence with regard to the exodus narrative.[35] Indeed, it is very probable that large bands of Edomites occupied the territory as semi-nomads living in large tent villages. Their ability to control passes and mountains would make them a formidable force even though small in number and unimpressive in material culture. One should also be reminded of the fact that the movement of the Israelites through the territory constituted a very vulnerable domestic migration of men, women, children and animals. This was not a highly mobilized military expedition. The confrontation between the Edomites and Hebrews, therefore, should be viewed in that light.

Secondly, many scholars have not acknowledged the fact that Nelson Glueck himself modified certain features of his occupational hypothesis for Transjordan. In the second edition of *The Other Side Of The Jordan* Glueck states:

> In much of Transjordan, especially in the areas of some distance south of the south side of the Wadi Zerga (biblical River Jabbog), the Middle Bronze I period of the Age of Abraham seems to have been followed by a considerable decline in sedentary settlement during the Middle Bronze II and the late Bronze I-II periods, although not as radically as we had once assumed.[36]

---

[35]For a full discussion of this point see John Rea, "The Historical Setting of the Exodus and Conquest" (Unpublished Th.D. Dissertation, Grace Theological Seminary, Winona Lake, Ind., 1958), pp. 45, 183-190. Also see his "New Light on the Wilderness Journey and the Conquest," *Grace Journal,* II, No. 2 (Spring, 1961), p. 6 and Leon Wood, "Date of the Exodus," *New Perspectives on the Old Testament,* J. Barton Payne, ed., (Waco, Texas: Word Books, 1970), pp. 66-87.

[36]Nelson Glueck, *The Other Side of the Jordan,* (2nd edition, 1970), pp. 140-141.

Excavations in central and southern Transjordan have largely confirmed the qualified observations of Nelson Glueck. There is a growing corpus of information indicating that Late Bronze Age occupation was far more substantial than originally acknowledged by Glueck. Harding reports that

> Next in date is one of the most important finds, a tomb group of the Hyksos period (18th-16th centuries), in Amman. All the forms and wares most typical of the period are present, including black pricked ware, button-base vases, oil flasks, carinated bowls, etc., in addition to scarabs and bronze toggle pins. The importance of the group, which contains 95 pots, plus a mass of sherds, lies in its relation to Nelson Glueck's conclusions as to the non-occupation of Jordan during the period 1800-1300 B.C.; our group is probably about 1600 B.C. By its very nature, as a family vault, it is unlikely to be an isolated example, but without proper excavations in the country such assumptions must remain inconclusive.[37]

In addition to this, reports have come relating to the discovery of a Late Bronze-Early Iron Age tomb with objects and pottery very similar to the Fosse tombs of Tell Fara. Included in the objects discovered were 119 pots and some sherds of Mycenaean ware (fourteenth-thirteenth centuries B.C.).[38] A number of writers have now challenged some of Glueck's conclusions based on Middle and Late Bronze Age finds from Amman, Tell Safut, Sahab Na'ur, Medeba, Khirbet el-Mekhayyat, and Qla'et-Twal, as well as artifacts from the Heshbon region and the Bag'ah Valley.[39]

Furthermore, the excavations at Tell Deir 'Alla have produced significant evidence requiring some modification of Glueck's occupational gap. In a review of Glueck's *Explorations in Eastern Palestine,* attention was drawn to the fact that some of his con-

---

[37]G. L. Harding and W. L. Reed, "Archaeological News from Jordan," *The Biblical Archaeologist,* XVI, No. 1 (1953), p. 4.

[38]*Ibid.*

[39]For a discussion of the materials as well as an evaluation of Glueck's work, see Gerald L. Mattingly, "The Exodus-Conquest and the Archaeology of Transjordan: New Light on an Old Problem," *Grace Theological Journal* IV, No. 2 (1983), pp. 245-262.

J. J. Davis

Seti I tomb painting.

Main gateway to the temple of Amun at Karnak.

J. J. Davis

clusions were based on questionable pottery interpretation.[40] It was pointed out that Glueck operated under the assumption that the culture of Iron Age Transjordan was so similar to that of Palestine that the pottery of Transjordan could be compared with, and chronologically tied into, the known Palestinian repertoire. This was shown to be a questionable assumption.[41] It was also observed that he only published the pottery forms with which he was familiar,[42] another curious procedure. Of special significance is the fact that Deir 'Alla was occupied during the whole Late Bronze Age, a fact frequently overlooked by those advancing the late date of the exodus. If it is true that what Glueck called Iron Age pottery was in reality Late Bronze Age pottery, a significant difference would emerge with regard to the occupational character of some sites.[43]

Finally, the character and cultural interests of the inhabitants of Late Bronze Age Transjordan appear to be quite sophisticated (which is, of course, what is implied in Scripture).

> . . . Deir 'Alla also indicated that Glueck underestimated the sophistication of the Late Bronze Transjordanians, for the sanctuary has imports from all over the known world including gifts from Egypt. The same is also true of the Amman airport temple, which is also detached from a settlement. The precise dates of the temples remain unknown but the evidence derived from them points to the existence of tribes who had a taste for and a knowledge of the "civilized" countries around them.[44]

One needs to be reminded, in connection with Edomite control of southern Transjordan, that it was not so much the superior military strength of these peoples that prevented the Israelites from passing through their territories, as it was the direct command of God not to fight (cf. Deut. 2:4, 5, 9).

The third major argument upon which the late date of the ex-

---

[40]H. J. Franken and W. J. A. Power, "Glueck's *Explorations in Eastern Palestine* in the Light of Recent Evidence," *Vetus Testamentum*, XXI (1971), pp. 119-123.

[41]*Ibid.*, pp. 119ff.

[42]*Ibid.*

[43]*Ibid.*, p. 123.

[44]*Ibid.*

odus is based relates to the numerous thirteenth-century destruction layers in Palestinian mounds. Archaeological evidence indicates that about 1230 B.C. a number of important sites were destroyed, such as Lachish, Bethel, Debir and Hazor. The correlation of these destruction layers is indeed impressive, assuming of course, that the thirteenth-century date of the conquest is already well established.

J. M. Miller, however, has demonstrated that the identification of destruction layers is at best an ambiguous form of archaeological evidence.[45] There is nothing in the destruction layers themselves that would demand that they were caused by Israelite, as opposed to, for example, Egyptian invading groups. It might also be noted that it is generally assumed that all the cities conquered by Joshua, with their kings, received the full force of destruction as did Jericho, Ai and Hazor. It would appear from Scripture, however, that very few cities were destroyed in the same manner as Hazor and Jericho (cf. Josh. 11:13).

Furthermore, some recent studies would seem to indicate that the early date (1445 B.C.) can be correlated with certain stratagraphic detail.[46]

It also appears that the southern campaign of Joshua (recorded in Joshua 10) was nothing more than a series of lightning-like raids against principal military centers to effect an immobilization of major forces in that region.

The task of occupation and colonization was given to various tribes that would occupy these territories at a later time.[47] The Bible does not make any mention of a battle at Shechem (Tell Balatha) and this is in remarkable agreement with the archaeological data from that site.[48]

---

[45]"Archaeology and the Israelite Conquest of Canaan: Some Methodological Observations," *Palestine Exploration Quarterly*, 109 (1977), pp. 87-93.

[46]See Bruce K. Waltke, "Palestinian Artifactual Evidence Supporting the Early Date for the Exodus," *Bibliotheca Sacra*, 129 (1972), pp. 33-47. Bimson, however, has challenged some of his reconstructions. See Bimson, *op. cit.*, pp. 189-191. Also see Leon Wood, "The Date of the Exodus," in J. Barton Payne (ed), *New Perspectives on the Old Testament* (Waco, Texas: Word, 1970), pp. 67-86.

[47]See John J. Davis and John C. Whitcomb, *A History of Israel: From Conquest to Exile* (Grand Rapids: Baker Book House, 1980), pp. 70-72.

[48]*Ibid.*, pp. 58-60.

In many cases it is possible to account for thirteenth-century destruction levels on the basis of biblical data other than that which is found in the Book of Joshua. For example, it is clear that Debir was twice attacked by the Hebrews, once during Joshua's campaign (Josh. 10:38), but also later by Caleb and the tribe of Judah (Judg. 1:10-15).

The site of Bethel has been used by Albright and others as a strong proof for the late date of the exodus based on a very obvious thirteenth-century destruction level; however, it appears from the Joshua narrative that the city of Bethel was probably not destroyed during that time. The biblical text merely makes reference to the fact that men from Bethel participated in the battle at Ai (cf. Josh. 8:17). There is no other statement to the effect that Bethel was burned or destroyed at that time; however, there is a record of a battle at the site of Bethel later when the house of Joseph went to the city and fought against it in an attempt to occupy this territory (cf. Judg. 1:22). This battle fits better the archaeological data relative to the thirteenth-century destruction level. It may well be that other thirteenth-century destruction levels are to be attributed to Egyptian activity rather than to that of the Israelites.

The Amarna Tablets, which were written about 1380 B.C. or shortly after the conquest period, may well reflect military activity not only on the part of the Hebrews, but on other invading groups as well. While it does not appear to be appropriate to equate the term *Hebrew* with Habiru of the Amarna letters, it is reasonable to assume that some of the activity attributed to the Habiru may well have been associated with the military activity of certain Israelite tribes. The Stele of Sethos I may well describe the defeat of the tribe of Manassah in its attempt to conquer the city of Beth-Shean (Judg. 1:27). Records from the reign of Sethos I (about 1320 B.C.) indicate that he encountered Habiru and defeated them.[49]

One of the most knotty problems with regard to occupational sequences and the Israelite conquest is the site of Et-Tell, com-

---

[49]Kathleen Kenyon, *Archaeology in the Holy Land* (3rd ed., rev.; New York: Praeger, 1970), p. 219. Also note the comments of Laird Harris on this data, *op. cit.*, p. 14.

monly associated with the biblical Ai. This site has been extensively excavated and still exhibits an occupational gap between 2100 and 1200 B.C. A variety of explanations has been suggested for this difficulty,[50] including a relocation of the site.[51]

A fourth argument offered in support of the late date of the exodus focuses on the relationship of the Hebrews to the Habiru of the Amarna Letters. As observed above, it is questionable on semantic and historical grounds to identify the term *Hebrew* with Habiru. However, that Habiru activity could well have included military activity of the tribes is a distinct possibility.

With this Jack Finegan would not agree, however.

> The identification of the Habiru of the Amarna Letters in the Biblical Hebrews is improbable, since the frantic correspondence of Abdi-Hiba indicates that Jerusalem was in imminent danger of serious conquest, and that city does not seem to have been a major objective of Joshua and was only permanently conquered in the time of David (II Sam. 5:6ff).[52]

In this discussion Finegan suggests that Jerusalem was not the target of Israelite military activity until the time of David. Such a contention, however, lacks a careful appraisal of important biblical data relating to Jerusalem in the time of Joshua and the later period of the Judges. Notice that the Book of Joshua records the fact that the king of Jerusalem joined the southern coalition of Amorite city-states in an attempt to punish Gibeon for its surrender to Joshua (10:1-5). As a result of his participation in this battle, he was captured along with the other four kings and was slain (Josh. 10:16-28; cf. 12:10).

Furthermore, the Book of Judges records the fact that the tribe of Judah attacked the city of Jerusalem during its colonization of that area (1:8). The military fortress of the city was probably

---

[50]See John J. Davis, *op. cit.*, pp. 57-58.

[51]David Livingston, "Location of Biblical Bethel and Ai Reconsidered," *The Westminster Theological Journal*, XXXIII, No. 1 (Nov., 1970), pp. 20ff. For a defense of the traditional identifications see W. Winter, "Biblical and Archaeological Data on Ai Reappraised," *The Seminary Review*, XVI, No. 3 (1970).

[52]*Op. Cit.*, p. 136.

destroyed, but the site was not occupied or controlled by the Israelites at that time (cf. 1:21; also Josh. 15:63).

The final argument used to support the thirteenth-century date of the exodus and conquest is based on negative evidence; namely, the apparent absence of extensive building in the delta region by Thutmosis III and his successors.[53] However, it is well known both from archaeological remains and important inscriptions that the Eighteenth Dynasty Pharaohs did have a keen interest in building projects in the northern part of Egypt. Along with two red granite obelisks erected by Thutmose III in front of the temple of Ra'-Heliopolis, a scarab has been discovered that refers to the birth of Amonhotep II as having taken place in Memphis just below Heliopolis. It appears that as a youth Amonhotep II spent considerable time in that area.[54]

It is evident that in the Eighteenth Dynasty there were two viziers in Egypt, one in Upper Egypt and one in the delta region.[55] Aling has documented a number of other evidences which point to considerable Eighteenth Dynasty activity in the delta region.[56] Since Eighteenth Dynasty pharaohs were very active in Palestinian campaigns, it would seem reasonable that they would have established garrisons and store-cities somewhere in the delta region to facilitate movement between Syro-Palestinian sites and Egypt itself.

### 4. Modifications of the Late Date

A number of scholars have suggested alternative dates and proposals to the generally accepted late date. Rowley, for example, establishes a chronology which places the exodus from Egypt approximately 1230 B.C. followed by a brief wandering of only two years, during which time the tribes which participated in the

---

[53]*Ibid.*, pp. 118-119.

[54]James B. Pritchard, ed. *Ancient New Eastern Texts*, "Pharaoh as a Sportsman," trans. by John A. Wilson (3rd ed. with supplement; Princeton: Princeton University Press, 1969), p. 244 (hereafter referred to as ANET). Note also William C. Hays, *The Scepter of Egypt* (Cambridge, Mass.: Harvard University Press, 1959), II, p. 141.

[55]John Rea, *op. cit.*, p. 12.

[56]Charles F. Aling, *Egypt and Bible History*, pp. 97-100.

exodus received the law.[57] More recently Joseph Callaway, who directed the excavations at Et-Tell, has concluded that the conquest under Joshua must have taken place in the twelfth rather than the thirteenth centry B.C. as proposed by most critical scholars.[58] His conclusions on this matter have been influenced primarily from the archaeological data of Et-Tell. At this site there is an apparent lack of occupation between the end of the Early Bronze Age and the beginning of the Iron Age; therefore, the conquest under Joshua, according to this view, could not have occurred until the twelfth century B.C.

The difficulty with both these proposals is that they run into deep tension with obvious chronological information supplied by Scripture. Of equal concern with regard to Callaway's suggestion is that on methodological grounds, the chronology of the conquest appears to be established by a problem site. It would be preferable to start with the clearly articulated biblical information and then evaluate the problem of Ai in the light of that rather than to reorient biblical history to suit the demands of the negative evidence at Et-Tell. At the present, there are no easy answers to the problem of Ai and the date of the conquest.

5. The Early Date

The early date of the exodus (1445 B.C.) is primarily established upon two biblical texts and the resulting relationship of that chronology to Egyptian history. According to I Kings 6:1, the exodus from Egypt took place 480 years prior to the fourth year of Solomon. Since the fourth year of Solomon is usually calculated at 966/5 B.C., this would point to an exodus date of approximately 1446/5 B.C. The implications of the language of I Kings 6:1 appear to be very clear.

Some have attempted to discredit the text as a late edition and therefore worthless; however, it is interesting to observe that the name of the month which appears in that text is the archaic form

---

[57]See H. H. Rowley, "Israel's Sojourn in Egypt," *Bulletin of the John Rylands Library,* XXII (1938), p. 263.

[58]"New Evidence on the Conquest of Ai," *Journal of Biblical Literature,* LXXXVI (1968), pp. 312-320.

and not the later one. Furthermore, the number 480 is well attested in all major manuscripts.

The popular interpretation of that number by those defending the late date changes its status as a chronological notation to a vague illusion to twelve generations. R. K. Harrison writes:

> However, while such a figure represents the unanimous testimony of the manuscripts, it can be questioned on other grounds, particularly when it is examined against the background of oriental symbolism. The number 480 can be resolved into units of twelve generations of forty each. A double cycle of motif may be involved in consequence, having the effect of relating the concept of a generation to each of the twelve tribes.[59]

Such an explanation, however, must be rejected on several grounds. First, if one is able to manipulate a number whose functions are clearly delineated in a sober historical context, then every number in Scripture becomes subject to the whims of an interpreter. Second, there is nothing in the text that states or even implies the idea of twelve generations. While such a supposition might be mathematically possible, it is highly questionable on exegetical grounds. Third, as Gleason Archer points out,[60] a true generation span is more likely to have been twenty-five years rather than forty.

Of equal importance in the discussion of the early date is the statement attributed to Jephthah in which he places three hundred years between Israel's sojourn at Heshbon and the second year (approximately) of his judgeship (Judg. 11:26). Jephthah's statement is in remarkable agreement with the data given in I Kings 6:1.

> Jephthah was eighth judge of Israel. Following him came four other judges, Samuel's time of leadership, the kingships of Saul and David, and four years of Solomon's reign, all prior to beginning of the building of the temple. The total years represented by these successive leaders must be added to the date

---

[59]R. K. Harrison, *Introduction to the Old Testament* (Grand Rapids: Eerdman's Publishing Co., 1969), p. 317.

[60]"Old Testament History and Recent Archaeology — from Moses to David," *Bibliotheca Sacra,* CXXVII, No. 506 (1970), p. 106.

> of c. 966 B.C., when the construction of the temple began, to arrive at Jephthah's date. This works out to approximately 1100 B.C., which is just 300 years after 1400 B.C., the time of the conquest on the basis of the early date. There is simply no way to harmonize Jephthah's statement with the late date, apart from the denial of its historical accuracy.[61]

Those who take the late date of the exodus are forced to compress this period into a total of 180 years, an extremely brief time to include all the events that are described up to the time of Hephthah.[62] In an attempt to handle the problem of Jephthah's statement, Cundall and Morris make the following observation: "The reference to 300 years may be an editorial amplification of the remainder of the verse, or it may be a broad generalization for approximately seven or eight generations, or it may represent Jephthah's rough guess, since he would hardly have access to reliable historical records.[63] It is scarcely possible, however, that Jephthah should make such a historical blunder in the midst of important negotiations. His knowledge of the Torah is evident from the context of Judges 11.

It is also doubtful that Jephthah could have exaggerated this number in his argument to the king and have gotten away with it. Surely the King of Ammon had some knowledge of the historical precedence involved in Israel's occupation of the territory in Transjordan (cf. Judg. 11:13). Again it would be well to point out that the numerical information given in the passage in question does not appear in a poetic section and therefore should be regarded in its most literal sense.

Another form of evidence also exists which indirectly supports the early date of the exodus. This evidence is drawn from the excavations at Jericho (Tell es-Sultan) by both John Garstang and Kathleen Kenyon. Garstang, who worked at Jericho between 1930 and 1936, concluded that city III (Middle Bronze II) was

---

[61]Leon Wood, *A Survey of Israel's History* (Grand Rapids, Zondervan Publishing House, 1970), p. 89.

[62]A. E. Cundall and L. Morris, *Judges and Ruth* (Chicago: Inter-Varsity Press, 1968), p. 145.

[63]*Ibid.*, pp. 145-146.

J. J. Davis

Sphinx of Rameses II at Alexandria.

occupied down to the year 1550 B.C. by the Hyksos.[64] He also discovered another city layer which he called City IV and related this to the Late Bronze Age period, or the period of the conquest. In addition to that, he felt he had discovered the walls of Jericho, which he dated to Joshua's period. A great deal of evidence was recovered to indicate some form of Late Bronze Age occupation at the site. Approximately 320 objects from that period, including two scarabs from Amenhotep III (1410-1372 B.C.), were recovered.

The later excavations of Kathleen Kenyon (between 1952-1958) required a re-identification of the walls discovered by Garstang. Rather than belonging to the Late Bronze Age period, they represented a much earlier building phase (Early Bronze).[65] Of particular interest is the fact that very little Mycenaean pottery from the Aegean area appears at Jericho. According to Garstang, out

---

64John Garstang and J. B. E. Garstang, *The Story of Jericho* (London. Marshall, Morgan & Scott, Ltd., 1948), pp. 107-108.

65Kathleen Kenyon, *Digging Up Jericho* (London: Ernest Benn Limited, 1957), pp. 170-172.

of 150,000 pieces of pottery, only one was identifiable as Mycenaean.[66] Mycenaean pottery began to appear in Palestine in 1400 B.C. or shortly thereafter. The fact that very few samples appear at Jericho is interesting and perhaps very instructive, for Mycenaean pottery is not unknown to the Jordan Valley.[67] The lack of this pottery might indicate that there was little occupation of the site after the middle of the fourteenth century B.C.

Kenyon suggests that the latest occupation in the Bronze Age should be dated to the third quarter of the fourteenth century B.C.[68] But this date appears to be rather late in the light of the foregoing evidence. Garstang, on the other hand, suggested that the limits for City IV of Jericho should be between 1400 and 1385 B.C.[69] The tremendous erosion of the Late Bronze Age layers which took place because of a long period of abandonment might be a silent witness to the violent destruction of that city by Joshua in approximately 1400 B.C.

Waltke argues that the pottery found in the remains of the Late Bronze Age city should be associated with the Late Bronze IIA period (1410-1340 B.C.) Since no Egyptian scarabs were discovered later than the reign of Amenhotep III, he maintains that the destruction must have occurred before the reign of Akhenaton. Also, the fact that Jericho is not mentioned in the Amarna Letters may imply its destruction and abandonment.[70] Supporting evidence for the early date of the exodus and conquest also comes from the well-known Stele of Merneptah,[71] the Nineteenth-Dynasty king who succeeded Ramses II. In this victory stele he claims to have encountered the people of Israel and defeated them.[72] This information implies that Israel was already in Palestine and had, to some degree, expanded its land holdings toward the west. If one takes the late date of the exodus, he is forced to conclude that Joshua and the armies of Israel encountered the

---

[66]John Garstang and J. B. E. Garstang, *op. cit.*, p. 122.

[67]See R. Laird Harris, *op. cit.*, p. 13.

[68]*Op. Cit.*, p. 262.

[69]*Op. Cit.*, p. 135.

[70]Bruce K. Waltke, *op. cit.*, pp. 39ff.

[71]ANET, "Hymn of Victory of Mer-ne-Ptah," trans. by John A. Wilson, pp. 376-378.

[72]*Ibid.*, p. 378.

armies of Ramses II or Merneptah, either of which would have been a formidable force. Noteworthy is the fact that such an encounter with the Egyptians is nowhere mentioned in the books of Joshua or Judges. The early date assumes the entry of Israel into Canaan somewhere around 1400 B.C., approaching the reigns of Amenhotep III and Amenhotep IV, both of whom were very weak in their domination of Palestine. In this we may see the hand of Providence in the rapid decline of Egypt at the very moment Israel was entering and colonizing the Promised Land.

### 6. The Importance of this Issue

The date of the exodus is not an inconsequential historical matter when it comes to the interpretation of Scripture. The date that one adopts will influence all earlier chronology. In essence this date constitutes a bench mark for all pre-Solomonic chronology and the cultural backgrounds that will be associated with the various periods.

Also at stake here is the locus of authority. The Bible speaks very clearly to the issue of the date of the exodus and if these statements represent revelatory authority, then they are reliable and should constitute the foundation for chronological thought. If these data are not found to be reliable, then all biblical numbers and chronological notices can be regarded as suspect.

On the sheer basis of the history of archaeological research, one should be most hesitant to grant to the science of archaeology a sense of absolute and final authority. Archaeological conclusions have undergone constant change as the result of new discoveries. Furthermore, the clear trend in archaeological research has been consistently in the direction of affirming the reliability of biblical historiography. Archaeology, of course, by its very nature is an incomplete science with conclusions that often rest on the most fragmentary forms of information.[73]

### 7. Summary and Conclusion

On the basis of the above considerations it will be observed that dominating the studies of the Book of Exodus are two basic

---

[73]On the apologetic value of archaeology see John J. Davis, "Archaeology and Apologetics," *Seminary Spire*, XI; No. 4 (1983), pp. 7-9.

views of the date of the exodus. The one date, espoused predominantly by liberal critical scholars (although not exclusively so), is that the exodus occurred sometime in the early thirteenth century B.C., presumably during the reign of Ramses II. The other alternative, strongly suggested by biblical chronology, is that the oppression of Israel began during the period of the Hyksos and continued into the reign of Thutmose III, who perhaps was Israel's most severe taskmaster. The exodus, then, would have occurred shortly after his death and during the reign of Amenhotep II. The latter view seems preferable in light of the fact that it is more faithful to Scripture, and provides a credible background for integrating the events of the exodus and conquest with Egyptian history and culture.

This problem deserves, and probably will get, continued serious treatment in years to come. It is not likely that all problems will be solved in the near future, but it is the task of the Bible student to consider the various proposals with their theological implications.

### B. *Egypt: The Eighteenth Dynasty*

The last years of the Middle Kingdom period were, to a certain degree, dark, obscure and confused. One thing is clear, however—in these latter years Semites had infiltrated the Delta region in sufficient numbers so as to have gained access to the throne of Egypt. This is evidenced in a number of Semitic names that are identified with pharaonic rule.[74] This period of history, including the Fifteenth, Sixteenth, and Seventeenth Dynasties, is commonly known as the Second Intermediate Period or the period of Hyksos domination. According to Manetho, the fourth-century B.C. historian, the Hyksos took over Egypt by a violent invasion, a view which has generally been accepted by scholars down to the present day. Van Seters, on the other hand, has proposed that Egypt was taken over by an Amorite coup d'état and

---

[74]John Van Seters, *op. cit.*, pp. 87-96. Also compare G. Steindorff and K. Seele, *op. cit.*, p. 23.

Oriental Institute, Chicago

A nineteenth-century B.C. tomb painting which depicts the Semites entering Egypt.

did not suffer a major military invasion from the north as had previously been suspected.[75]

After approximately 150 years of rule, war broke out between the native Egyptians at Thebes under the leadership of Sekenenre, and Apophis, the Hyksos king at Avaris. A rather humorous tale exists concerning the conflict between these two kings. It seems that Apophis complained that the noise of the hippopotami in the pool down at Thebes was preventing him from getting a good night's sleep; the hippos were more than 400 miles away![76]

More serious evidence of the conflict between the native Egyptians and the Hyksos is found in the mummy of Sekenenre which exhibits very severe wounds in the head.[77] The struggle begun by Sekenenre was continued by his sons Kamose and Ahmose.[78] Ahmose is generally regarded as the first king of the Eighteenth Dynasty, which probably was to become the greatest age in all Egyptian history. Ahmose was succeeded by his son, Amenhotep I, who was followed by his daughter's husband, Thutmose I. Thutmose campaigned vigorously in the south to Nubia and as far north as the Euphrates River, thus reestablishing Egyptian control over Syro-Palestinian territory.

When Thutmose I died, there was no surviving male heir so his daughter Queen Hatshepsut seized the throne and ruled Egypt for approximately twenty-one years, even though during much of that time there was a legitimate heir to the throne in the person of Thutmose III. Because of his young age, however, and the powerful influence of Hatshepsut, he had to watch from the sidelines. It is the view of some that Queen Hatshepsut was the one responsible for caring for Moses in the early years.

Following her rule, Thutmose III finally regained the throne

---

[75]*Op. cit.*, pp. 192-193. For a recent defense of the traditional viewpoint suggested by Manetho (i.e., that the Hyksos entered Egypt by force) see Donald B. Redford, "The Hyksos Invasion in History and Tradition," *Orientalia,* XXXVIII, No. 1 (1970), pp. 1-17.

[76]ANET, "The Hyksos in Egypt," trans. by John A. Wilson, pp. 230-232.

[77]G. Steindorff and K. Seele, *op. cit.* fig. 7, p. 28.

[78]ANET, "The War Against the Hyksos," and "The Expulsion of the Hyksos," trans. by John A. Wilson, pp. 232-234.

as sole ruler and was destined to become one of Egypt's greatest. When he took the throne, he expressed to the fullest extent his resentment for having been kept so long in a minor position by destroying the representations and the name of Hatshepsut wherever these appeared on monuments in Egypt. This king renewed military activity in Syro-Palestine in the form of at least sixteen campaigns taking him as far north as the Euphrates. In this regard he continued the policies of his grandfather, Thutmose I, who had initiated the subjugation of Asiatic provinces for Egypt.

If the early date of the exodus is the correct one, Thutmose III would likely be the candidate for the Pharaoh of the oppression. This king was on the throne at the time of Moses' flight from Egypt and died approximately thirty or forty years later, thus permitting Moses to return. It may well have been that the vengeance sought upon Moses was not due only to Moses' murder of an Egyptian official, but also to his possible association with Hatshepsut.

Following the death of Thutmose III, his son, Amenhotep II, took the throne and ruled for at least twenty-six years. This king, according to the early date of the exodus, would have been the Pharaoh of the exodus and the one who lost his firstborn son in the final judgment of God (Exod. 12). Some have seen a relationship between the death of Amenhotep's firstborn son and the well-known "Dream Stela" of Thutmose IV, his son and successor to the throne. In this document the god Har-em-akht promised the throne to Thutmose IV on the condition that he restore the exposure of the great sphinx which apparently had been largely covered by drifting sand. It is their view that this Dream Stela represents an attempt at legitimatizing his right to the throne, since he was apparently not the firstborn son.[79]

---

[79]ANET, "A Divine Oracle Through a Dream," trans. by John A. Wilson, p. 449. For a detailed discussion of this point see Merrill F. Unger, *op. cit.*, pp. 142ff. and Gleason Archer, *A Survey of Old Testament Introduction* (Chicago: Moody Press, 1964), p. 218. Charles A. Aling has convincingly argued against this idea and has suggested that Webensenu was probably the firstborn son of Amenhotep II and his brother Khaemwaset was next to

Amenhotep II was a very energetic and skillful king. He is known to us in Egyptian history as a capable warrior and sportsman who distinguished himself in rowing, horsemanship, and archery. The mummy of this king was found in 1898 in the Valley of the Kings at Thebes along with his famous bow which he boasted that no other man could draw.

His successor to the throne, Thutmose IV, is somewhat of an enigma in Egyptian history. He carried out the usual campaigns to the north but relatively little is known of this Pharaoh. Following him to the throne was his son, Amenhotep III, who was an outstanding king, at least in the early phases of his reign. The last part of his reign and that of his son Amenhotep IV (Akhenaton) constituted a period of decline, confusion and weakness in Egypt, commonly known as the Amarna Period.

What is of significance is the fact that (according to the early date) the exodus from Egypt took place during the zenith of Egyptian power, prestige and glory. This fact, coupled with the idea of the unique nature of God's intervention for His people, made this one of the most memorable events in Hebrew history.

## II. The Biblical Record

### A. *The Title of the Book*

The Hebrew title of Exodus is *w$^{e}$ēlleh $s^{e}$môt* ("and these are the names of") or, in shortened form, *$s^{e}$môt* ("the names of"). This title is based on the opening words of Exodus 1:1, whereas the English title is founded on the Latinized form of the Septuagint title, *Exodus.* The Septuagint apparently derived this title from the principal theme of the book as described in Exodus 19:1.

The Book of Exodus is a vital connecting link between the patriarchal narratives of Genesis and the remaining parts of the Pentateuch. In the Hebrew text, the book begins with the *waw* consecutive usually translated "now" in the English versions. In

---

succeed his father. See "The Sphinx Stele of Thutmose IV and the Date of the Exodus," *Journal of the Evangelical Theological Society*, XXII, No. 2 (1979), pp. 97-101.

this particular instance it probably reflects some connection with the preceding material in Genesis (although grammatically it would not necessarily have to imply this). Strengthening this fact is the observation that the opening verse of this book is a repetition of Genesis 46:8.

## B. *Author and Date of Composition*

### 1. Liberal-Critical Views

Critical scholars have by and large handled the Book of Exodus much as they have the Book of Genesis; that is, attributing the composition to various sources from the eighth century B.C. to the second century B.C. The traditional Wellhausenian approach saw in the Book of Exodus at least five major sources: J (yhwh), E (*elohim*), D (Deuteronomic school), P (priestly school), and R (redactors).

In more recent days, O. Eissfeldt has added L (a lay source) in his *Einleitung in das Alte Testament.* Such a viewpoint obviously denies any form of Mosaic authorship and would be unacceptable to anyone who takes the statements of Scripture seriously.

It is strange indeed that P, which was supposed to have been written from a priestly point of view, does relatively little to enhance the priesthood in the Book of Exodus. It was Moses, the great leader of Israel, who was the hero, while the one who encouraged the people to idolatry was Aaron, the priest, and he was the one who was the object of very pointed criticism (cf. Exod. 32:19ff.). The documentary theory of the Pentateuch and the developments within the current school of form criticism have been adequately analyzed and evaluated by Harrison,[80] Archer,[81] Allis[82] and Young.[83]

---

[80] R. K. Harrison, *op. cit.*, pp. 495ff.

[81] Gleason Archer, *op. cit.*, pp. 73ff.

[82] Oswald T. Allis, *The Five Books of Moses* (Philadelphia: The Presbyterian and Reformed Publishing Co., 1949).

[83] E. J. Young, *An Introduction to the Old Testament* (Grand Rapids: Eerdmans Publishing Co., 1969).

## 2. Moses and His Contemporaries

In view of the fact that "Moses was learned in all the wisdom of the Egyptians and was mighty in words and in deeds" (Acts 7:22), it is not unreasonable to assume that he had the intellectual capacity and training to be the primary author of the Exodus material. His training and experience as a young man in the royal court of Egypt, a fact to be studied later in more detail, would have eminently qualified him for the task of writing.

The strongest evidence for Mosaic authorship is to be found in the biblical text itself. In many places it is clearly asserted that Moses had a record made or that he himself wrote an official record of a particular event (cf. Exod. 17:14; 24:4, 7, 12; 34:27; Num. 33:1-2; Deut. 31:9, 11).[84] Of special importance is the fact that the New Testament writers also ascribed authorship to Moses (cf. John 5:46-47; 7:19; Acts 3:22; Rom. 10:5). We must accept the unified testimony of Scripture both from the Old and the New Testaments or charge the prophets, Christ and the apostles with falsehood or error, either of which is unacceptable in the view of the scriptural teaching of inspiration.

Other indirect evidences are also available to support the claims for Mosaic authorship. The great abundance of details reflecting an eyewitness account would seem to support such a proposition (cf. Exod. 15:27 where the exact number of fountains and palm trees is given). The author demonstrates a thorough and accurate knowledge of Egyptian customs. He shows a familiarity with Egyptian proper names and appropriately refers to the king of Egypt as Pharaoh, which title was characteristic of the Eighteenth-Dynasty period onward. The title "Pharaoh" literally means "great house" which was originally used to describe the household of the king, but in the Eighteenth Dynasty was applied to the king himself. The writer of the Exodus narratives also demonstrates a thorough knowledge of the geography of Egypt and Sinai.

---

[84]Elsewhere in the Old Testament this material is attributed to Moses (cf. Josh. 1:8; 8:31; I Kings 2:3; II Kings 14:6; Ezra 6:18; Neh. 13:1; Dan. 9:1-13 and Mal. 4:4).

## C. *Literary Quality of the Text*

The literary style of the Book of Exodus is quite distinct from that of Genesis. In the first book of the Torah there are many narratives focusing primarily on personalities and events associated with them (e.g. Adam, Abel, Noah, Abraham, Isaac, Jacob, and Joseph), but in the Book of Exodus the only outstanding individual to receive such treatment is Moses himself.

The emphasis is on revelational matters relating to the divine perfection as expressed in God's covenant faithfulness, giving of the law and instructions for construction of the tabernacle. The original text of Exodus, unlike other books of the Old Testament, is quite free from transcriptional errors.

There are the usual number of examples of dittography, haplography, and other scribal mistakes, but these are of little consequence to the meaning and the significance of the text as a whole. The text is an example of classical Hebrew prose and generally reads with considerable consistency and smoothness. It is apparent at some points that additions were made by either Joshua or Eliezer, or perhaps one of the priests closely associated with Moses. The general authorship, however, must be ascribed to Moses himself with only minor additions and changes made after his death.

## D. *Themes and Theology*

No other event is alluded to more frequently by Old Testament writers than Israel's redemption from Egyptian bondage. This second book of the Pentateuch establishes a foundational theology by which God reveals his attributes, name, redemption, law and the ways of worship. The covenant faithfulness of the Lord is put on display in a marvelous exhibition of supernatural deliverance.

The sovereignty of God is also exhibited over the forces of nature and the political systems of men. The powerful existence of God is placed in contrast to the impotent deities of Egypt who could do nothing in the face of divine authority and power. The events of the ten plagues should have impressed upon Israel God's view of idolatry.

The holiness of God is also a very important theological theme in the book. Early in Moses' experience he was reminded that the ground upon which he stood was in the presence of the Lord, and was, therefore, "holy ground" (Exod. 3:5). This is the first appearance of the word "holy" as an adjective in the Pentateuch. Since the Lord was holy, it was expected that his people would also reflect that character (Exod. 19:6). The Hebrews were dramatically reminded of the holiness of the Lord by the nature of the innermost part of the sanctuary, which was designated the "holy of holies."

The God of Exodus is also a God of perfect fidelity. He had promised that Abraham would have many descendants and after a period of 430 years, the Hebrews numbered nearly 2,000,000. The redemption from bondage promised to Abraham also saw its fulfillment in the deliverance from Egypt. Redemptively, this book anticipates the even greater salvation provided by the Lord Jesus Christ.

The inclusion of codified law in Exodus gives insight into foundational ethics and morals within the framework of Israel's covenant community. It provided for orderliness and discipline, knowing well the inclinations of sinful man to rebel against God and society.

The events of the Book of Exodus are exciting, imaginative, and challenging. They provide inspiration to the young and comfort to the old.

## III. Basic Outline: Exodus

A. *Bondage in Egypt* (1:1–12:51)
   1. The Years of Oppression (1:1-22)
   2. The Birth of a Deliverer (2:1-25)
   3. The Call of Moses (3:1–4:17)
   4. A Challenge and a Crisis (4:18–5:23)
   5. Comfort from God (6:1-30)
   6. River of Blood (7:1-25)
   7. The Finger of God (8:1-32)
   8. When the Gods Were Silent (9:1–10:29)
   9. An Ordinance Forever (11:1–12:51)

B. *Journey to Sinai* (13:1–20:26)

1. Birth of a Nation (13:1–14:31)
2. Pilgrimage to Sinai (15:1–18:27)
3. Thunder, Clouds and Smoke (19:1–20:26)

C. *The Book of the Covenant* (21:1–24:18)

1. The Law of the Slave (21:1-11)
2. Laws Relating to Personal Injury (21:12-36)
3. Laws Concerning Theft (22:1-4)
4. Laws Concerning Property Damage (22:5-6)
5. Laws Concerning Dishonesty (22:7-15)
6. Laws Concerning Immorality (22:16-17)
7. Laws Relating to Civil and Religious Obligations (22:18–23:9)
8. Ceremonial Laws (23:10-19)
9. Laws Relating to Conquest (23:20-33)
10. Ratification of the Covenant (24:1-8)
11. The Glory of the Lord (24:9-18)

D. *The Tabernacle* (25:1–40:38)

1. Instructions for Building (25:1–31:18)
2. Apostasy and Covenant Renewal (32:1–34:35)
3. Construction of the Tabernacle and its Furniture (35:1–40:38)

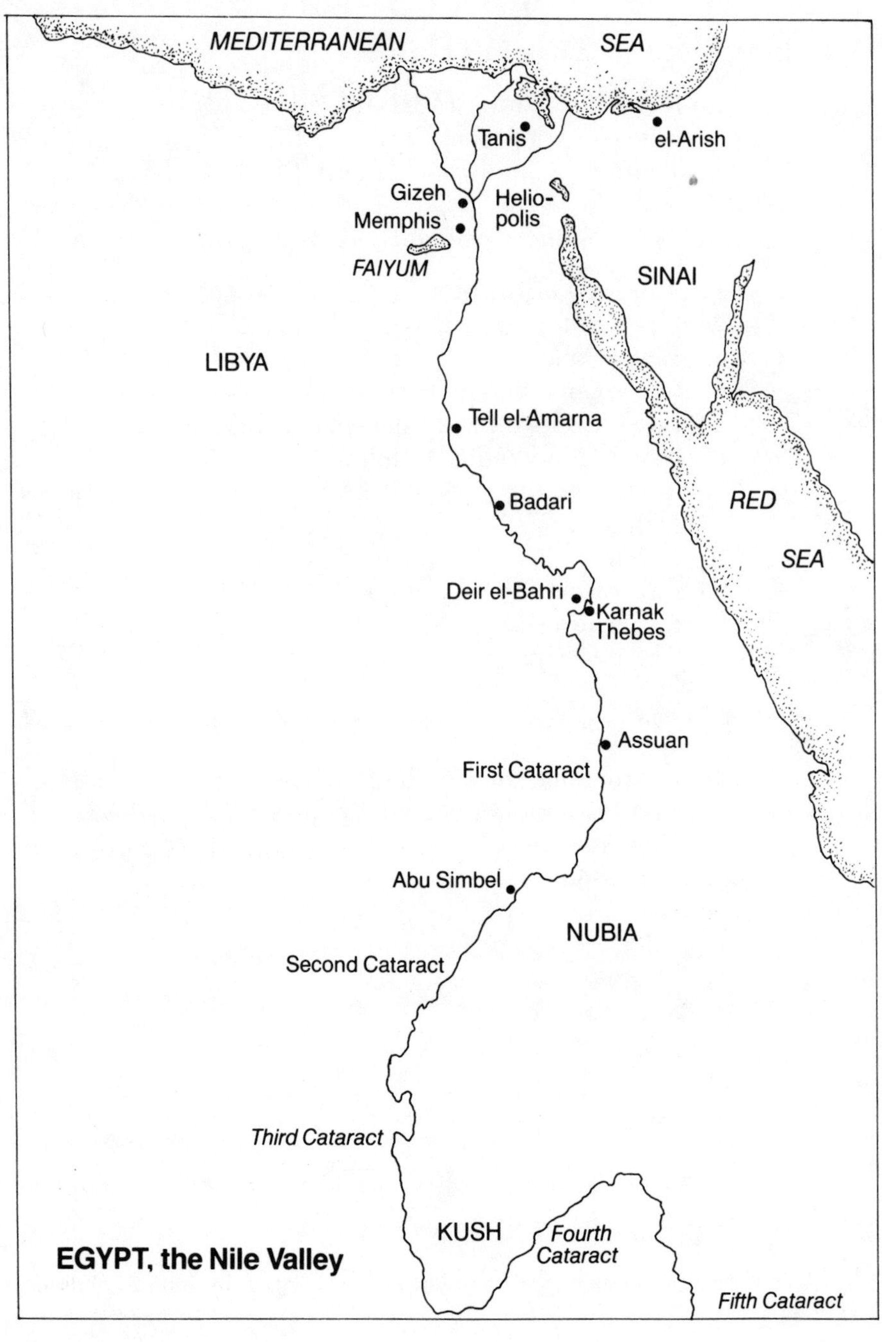


**EGYPT, the Nile Valley**

**Chapter 2**

# *A Dilemma and a Deliverer*

(Exodus 1–2)

> Then he took a stick of green tamarisk against him. Then he belabored all his limbs with it, and his donkeys were taken away and driven into his estate. Thereupon this peasant wept very greatly because of the pain of what had been done to him. Then this Thut-nakht said: "Do not be so noisy, peasant! Behold, thou art at the home of the Lord of Silence!" Then this peasant said: "Thou beatest me, thou stealest my goods, and now thou even takest away the complaint from my mouth! Oh Lord of Silence, mayest thou give me back my property!"[1]

The words of an Hebrew slave? No. These are the complaints of a peasant who lived in a salt field known today as Wadi Natrun, a small oasis west of the Delta region. He came to Egypt in order to exchange his products for corn and other foods. On the way he was humiliated and robbed by a man identified as Thut-nakht. The cry of this peasant may well have approximated the cry of the Hebrew slave many years later who was also humiliated at the hand of the Egyptian. Exodus 1 and 2 present one of the dark periods of Hebrew history, only exceeded in natural sorrow by the humiliation of Jerusalem and the destruction of its temple in 586 B.C. These chapters should not be regarded as a mere expression of national gloom, however, for they are also the revelation of God's providential work in preparing for deliverance and redemption.

## I. Bondage in Egypt (1:1-22)

### A. *Introduction* (1:1-7)

The first seven verses of Chapter 1 represent a repetition of information given in the Book of Genesis (35:22-26; 46:27; 50:26). The verses are a significant introduction to the chapter and the book, for they help to link together the historical infor-

---

[1]*ANET*, "The Protests of the Eloquent Peasant," trans. by John A. Wilson, p. 408.

mation of the last chapters of Genesis with the events of Exodus 1.

According to 1:1-5 all the sons of Jacob were involved in the descent to Egypt. This might appear to be an insignificant point but in the light of liberal criticism which has seriously questioned the total participation of all the tribes in the exodus, it is important to reemphasize this fact.[2] The sons are arranged according to their mothers, as in Genesis 35:23-26, with the sons of the two maidservants appearing last. The number of males that accompanied Jacob is given as 70 in verse 5. This is in agreement with a similar number which appears in Genesis 46:27 and Deuteronomy 10:22; however, the Septuagint reading of this text and Acts 7:14, which is apparently a quotation from the Septuagint text, reads seventy-five souls. It is interesting to observe that the Dead Sea Scrolls have the same reading as the Septuagint and may demonstrate the accuracy of the Septuagintal reading, at least at this point. What is important to the overall impression of the text, however, is the fact that it illustrates the tremendous increase which reflected divine covenantal blessing upon these people in spite of the adversity which is described throughout the chapter (cf. Gen. 15:14 and 46:3). Notice that in Genesis 46:26 the figure of the descendants of Jacob is given as only sixty-six. This is due to the fact that Jacob, Joseph and his two sons were not included in the calculation. Moses, later on, added these thus making the total seventy. The number seventy-five is probably inclusive of the five grandsons of Joseph.

The information of verse 7 is important because it appears to imply a considerable lapse of time during which the children of Israel were "fruitful and increased abundantly and multiplied and became exceedingly mighty and the land was filled with them." The Hebrew expressions in this verse are strangely reminiscent of the expressions used in Genesis 1:28, and probably indicate that by this time the children of Israel numbered close to two million (assuming the 603,000 of Num. 1 represented approximately one-fourth the total population).

---

[2]Further support for the fact that all tribes were present in Egypt is found in Gen. 46:6-27; 49:1ff.; Exod. 12:41 and the use of the number twelve in Exod. 24:4; 28:9-21; 39:6-14.

B. *The Bondage Described* (1:8-22)

After this long period of time, during which Joseph had died (v. 6), a new king arose over Egypt who knew not Joseph (v. 8). The identity of this king has been the focal point of a great deal of speculation. George Ernest Wright, who accepts the late date of the exodus, suggests that Seti I, the father of Rameses II, was the king here involved.[3] Many scholars identify this new king with one of the New Kingdom pharaohs.[4] A third view is that this ruler was one of the Hyksos kings.[5] This view better fits the biblical chronology which suggests that Joseph entered Egypt some time in the Middle Kingdom period (1445 B.C. + 430 years, Exod. 12:40). From the context itself, it appears that the statements made by this king make an Eighteenth Dynasty association rather unlikely. It is doubtful that a New Kingdom Pharaoh, who had just been victorious over the Hyksos peoples, made the statement that the Semitic shepherds in the Delta were "more and mightier than we" (v. 9). The Hebrew text seems to support this identification as well. John Rea observes:

> The text says, "A new king rose over Egypt," *wayaqom melek hāḏāš 'al miṣrāyim*. In Hebrew the verb *qûm* plus the preposition *'al* often have the meaning 'to rise against' (e.g., Deut. 19:11; 28:7; Judges 9:18; 20:5; II Sam. 18:31; II Kings 16:7); but they never have the meaning of assuming the throne of a nation in a peaceful, friendly manner. It is certainly true that the Hyksos arose *against* Egypt. Furthermore, the Hyksos may well have had reason to hate the descendants of Jacob because of the episode at Shechem (Gen. 34) and Jacob's later fighting with the Amorites (Gen. 48:22), Amorites being one of the main elements of the Hyksos people" (Albright, *From the Stone Age to Christianity*, p. 202, note 4).[6]

This identification also has in its favor the time required to fulfill the prediction given to Abraham in Genesis 15:13. It is there stated that the descendants of Abraham would ". . . be a

---

[3]*Op. cit.*, p. 60.

[4]Merrill F. Unger, *op. cit.*, p. 144.

[5]John Rea, "The Time of the Oppression and the Exodus," *Grace Journal*, II, No. 1 (Winter, 1961), pp. 7 ff.

[6]*Ibid.*, pp. 7-8.

sojourner in a land that is not theirs, and shall serve them; and they shall afflict them four hundred years."

Many have associated Joseph and his family with the Hyksos rule in Egypt and in this have sought a favorable context in which to explain Joseph's rise to power; however, opposed to this view are the biblical statements indicated above. This question is often asked, "Why would the Hyksos, a largely Semitic people, oppress the Hebrews who were also Semitic?" To this question several answers might be given. In the first place Israel had grown to significant proportions and could well have been a threat to the security of the Hyksos capital which was located in the general vicinity of Goshen. Secondly, since Israel was already in the land when the Hyksos arrived, it would be natural for the Hyksos to suspect an alliance between the native Egyptians and the Hebrews (cf. v. 10). What is usually not considered by those who advocate Joseph's rise under the Hyksos is the fact that when the Hyksos were driven out of Egypt, the Israelites were not. It would seem that if friendly relations indeed were sustained between the Israelites and the Hyksos, the Israelites would have suffered the same fate as their friends. In the light of the above interpretation, therefore, verse 10 would read, "Come on, let us [Hyksos] deal wisely with them [Israelites], lest they multiply, and it come to pass, that, when war occurs, they join also unto our enemies [the Egyptians], and fight against us [Hyksos], and so get them up out of the land."

In order to prevent the Israelites from becoming a threat to Hyksos security, they decided to set "taskmasters" (Heb. *śārê missîm*, "officers or chiefs of the labor gangs," v. 11). By placing large numbers of the Israelites in labor gangs, it would break down their will to become independent, and prevent any security threat to the Hyksos. Furthermore, it would enable them to expand their building projects in the Delta region. The word for "afflict" (Heb. *ʿānāh*) is also used in Genesis 15:13 (cf. Isa. 53:7). The labor gangs were employed mainly in the service of Pharaoh to build "treasure cities" (Heb. *ʿārê miskᵉnôṯ*). This same expression also occurs in I Kings 9:19; II Chronicles 8:6; 17:12. These store cities may have been like those of Solomon and Jehoshaphat, designed to store goods both of domestic and military nature. While the name of the Pharaoh is not given, the names of the cities are: namely, Pithom and Ra'amses. "Egyptologists and biblical scholars are both agreed that the names were derived from Pi-Tum, i.e., Pi Atum or Per Atum, and Pi-Ramesses or more correctly Per Ramessu. The use of the word Pi or Per is significant. It has a wide application in Egyptian texts being derived from 𓉐, *pr*, 'house.'"[7] Pithom has been identified with three sites.[8] The first is Tell el-Maskhutah, which is an eleven-acre town located in the eastern reaches of Wadi Tumilat. The Swiss Egyptologist Edouard Naville championed this identification with the biblical Pithom, but modern scholarship has largely abandoned this view. Also located in Wadi Tumilat is Tell er-Retaba where a temple of Atum was discovered. This is archaeologically significant since the name Pithom is probably derived from an Egyptian word meaning "house of Atum." The third candidate, strongly supported by Uphill is Heliopolis,[9] located some distance southwest of Tell er-Retaba and Tell el-Maskhutah. Of the options available, it would appear that the best possibilities are Tell er-Retaba and Heliopolis since both were centers of sun worship.

The city of Ra'amses, on the other hand, has been identified with five different sites: (1) Tell er-Retaba (2) Pelusium, (3) Tanis, (4) Qantir, (5) Tchel.[10] While earlier scholars favored the site of Tanis, more recent evidence seems to have firmly established that the city of Ra'amses was situated in the region south of Tanis at Qantir.[11] Since Qantir gives evidence of occupation as early as the Middle Kingdom, it serves well as a candidate for the biblical Ra'amses.[12]

While the Hyksos were successful at having store cities built, they were not able to restrict or diminish the growth of Israel. Verse 12, which probably implies another time gap, indicates that the more the Hyksos afflicted them the more they multiplied

---

[7] E. P. Uphill, *op. cit.*, XXVII, No. 4, pp. 291-292.

[8] See E. P. Uphill, "Pithom and Ramses: Their Location and Significance," *Journal of Near Eastern Studies*, XXVII, No. 4 (1968), pp. 291-299.

[9] *Ibid.*, pp. 296ff.

[10] E. P. Uphill, *op. cit.*, p. 299.

[11] See Charles F. Aling, "The Biblical City of Ramses," p. 129.

[12] See John Van Seters, *op. cit.*, pp. 127ff.

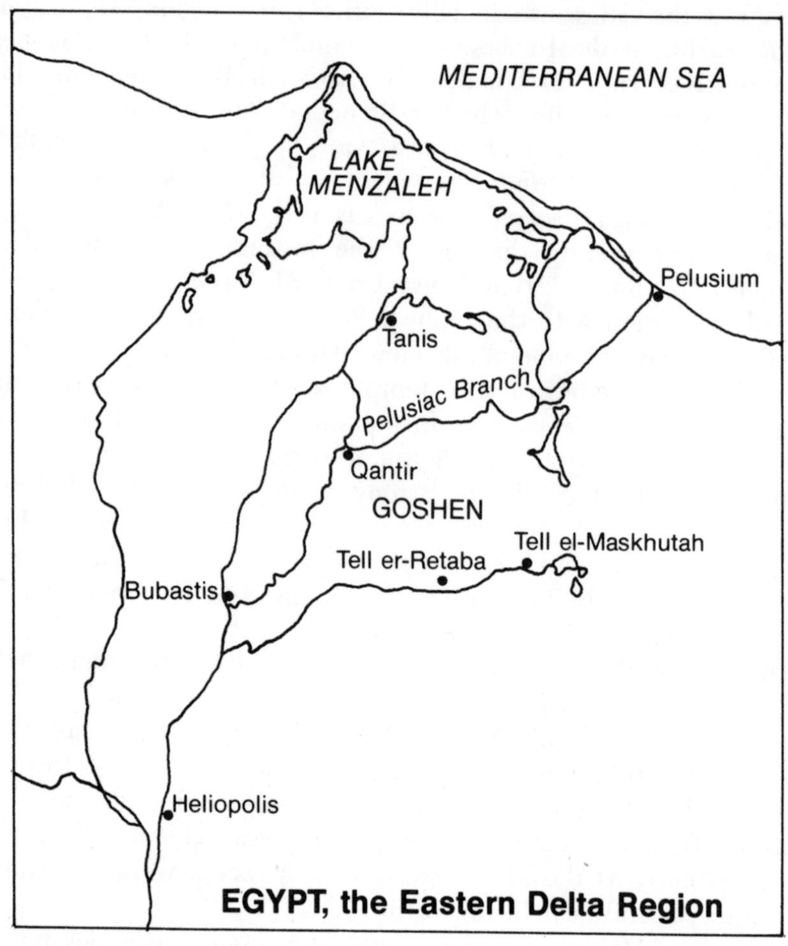

EGYPT, the Eastern Delta Region

and grew. This verse along with verse 7 quite obviously describes something most unusual biologically. Assuming that the original group to enter Egypt was at least 140 persons (the number 70 of verse 5 includes males only), the original population would have had to have doubled fourteen times to produce the number who took part in the exodus (about 2,000,000). This apparently reflects special divine blessing and intervention as promised in the Abrahamic covenant (cf. Gen. 12:2; 15:5). It might be observed at this point that the tremendous increase in population implies a considerable period of bondage in Egypt. This is in agreement with the 430 years of Exodus 12:40 and the 400 years of Genesis 15:13. However, it is quite problematic if one takes a reduced view of the oppression, that is, a period of about 200 years. This is done by some who accept the Septuagint reading of Exodus 12:40, which includes in the 430 years the patriarchal period in Canaan as well as the oppression period in Egypt. This problem will be discussed at a later point.[13]

The identity of the oppressors in verse 13 is not left in doubt, for it definitely states that the *Egyptians* made the children of Israel to serve with rigor. This servitude not only involved them in building projects but agriculture as well (v. 14). We might assume that between verses 12 and 13 the Hyksos were driven from the land of Egypt, and perhaps there was a brief relaxation of servitude. The Pharaoh of verses 13 and 14 may have been Ahmose I (1570-1548 B.C.), the first king of the Eighteenth Dynasty. Labor under this king involved hard work in ". . . mortar, and in brick, and in all manner of service in the field . . ." (v. 14). The lot of the Israelites must have been extremely difficult at this time, for hour upon hour they would work out in the blistering hot sun in Egypt in the fields sowing seed and working in irrigated areas (cf. Deut. 11:10). Josephus speaks of the children of Israel being employed specifically to dig canals.[14]

Assuming another brief time gap, the "king of Egypt" mentioned in verse 15 would probably be identified with either Amenhotep I (1548-1528 B.C.) who ruled for about twenty-one years or his successor Thutmose I (1528-1508 B.C.). Previous plans of subjugation having been only partially effective, the king decided to take more drastic measures and attempt to exterminate young male babies in order to keep the population of the Israelites under control. To do this the king contacted two "Hebrew midwives," or as the original text might read, "midwives of the Hebrews." It might be assumed by some that these would have been Egyptians since one would scarcely have expected Hebrew women to aid Pharaoh in the annihilation of Hebrew babies; however, both the names are of Semitic character, and the fact that they "feared God" (v. 17) would mitigate against this kind of identification. W. F. Albright states that both these

---

[13]See pp. 148 ff.

[14]*Antiquities,* II:9:1.

names are good northwest Semitic names of the second millennium B.C.[15] The name of the first midwife, Shiphrah, appears in nearly the same form in the Brooklyn Museum Papyrus, dated about 1740 B.C.[16] The second name, Puah, has the Canaanite meaning "last girl," equivalent to the Ugaritic *Paghitu.*[17]

It should not be concluded that these were the only midwives among the Hebrews. They were, in all probability, the chief midwives. The Hebrew word "midwife" (*mᵉyalleḏeṯ*; literally means "one who helps to bear." The midwife aided at childbirth by taking the newborn child, cutting its umbilical cord, washing the baby with water, salting, and wrapping it (cf. Ezek. 16:4). The first mention of midwives was during the time of Jacob when they attended on Rachel (Gen. 35:17) and Tamar (Gen. 38:28). In Mesopotamia, Egypt, and among the Hebrews, women often crouched down in childbirth upon a pair of bricks or stones or on a birth stool of similar pattern. This procedure is well illustrated from ancient sources. The Egyptian Papyrus Westcar, written in the Hyksos period, records how three goddesses delivered a priest's wife of three sons: One each took a child on her arms, they cut the umbilical cords, washed the children, and put them on a cloth on a little brick bench, then went to announce the births to the waiting husband.[18] The Hebrew word for "stools" in verse 16 is *hā'oḇnāyim* meaning "two stones" undoubtedly referring to the procedure described above. The two midwives, however, "feared God" and refused to follow the dictates of the king. Like Peter in the New Testament, they felt it more important to obey God rather than man (cf. Acts 4:19; 5:29).

It became obvious to Pharaoh that this plan for extermination was not working, and the midwives were called in. They indicated that the situation among the Hebrew women was of such a nature that they could not control it. The Egyptian women

---

[15]*From the Stone Age to Christianity* (Garden City, N.Y.: Doubleday & Co., 2nd edition with a new introduction, 1957), pp. 13-14.

[16]W. F. Albright, "Northwest Semitic Names in a List of Egyptian Slaves from the Eighteenth Century B.C.," *Journal of the American Oriental Society,* LXXIV (1954), pp. 222-232.

[17]*Ibid.*

[18]Adolph Erman, *Literature of the Ancient Egyptians* (1927), pp. 44-45, quoted by K. A. Kitchen, "Midwife," *The New Bible Dictionary,* p. 821.

needed the care of the midwife to a greater degree than the Hebrew women who were "lively" and capable of delivery without the aid of the midwife. Because of their faith, God blessed the midwives with families of their own and, in addition, the people of Israel continued to grow and become mighty (vv. 20-21). The frustration and anger of Pharaoh is very vividly expressed in verse 22 when he demanded all the people of Egypt to participate in the extermination of male children born to the Hebrews. His rage and fear are reminiscent of that expressed by Nebuchadnezzar who is described as being "full of fury" (Dan. 3:19) over the insubordination of those who were faithful to God. The Pharaoh of verse 22, as in previous passages, is not identified. It is possible, however, that by this time he would be identified as Thutmose I (1528-1508 B.C.).

## II. The Birth of a Deliverer (2:1-25)

The birth of Moses was for Israel a most important event, although not recognized as such when it occurred. Since Moses was eighty years old at the time of the exodus in 1445 (7:7), his birth date would have been in 1525 B.C. Moses was not the first child in the family, however. Preceding him was his older sister, Miriam (v. 4), and Aaron who was three years older than he (7:7). The expression "a daughter of Levi" must refer to a descendant of Levi rather than daughter in the literal sense (cf. Exod. 6:20; Num. 26:59).

Because of the decree of Pharaoh, mentioned in 1:22, Moses' mother had to conceal him for three months until finally the pressure became too great, and she could no longer hide him (v. 3). The child is described in verse 2 as being "beautiful" (cf. Acts 7:20). The faith of Moses' parents and their fearlessness are alluded to in Hebrews 11:23. The hiding place selected for him was along one of the tributaries of the Nile River where his mother prepared for him an "ark" of "bulrushes" (v. 3). Both the word for ark (Heb. *tēḇāh*) and the word for bulrushes (Heb. *gome'*) are Egyptian terms, the first coming from the Egyptian *tebet.* It is used only here and in Genesis 6 and 7 with reference to the ark of Noah. The word for bulrushes is probably derived from the Egyptian *qama,* which designated the papyrus plant. This box-like container was covered with "slime," the same word used in Genesis 11:3 for "asphalt" or "bitumen." The ark was placed among the "flags" (Heb. *sûp* – "reeds"). In all probability the reeds here were papyrus plants. His sister Miriam was left to care for the child after his mother left (v. 4). What looked like a potentially disastrous situation turned out, under the providence of God, to be the means by which God could prepare Moses for the great challenge which was ahead. The tragic events brought about by Pharaoh and the resulting good which was accomplished are reminiscent of the words of Joseph in Genesis 50:20: "Ye thought evil . . . God meant it unto good."

The ark was spotted by the daughter of Pharaoh who had come down to the river along with the maidens to wash herself (v. 5). The identity of this daughter of Pharaoh is subject to speculation. If Thutmose I were the Pharaoh of 1:22 then his daughter, the famous Queen Hatshepsut who later assumed kingship, may have been this daughter. This view has been suggested by a number of writers.[19] While this view is entirely possible, it is equally possible that Moses was reared in one of the royal *harims* which were common to the New Kingdom period.

> Modern knowledge of ancient Egypt yields a rich background for the early life of Moses in Egypt. The pharaohs of the New Kingdom period (c. 1570-1085 B.C.) maintained residences and *harim* not only in the great capitals of Thebes, Memphis, and Pi-Ramesse (Ra' amses) but also in other parts of Egypt, especially in pleasure resorts. . . . Papyrus documents indicate that this *Harim* was no prison of enforced idleness for its inmates in pharaohs absence; the royal ladies supervised a hive of domestic industry, spinning and weaving done by servants (Gardiner, *J.N.E.S.*, XII, 1953, pp. 145-149, especially p. 149). . . . Anciently, children of *harim*-ladies could be educated by the Overseer of the *harim*. . . . In due course princes were given a tutor, usually a high official at court or a retired military officer close to the king. . . .[20]

When Pharaoh's daughter saw the box-shaped ark, she opened it, saw the child, and had compassion on him (v. 6). Arrangement was made for the child to have a nurse of the Hebrew

---

[19]Merrill F. Unger, *op. cit.*, pp. 144-145; Joseph P. Free, *Archaeology and Bible History* (Wheaton: Van Kampen Press, 1950), p. 86, n. 9; and Francis D. Nichol, ed., *The Seventh-Day Adventist Bible Commentary* (Washington, D.C.: Review and Herald Publishing Assoc., 1953), I p. 502.

[20]K. A. Kitchen, "Moses," *op. cit.*, p. 844.

Temple of Queen Hatshepsut at Deir el-Bahri.

J. J. Davis

women, which providentially turned out to be the mother of Moses (vv. 7-8). After the child grew, which is interpreted by some to mean the weaning period of about two or three years,[21] or perhaps as much as twelve years,[22] he was brought back to Pharaoh's daughter to receive the full training as one who was a member of the royal household. The description of this is found in verse 10: "he became her son." It would appear that there is a contradiction between the statement given here and that which appears in Hebrews 11:24 where it is stated that he "refused to be called the son of Pharaoh's daughter." The verse at hand merely indicated the fact that he had rejoined the royal court and having done this was in a position to receive all the privileges and opportunities of a member of that court. The refusal of Moses may have been an official position taken by him in later life when he had to choose between a career in Egypt or a concern for his own people. It is possible that even as a lad he may have refused some of the privileges of a member of the royal court, especially when those privileges violated his own spiritual conscience.

The name given to Moses was *mōšeh.* The explanation for the name is given in verse 10 as being "Because I drew him out of the water." Considerable debate has revolved around the antecedent of the pronoun "she" in verse 10. Who is it that gave Moses his name? And was that name a Hebrew or an Egyptian name? Many feel that the name was quite clearly Egyptian though the form in which we know it today is Hebrew.[23] K. A. Kitchen, on the other hand, feels that the name is most likely Hebrew and was given to Moses by his mother.[24] He argues that the pun found in verse 10 dealing with the meaning of the name would come naturally to a Hebrew speaker but not to an Egyptian. Those who hold that the daughter of Pharaoh gave an Egyptian name to Moses would point out that the name "Moses" may have been a longer name in the light of the common practices of

---

[21]C. F. Keil and F. Delitzsch, *The Pentateuch, Biblical Commentary on the Old Testament* (Grand Rapids: Wm. B. Eerdmans Publishing Co., 1949), I, p. 429.

[22]Francis D. Nichol, *op. cit.*, p. 503.

[23]*Ibid.*, p. 504.

[24]"Moses," *op. cit.*, p. 843.

that period (e.g., Ahmose, "the one born of [the moon-god] Ah"; Kamose, "the one born of the [deified soul] ka."). Moses may have had a longer Egyptian name such as *Hapmose* or *Irumose* meaning "the one born of the Nile." Thus in refusing to "be called the son of Pharaoh's daughter" Moses was actually refusing reference to an Egyptian deity.[25]

Between verses 10 and 11 there is probably a time gap of about forty years (cf. Acts 7:23). These forty years represented the period of Moses' training, which, according to Acts 7:22, exposed him to "all the wisdom of the Egyptians." The question might be asked, "What kind of boyhood did Moses actually have?" Fortunately, through archaeology and related studies, some light can be shed on this period of silence. Children were generally carefree and played much like children do today. They used sticks and stones and made objects of mud and bits of broken pottery. Among the more wealthy children, however, some toys were probably used. A few of these have survived. They are ". . . tops, miniature weapons, and several elaborate mechanical toys. One of these has a row of little dancing dwarfs on a platform; they are made to jog up and down by means of a string. An expensive toy, this one, for some nobleman's son – who probably left it lying in the dust after five minutes, and went back to his mud pies."[26] Swimming, horseback riding, hunting, playing with household pets would all be part of the experiences of a young boy in Egypt. Something is even known of the hair styles of the ancient Egyptians.

> The girls let their hair hang loose or braided it into pigtails, but boys had an unusual coiffure – the head was shaved except for one long lock on the side, which was braided. The distinctive side lock is known from the reliefs, and it was actually found on a mummy, that of a boy about eleven years old.[27]

As Moses grew older, however, he would become more and more involved in formal education which in Egypt included reading

---

[25]Francis D. Nichol, *op. cit.*, p. 504

[26]Barbara Mertz, *Red Land, Black Land* (New York: Dell Publishing Co., 1966), p. 57.

[27]*Ibid.*, p. 63.

and writing of the hieroglyphic and hieratic scripts, the copying of text, instruction in writing letters and other formal documents. He would have learned such sports as archery and horseback riding which were favorite pastimes of a number of the Pharaohs of the Eighteenth Dynasty.[28] He probably had opportunity to learn something of the languages of Canaan, for some Egyptian officials were capable of speaking these languages as well as knowing the geography of that land.[29] The discovery of "proto-Sinaitic" inscriptions from the early fifteenth century B.C. indicate that Semitic captives used by the Egyptians to work the turquoise mines of the Delta Region knew not only the languages of Canaan but had developed some type of script.[30] This information not only gives us a better perspective on the boyhood of Moses but makes his authorship of the Pentateuch all the more credible. From a theological point of view, we see in these passages a remarkable example of the excellency of the providence of God as all things are worked out in accordance with His will (Rom. 8:28).

When Moses had reached the age of 40 years, he had a crucial decision to make – whether to become an Egyptian without reservation or to join his people. According to Hebrews 11:25 he decided to "suffer affliction with the people of God" and presumably he knew something of his responsibility as a deliverer even at that stage in his life (cf. Acts 7:23-25). The slaying of the Egyptian (v. 12) was an important turning point in his life. While his deed cannot be condoned, it certainly expressed his deep love for the people of God, and was, in effect, an outward expression of his righteous indignation for the plight of those people. The decision made here not only reflected his deep love for the people of Israel but it also indicated a complete rejection of the pleasures which Egypt had to offer. Moses "esteemed the reproach of Christ greater riches than the treasures in Egypt . . ." (Heb. 11:26). This decision has been illuminated by

---

[28]See *ANET*, "Pharaoh as a Sportsman," trans. by John A. Wilson, pp. 243-245.

[29]See *ANET*, "A Satirical Letter," trans. by John A. Wilson, p. 477.

[30]W. F. Albright, "The Early Alphabetic Inscriptions from Sinai and Their Decipherment," *Bulletin of the American Schools of Oriental Research,* No. 110 (1948), pp. 12, 13, 22.

Carter's discovery of the tomb of Tutankhamun which produced some of the greatest treasures ever discovered in ancient Egypt.

While the intentions of Moses may have been good, the specific act was ill-advised at this time since his own people had not been assured of his leadership (cf. v. 14). Word of this deed reached the ears of Pharaoh who immediately took steps to slay Moses (v. 15). This Pharaoh, in all probability, is to be identified with Pharaoh of the oppression (v. 23); that is, Thutmose III (1483-1450 B.C.). Because of Pharaoh's anger, Moses was forced to leave the land of Egypt and flee eastward to the land of Midian (v. 15). Such an escape was not unusual, for it was employed by Sinuhe about 400 years earlier,[31] and by run-away slaves later in the thirteenth century B.C.[32] While in the land of Midian, Moses had the opportunity to help the daughters of a Midianite priest. Later he married one of them, Zipporah, who bore him a son named Gershom (vv. 21-22). The long years in the desert were not wasted years but times of further maturity and reflection in the things of God (cf. Acts 7:29 ff.). Moses needed the discipline of physical toil and the lessons this kind of occupation conveys.

God was preparing Moses to be a leader of men, so for forty years he received experience by leading the flocks of the Midianite priest. The people with whom he stayed were not complete aliens however, for the Midianites were descendants of Abraham by Keturah (Gen. 25:1-2) and may have remained to some extent worshippers of the true God. The man with whom he stayed (Reuel) may have been a priest of the true God (cf. 18:12-23). The identity of this "priest of Midian" is referred to a number of ways in Scripture. In verse 18 he is named Reuel (cf. Num. 10:20). Later he is given the name Jethro (3:1; 18:1), and Raguel (Num. 10:29). At one place he is identified as a Midianite (Exod. 18:1). Later, however, he is associated with the Kenites (Judg. 1:16).[33]

---

[31]*ANET*, "The Story of Si-Nuhe," trans. by John A. Wilson, p. 19.

[32]*ANET*, "The Pursuit of Runaway Slaves," trans. by John A. Wilson, p. 259.

[33]For a full discussion of this problem see James Crichton, "Jethro," *The International Standard Bible Encyclopedia*, James Orr, ed. (Grand Rapids: Wm. B. Eerdmans Publishing Co., 1939), III, pp. 1674-1675.

At the end of the forty years (Acts 7:30), the king of Egypt died. Presumably this describes the death of Thutmose III who oppressed Israel so severely. With the death of this king Moses was then able to return to the land of Egypt and resume fellowship with his own people. The chapter concludes with reflections upon God's deep concern for His people. Nearing the conclusion of over 400 years of subjugation, humiliation and frustration, the Lord now begins to initiate the plan of redemption and freedom for His covenant people.

J. J. Davis

Pylon gateway at Amun, Karnak erected by Thutmose III.

Chapter 3

# *The Call of Moses*

(Exodus 3–6)

Because of the completeness of the historical profile of Moses, we are able to achieve a rather full understanding of both the man and his mission. Not only are his heroic acts part of the biblical record, but his weaknesses and failures are also clearly revealed. In the first two chapters of Exodus two themes emerge: the plight of the children of Israel in Chapter 1 and the preparation of the deliverer in Chapter 2.

For forty years Moses had enjoyed the privileges and prestige of a prince in Egypt. Participation in certain royal processions and enjoyment of entertainment would have been a normal part of his daily experience. The time had come, however, when one of the biggest decisions of his life had to be made and that related to identification. Should he remain in the royal court and enjoy all the luxuries afforded him there or cast his lot with the people of God? The poverty and daily humiliation of his own people was something that he could not ignore. Perhaps the godly influence of his mother in those early years of his life began to weigh heavy upon his conscience. Whatever the influencing factor, Moses, by faith, turned his back on the opportunities and riches that could have been his and joined the Hebrews (cf. Heb. 11:24, 26).

His zeal and enthusiasm for his people, however, led him to act rashly and to murder an Egyptian. Rather than endearing him to his own people, this event created misunderstanding and bad will (cf. Exod. 2:14). Furthermore, the wrath of Pharaoh was kindled against him, thus necessitating his flight to Midian (Exod. 2:15). While the immediate reaction to this turn of events must have been disappointment and frustration, Moses, in later years, probably realized that all this was practical preparation for leadership. By virtue of the fact that he was a prince in the royal court, he had learned to read and write, but now as a refugee he would learn the ways of spiritual and intellectual maturity.

After forty years (Acts 7:29-30), Moses was finally able to return to Egypt. The question that must have loomed large in his mind was, what could a man of eighty do for his people now? The answer to this question was to come from God Himself and in a most unusual way.

## I. The Call of Moses (3:1—4:17)

### A. *The Burning Bush* (3:1-6)

Compared to all the privileges enjoyed in the royal court, life in the desert must have been lonely and, at times, very depressing. For forty years in Egypt he had learned the skills of the educated man. In the desert for forty years he was taught the qualities of spiritual leadership: patience, maturity, and sensitivity to the divine will. In 3:1 Moses is described as leading the flock of his father-in-law, Jethro, to the west side of the desert to Horeb. Later on he would have the great privilege of leading not a flock of sheep to this mountain, but the flock of God, and there receive one of the greatest revelations ever given.

Horeb and Sinai are two names for the same mountain (cf. Exod. 19:11; Deut. 4:10). Mount Horeb has been traditionally identified with one of the larger mountain peaks in the south-central part of Sinai called Jebel Musa, "the mountain of Moses." This mountain is 7,632 feet high and rises some 5,000 feet above the surrounding valleys. However, many scholars feel that the neighboring mountain peak, Ras es-Safsaf, is a better candidate for Mount Horeb. This mountain stands 6,640 feet high and is easily viewed from the desert of Sinai.[1] In view of the fact that Horeb is called "the mountain of God," it seems apparent that this material, along with the associated narratives, was written at a later period in Israel's journeys. Some have suggested, however, that this mountain was a sacred mountain even prior to the call of Moses.[2]

The special call of Moses to the task of leadership came by

---

[1]Francis D. Nichol, *op. cit.*, p. 509.

[2]See discussion in John P. Lange, "Exodus," *Commentary on the Holy Scriptures*, trans. by C. M. Mead (Grand Rapids: Zondervan Publishing House, 1960), p. 9.

means of "the angel of the Lord" (v. 2), which, in fact, was an appearance of the Lord himself, the second Person of the Godhead. The manner in which the angel of the Lord appeared to him was quite unique. This was accomplished ". . . in a flame of fire out of the midst of a bush." Some modern interpreters have attempted to explain this experience as something purely subjective and visionary. Honeycutt suggests that:

> Such a revelation, however, may well have been mediated through a visionary experience. The visionary experience would likely have assumed its descriptive character from the cultural ideas common to the era in which Moses lived. For Moses, the bush burned with the flaming presence of the angel of the Lord. But it may well have been an inner experience, and one standing next to Moses may have seen nothing extraordinary.[3]

Such a viewpoint, however, seems both unnecessary and unnatural to the language of the context. Nowhere is it specifically stated that this was a vision. Such a concept is capable of expression as exemplified in Genesis 15:1 where the word of the Lord came to Abram in "a vision" (Heb. *bammaḥ*$^{a}$*zeh*). The phenomenon of the burning bush is something which has been subjected to considerable discussion because of its obvious uniqueness. Various attempts have been made to provide a rational or scientific explanation. Werner Keller, quoting Harold N. Moldenke, records the following explanation:

> . . . among the commentators who think that a natural explanation can be found, some think that the phenomenon of the bush that "burned with fire" and yet "was not consumed" can be explained as a variety of the gas plant or *Fraxinella*, the *Dictamnus Albus L.* This is a plant with a strong growth about three feet in height with clusters of purple blossoms. The whole bush is covered with tiny oil glands. This oil is so volatile that it is constantly escaping and if approached with a naked light bursts suddenly into flames. . . .[4]

---

[3]Roy L. Honeycutt, Jr., "Exodus," *The Broadman Bible Commentary*, Clifton J. Allen, ed. (Nashville: Broadman Press, 1969), p. 328.

[4]*The Bible as History* (New York: William Morrow and Co., 1956), p. 131.

Another writer attempts to explain the flames on different grounds:

> The flames may have been the crimson blossoms of mistletoe twigs (*Loranthus Acaciae*) which grow on various prickly Acacia bushes and Acacia trees throughout the Holy Land and in Sinai. When this mistletoe is in full bloom, the bush becomes a mass of brilliant flaming color and looks as if it is on fire.[5]

This explanation characterizes many which are found in both older and more recent commentaries. Many cite various kinds of berries, angles of sunlight, or the appearance of "golden sunlight on colorful leaves"[6] as being that which created the illusion of a burning bush. The most bizarre of the interpretations found thus far by this author is as follows:

> Electrical energy of an extremely high voltage would readily produce the phenomenon which Moses witnessed as fire burning in the bush without consuming it. This does not detract one iota from this miracle; but it demonstrates that the presence of the angel of the Lord was accompanied by electrical phenomena surrounding deity.[7]

It is the view of this writer that the above explanations are both unnecessary and do not really complement the meaning of the biblical text. Such events are clearly described as being unusual and supernatural. The particular method which God may or may not have used is of little or no importance to the meaning of the text. What is clear is that Moses saw a bush; it was on fire, but it did not burn. The event must have been something out of the ordinary, for Moses turned aside to examine this more closely (v. 3). If it were merely berries or leaves, such would not have attracted his attention. Several years ago this writer was most amused and amazed at being shown, in one "holy place," some of the "original ashes" from Moses' burning bush!

---

[5]Smith, quoted by Werner Keller, *ibid.*, p. 131.

[6]Carl S. Knopf, *The Old Testament Speaks* (New York: Thomas Nelson and Sons, 1933), p. 83.

[7]Howard B. Rand, *Primogenesis* (Haverhill, Mass.; Destiny Publishers, 1953), p. 142.

From this burning bush the angel of the Lord spoke to Moses in a voice which he heard clearly and to which he responded (v. 4). The command was not to draw near that place, but to remove his sandals because he stood on holy ground (v. 5). The event here is reminiscent of that which Joshua experienced approximately forty years later (cf. Josh. 5:15).[8] The identity of this visitor was made clear in the words that are recorded in verse 6. Moses recognized the fact that he was in the presence of deity and feared to look upon the face of God (cf. Exod. 33:20; Judg. 6:22-23; 13:22).[9]

B. *Moses' Commission* (3:7-12)

The revelation of God in this portion is instructive and theologically important. We are immediately reminded that this was, in fact, a self-revelation of God to Moses. We do not have record here of a long search on the basis of a trial and error method in which Moses "discovered" theological truth. The holiness of God is emphasized (v. 5). While He is a God of power and transcendent glory, He is also immanent and therefore the God of history (v. 6). The section presently under consideration reveals additional information concerning the One who was challenging Moses. According to verse 7 He was a God sensitive and aware of the deep need of His people. He was a merciful God. He had *seen* their affliction and *heard* their cry and *knew* their sorrows, and the means by which God would care for the tragedy of His people would be to "come down" to deliver them out of the hand of the Egyptians (v. 8). The description here is that of a God who acts not above history, but in and through history. This expression was fully understood by the ancient

---

[8]The explanation given for the removal of Moses' shoes by Howard Rand is: "It would have been very dangerous for Moses to have approached this bush while his shoes insulated him from the ground. The removal of his shoes 'grounded' his body and prevented high inductive currents, generated by the presence of the Glory of the Lord in the bush, from harming him." *Op. cit.*, p. 142.

[9]For an excellent study on this whole subject see E. J. Young, "The Call of Moses," *Westminster Theological Journal*, XXIX, No. 2, (1967), pp. 117-135 and XXX, No. 1, (1967), pp. 1-23. See also R. C. Foster, "The Choice of Moses," *The Seminary Review*, X, No. 1 (1963), pp. 1-10.

Hebrews as meaning the immanent expression and working of God's power.

The specific nature of Moses' call is revealed in verse 10. His primary responsibility was to appear before Pharaoh in order that the people of Israel might be freed from Egyptian bondage. The implications of this responsibility were immediately clear to Moses. He knew well the power and the fury of the arrogant Pharaoh. Such a demand would indeed place him in a most precarious position. The confident, impulsive Moses of many years ago now bowed in humility and in reticence before the challenge from God. His reaction is reminiscent of that of Jeremiah: "Ah, Lord God! Behold, I cannot speak; for I am a child" (Jer. 1:6). The response of Moses in verse 11 represents the first of five occasions in which he attempted to demonstrate sufficient weakness so as not to be responsible for the call which God had given to him (cf. 3:13; 4:1, 10, 13). It is interesting and instructive that God did not attempt to debate the issue, but merely reminded Moses that he was a child of God and as such had the presence of the Lord which made him all he needed to be to meet this challenge (v. 12).

### C. *The Name of God* (3:13-14)

The second difficulty faced by Moses is expressed in verse 13 when he would be asked, "What is his name? what shall I say unto them?" Moses wanted to know upon what authority his call should rest. How should he validate that call before the people of Israel? God then identified himself as "I AM THAT I AM" (v. 14). Moses was commanded to tell the people of Israel that "I AM" had sent him unto them. The key expression in verse 14 is "I am that I am" (Heb. *'ehyeh 'ašer 'ehyeh*). The verb *'ehyeh*, as pointed in the Masoretic text, is considered a Qal imperfect first person singular of the root *hāyāh* (*hwh* – "to be, become"). This clause is extremely important because the verb forms reveal the essential idea of the tetragrammaton *yhwh* commonly translated "Jehovah" in English versions. The Hebrew word *yhwh* is, in fact, the third person form of the root *hāyāh* (*hwh*). If the simple Qal sense is maintained, it carries the fundamental idea of the self-existence of God, and simply means "I am the One who is." This has long been the view of most conservative scholars.[10] This interpretation is supported by the rendering of the Septuagint which reads *egō e'imi o' ōn.*

On the other hand, there is a large group of scholars who regard the stem of the tetragrammaton *yhwh* as being the Hif'il rather than the Qal. This, of course, gives to the name a causative sense and would be translated as "He who causes to be" rather than "He who is." This viewpoint is perhaps best expressed by David N. Freedman who considers the whole subject to revolve around four basic assumptions:

> (1) that the tetragrammaton was pronounced *yahweh;* (2) that it is a verb derived from the root **hwy* **hwh,* which in accordance with recognized linguistic laws appears in Biblical Hebrew as *hyh;* (3) that it is a Hifil imperfect third masculine singular form of the verb; and (4) that it is to be translated, "He causes to be, brings into existence; He brings to pass, He creates."[11]

From the standpoint of grammatical possibility alone, it is entirely possible that this form could be a Hif'il; however, on the basis of the explanation given in Exodus 3:14 along with the Septuagint reading and the New Testament interpretation using the same Greek form (cf. Matt. 22:32; Mark 12:26; John 8:58), the simple Qal meaning "to be" is preferable. The usual objection to this approach is that such a concept of self-being or self-existence was too advanced for the "primitive theological mentality" of the Israelites during that period. Such an objection, however, is the product of an evolutionary view of Israel's religion and such a view must be abandoned in the light of archaeology and an enlightened understanding of Old Testament revelation.

---

[10]See discussion on this in C. F. Keil and F. Delitzsch, *op. cit.*, pp. 74-76.

[11]"The Name of the God of Moses," *Journal of Biblical Literature,* LXXIX, (1960), p. 152. See Also W. F. Albright, "The Name Yahweh," *Journal of Biblical Literature*, XLIII (1924), pp. 370-378. See also William R. Arnold, "The Divine Name in Exodus 3:14," *Journal of Biblical Literature,* XXIV (1905), pp. 107-165; S. Mowinckel, "The Name of the God of Moses," *Hebrew Union College Annual,* XXXII (1961), pp. 121-133.

D. *A Message of Deliverance* (3:15-22)

In the verses that conclude Chapter 3, we have a record of an expansion of God's call to Moses and an explanation not only of the character of the God who gave the call, but some indication of how God brought about the deliverance of His people. Moses was again reminded that the God to whom he was speaking was the same God that cared for Abraham, Isaac and Jacob (v. 15). The practical aspects of God's plan are revealed in verses 16 ff. Moses was to go and gather the elders of Israel together and inform them of the message he had received. Having gained national acceptance, Moses then would approach Pharaoh and present his demand, which in essence is given in verse 18. He was reminded of the fact that his message would not be received positively (v. 19). The Lord would respond to Pharaoh's resistance by producing "wonders" (v. 20) which would bring about a change in Pharaoh's attitude. Not only would Pharaoh change, but the peoples of Egypt would also change; in fact, so much so, that when the children of Israel left, they would "not go empty" (v. 21). Every woman would be able to borrow ("ask" – Heb. *šā'āl*, cf. Gen. 15:14; Exod. 12:35). What is of interest in verse 22 is not what was asked for (jewels of silver, gold and raiment), but what they did *not* ask for. No mention is made of food, weapons and armor, cattle, etc. (cf. 11:2 ff.; 12:35 ff.; Ps. 105:37). In a certain sense such objects were a small compensation for the 400 years of slavery and humiliation.[12]

E. *Doubts of the Deliverer* (4:1-17)

The essence of Moses' third objection is expressed in verse 1 and simply was that he feared the people would not listen to his voice or would perhaps deny that the Lord had actually appeared to him in special revelation. He probably feared that his brothers would not even remember him after such a long absense. In answer to his problem the Lord gave him three signs.[13]

---

[12]For a defense of the translation "borrow" in v. 22 see Julian Morgenstern, "The Despoiling of the Egyptians," *Journal of Biblical Literature,* LXVIII (1949), pp. 1-28. Also see George W. Coates, "Despoiling the Egyptians," *Vetus Testamentum,* XVIII, No. 4 (1968), pp. 450-457.

[13]Cf. Gideon, Judges 6:17-22, 36-40.

Metropolitan Museum of Art

Egyptian bronze mirror.

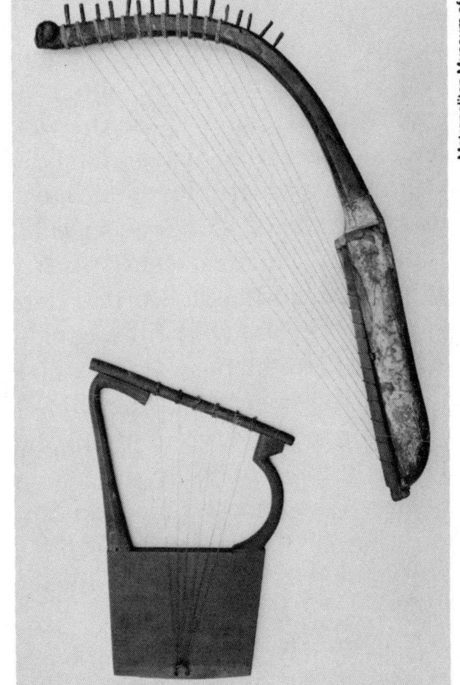

Metropolitan Museum of Art

Egyptian musical instruments. The lyre is made of wood and has bronze staples. The harp is from the XVIII to XIX Dynasty.

The first sign involved the changing of his rod (shepherd's staff?) into a serpent and then back to a rod again (vv. 2-5). That this was a genuine miracle and something out of the ordinary is evidenced in the fact that "Moses fled from it," indicating that he was surprised at the occurrence. The second sign (vv. 6-8) involved the infliction of his hand with leprosy and its immediate healing. The form of leprosy described was considered by the Greeks as *leuke* "the white disease." The third sign consisted of the gift of being able to turn the water of the river to blood (v. 9).

The fourth objection of Moses was that he did not possess the necessary "eloquence" to be effective in Pharaoh's court (v. 10). The Hebrew reads *lō' 'îš dᵉḇārîm 'ānōkî* – "I am not a man of words." Later in the verse he speaks of the fact that he was "slow of speech" and "slow of tongue." The Hebrew literally reads "heavy in mouth and heavy in tongue"; that is, he was not fluent in speech. The objections of Moses have generally been regarded as a superficial dodge from his responsibility; however, we do know from a famous Middle Kingdom document that eloquence in speech was not only a desirable quality, but was that which could bring about social justice and positive decision.[14] Moses knew well that any approach to the king would have to be done appropriately. However, his excuse was not entirely legitimate, for God had made provisions for him in the development of eloquent speech. For forty years he had been trained in the royal court, thus giving him the necessary skills to perform the task. Furthermore, the Lord reminded him that God the Creator was fully capable of meeting any inadequacies which he might possess (vv. 11-12). Apparently Moses did not find this answer satisfactory, and his fifth objection appeared in the form of a very brief but cutting statement, literally translated, "send, I pray, by the hand of the one you will send." The answer was almost rude and for the first time we have an expression of the anger of God (v. 14), for it now became apparent that Moses was not speaking out of weakness, but out of

---

[14]See *ANET*, "The Protests of the Eloquent Peasant," trans. by John A. Wilson, pp. 407-410.

a lack of obedience. The Lord provided Aaron, his brother, to help him in these areas (v. 14).

## II. A Challenge and a Crisis (4:18—5:23)

### A. *Moses' Return to Egypt* (4:18-31)

Moses, now fully assured of the call of God, returned to Jethro and requested permission to leave and return to Egypt (v. 18). Notice that he did not indicate the real object of his journey. Perhaps he feared that Jethro would refuse permission for his wife and his children to accompany him on such a dangerous venture, or maybe he wanted to prevent word of his movement preceding him to the land of Egypt. In any case, Jethro gave him his blessing. Moses was free to return to the land because "all the men are dead who sought thy life" (v. 19). He took his wife and his two sons (cf. 18:3-4). Gershom was the name of the one son mentioned in 2:22 and Eliezer was the name of the other son apparently born after his return to Jethro's home (cf. 2:22 which speaks of only one son born to him prior to the divine revelation at Horeb). It was further revealed to Moses that when he got to Egypt "wonders" would be performed before Pharaoh.

Also promised to Moses was the fact that God would "harden" Pharaoh's heart in order that he would not let the people go (v. 21). This has been a great problem to many commentators because it gives that appearance of the kind of sovereign action which prevents the operation of free human choice. The passage properly studied, however, is made clear – both in its Old Testament context and relationship to New Testament doctrine of God's elective purposes. Three different Hebrew words are used to describe this condition attributed to Pharaoh. The first is the verb *kāḇēḏ* which has the idea "to be heavy, insensible, or dull,"[15] and is used in 7:14; 8:15, 32; and 9:7, 34. The next word used is *qāšāh* which conveys the sense of "being hard, severe, or fierce." In the Hif'il stem it has the sense of "making

[15]Francis Brown, S. R. Driver and Charles Briggs, *A Hebrew and English Lexicon of the Old Testament* (Oxford: The Clarendon Press, Corrected Impression, 1952), p. 457.

difficult."[16] There are two occurrences of this term, one in 7:3 and the other in 13:15. The final term used is *ḥāzaq* which is one of the strongest terms employed, meaning "to be or grow firm, strong." In reference to its use in this context, it has the sense of "growing stout, rigid, or hard."[17] Two things should be observed in connection with this problem. One is that Pharaoh hardened his own heart and resisted the demands of God. This is clearly indicated in a number of the passages (cf. 7:13, 14, 22; 8:15, 19, 32; 9:7, 34-35; 13:15). He refused to acknowledge the power of Jehovah the God of Israel and, at times, did not even listen to the statements of the magicians themselves (cf. 8:19). There is a sense, therefore, in which Pharaoh blinded himself and in so doing incurred the wrath and judgment of God. On the other hand, it is clearly stated that God hardened Pharaoh's heart (cf. 4:21; 7:3; 9:12; 10:1, 20, 27; 11:10; 14:4, 8, 17). This act of God should be considered judicial and real. While it is true that God desires all men to repent and be saved (cf. Ezek. 33:11; I Tim. 2:4; II Peter 3:9), it is equally true that God reserves the right to judge sin and the sinner whenever He desires. The sinner is subject to the wrath of God at any point in his life. The fact of the matter is, God has the right to judge sin in any way He so desires the first time one commits a sin. It is really the mercy of God that allows the sinner to continue to live. That Pharaoh was part of a divine plan for the exodus is made clear by the Apostle Paul in Romans 9:17-18. The hardening of men's hearts who have resisted His will is one way that God judges men. Furthermore, it was also a way that God accomplished His purposes for the people of Israel. This is not only witnessed in the accounts of the exodus, but is quite clearly demonstrated in Joshua's victories over the enemies that inhabited Canaan (cf. Josh. 11:20). Joshua states that ". . . it was of the Lord to harden their hearts, that they should come against Israel in battle, that he might destroy them utterly. . . ." The Hebrew word for "harden" is *ḥāzaq*, the same term that is used in a number of the passages in the Exodus account. It must always be remembered that God reserves the right to judge sin

---

[16]*Ibid.*, p. 904.
[17]*Ibid.*, p. 304.

in any way that He sees fit. If this expression of God's holiness is not allowed, then the Bible student is in serious difficulty with a whole host of passages in the Old Testament which describe the destruction of peoples quite apart from their "natural" death.[18]

The particular demand that Moses was to bring to Pharaoh is again repeated in verses 22 and 23. The mention of Israel as Jehovah's "firstborn" is significant in this larger context. The first-born son was to the Egyptians not only special, but in many respects sacred. It is therefore most interesting that the people of God are regarded as firstborn in this passage (cf. Hos. 11:1).

As Moses continued his journey to Egypt, he was met by the Lord (v. 24). The Septuagint version of this verse reads, "the angel of the Lord," but the Masoretic text appears preferable at this point. His life was in danger because he had apparently neglected the rite of circumcision. This was performed by his wife Zipporah who used a sharp stone (cf. Josh. 5:2) but with great dissatisfaction, charging that Moses was a "bloody husband" (v. 25). It is generally the view of commentators that these words were an expression of reproach and unhappiness. They reflect the fact that Zipporah performed the rite grudgingly, not from a desire to obey the God of Moses, but primarily out of practical necessity to save his life.[19] Perhaps Moses had neglected this rite in order to accommodate the wishes of Zipporah. In any event, he was punished by God and was apparently desperately sick.

Among liberal commentators this event is interpreted quite differently. Many (e.g., Wellhausen) see in this marriage rite for the purpose of identification with a clan.[20] Other scholars have maintained that Moses was not circumcised prior to this time and see a close connection between circumcision and marriage. This view is based on some ethnological evidence from Africa and southwestern Asia. Noth, therefore, is tempted to think of the appearance of the son on the scene as a later ac-

---

[18]For further discussion of this problem see Keil and Delitzsch, *op. cit.*, pp. 453-457.

[19]Francis D. Nichol, *op. cit.*, p. 517.

[20]See Julian Morgenstern, "The 'Bloody Husband' (?) (Ex. 4:24-26) Once Again," *Hebrew Union College Annual*, XXXIV (1963), p. 66.

cretion and that, originally, the story dealt with Moses and Zipporah only.[21] Still others have suggested that the translation should not be "bloody husband" but "bloody bridegroom," a view originated by Eduard Meyer and followed by Georg Beer and Elias Auerbach.[22] According to this view the bridegroom becomes bloody in the night when he goes in to his bride. The deity then contended with Moses and was therefore about to kill him. To satisfy the wrath of God, Zipporah circumcised her son and put the blood on the private part of Moses to make the deity believe that it came from Zipporah. The question that should be asked regarding a view like this is, could the gods (of any kind) be so naive? After all, she already had one son. Can the gods be so easily cheated? This view hardly does anything to clarify the text.[23]

Once the child had been circumcised, God let Moses go (v. 26); that is, God healed him. It was probably at this time Zipporah and her two boys were sent back to Jethro by Moses (cf. 18:2-3). Following Moses' recovery he met Aaron and the two of them joined the elders of Israel (vv. 27-29). Moses was then introduced as God's leader for Israel, and this introduction was accompanied by special signs to confirm the message of Aaron. The result was that the people believed their report (vv. 30-31).

### B. *A Meeting with the King* (5:1-14)

Once Moses and Aaron had been accepted as representatives of the nation of Israel, the stage was set for their encounter with the king of Egypt. Where exactly Moses and Aaron met the Pharaoh we are not told. Presumably, however, they met the king somewhere near the Delta region, a situation that would not be unlikely in the light of the frequent visits of Egyptian monarchs to that area during the Eighteenth Dynasty. If the early date of the exodus is correct, this king would be Amenhotep II. Those following the late date would suggest Rameses II as the Pharaoh

---

[21]Compare Hans Kosmala, "The Bloody Husband," *Vetus Testamentum*, XII (1962), pp. 14-28.

[22]*Ibid.*, p. 16.

[23]For another study on this problem see H. P. Smith, "Ethnological Parallels to Exodus 4:24-26," *Journal of Biblical Literature* (1906).

encountered. The scene before us is decidedly a dramatic one. Here two men over eighty years of age stand before one of the greatest kings of the ancient Near East at that time. The abundance of red granite and massive limestone columns delicately painted with hieroglyphs would make an impressive sight. The forty years of training that Moses had received was a preparation for just this kind of mission. The request of Moses was based on a revelation from the Lord God of Israel, and that request was to let the people go that they should hold a feast in the wilderness. Pharaoh's response to this was completely negative. In fact, he challenged the whole proposition by saying, "Who is Jehovah, that I should obey his voice to let Israel go?" (v. 2). It is doubtful that Pharaoh would be completely ignorant of the name of the God of the Israelites. More likely he refused to recognize that name, or the request brought in that name. It must be remembered that the king in Egypt was not considered a mere representative of the gods, but was a god himself. Pierre Montet observes:

> The king was certainly far above ordinary mortals. In official stelae he was often called *neter nefer,* the perfect god. A courtier even described him as *neter aa,* the great god.[24]

In spite of the fact that the request of Moses and Aaron was a moderate one and did not immediately reveal the full plan of God, this was refused. The refusal of Pharaoh, however, did not discourage Moses and Aaron at this point. They continued their plea for freedom to go three days' journey into the desert and sacrifice to their God (v. 3). They argued that if they did not, they themselves would be punished. The king, however, did not see this as a legitimate request for sacrifice, but, on the contrary, as a mere maneuver on the part of Moses and Aaron to get the people of Israel out of work. The king demanded that they should return to their burdens (v. 4). His observation that ". . . the people of the land are now many" (v. 5) is in agreement with the statement that appears in 1:9. Israel indeed had grown to considerable proportions. That the court which Moses and Aaron visited was very close to the area of Goshen is implied in

---

[24]*Eternal Egypt* (New York: The New American Library, 1964), p. 57.

the language of verse 6, for Pharaoh communicated "the same day" with the taskmasters of the people (cf. v. 10 and 12:31). Three different terms are used to describe the officials who superintended the work of the Hebrews: (1) "officers of the labor gangs" (Heb. *śārê missîm* – 1:11); (2) "taskmasters" (Heb. *hannōg̱ᵉśîm* – 5:6, 10, 13, 14); and (3) "officers (Heb. *šōṭᵉrîm* – "scribes," 5:14-15). The first two groups were undoubtedly native Egyptians, the most important being the "officers of the labor gangs." The taskmasters were their subordinates. A larger group, probably serving as intermediaries between the groups above and the peoples of Israel, were the "officers" who were probably Hebrews, judging from the kind of treatment which they received (cf. v. 14).

Pharaoh's primary concern in this whole matter was possible delay or a diminishing of the productivity of these slaves, either of which was unacceptable. It is quite clear from ancient Egyptian records that great concern was expressed over continued

Metropolitan Museum of Art

Painting of brickmaking.

idleness.[25] The answer to the request of Aaron and Moses came in the form of additional work in order that such idleness would no longer be perpetuated (v. 9). To compound the problem for the enslaved Israelites the officers commanded that straw, which was used commonly in brick making, would no longer be provided by the government. The people had to gather their own supplies. This probably resulted in many more people working and perhaps to a much harder degree. It also brought about a great scattering of the people in order to get the necessary materials (v. 12). Straw and stubble were commonly used in the Nineteenth and Twentieth Dynasties. The straw itself is not so much a binding agent, but its chemical decay in the clay released an acid which (like glutamic or gallotannic acid) gave the clay greater plasticity for brick making.[26] It should be pointed out here that Moses *did not* present the Hebrews as making bricks without straw as is sometimes stated. The decree of Pharaoh clearly instructed them to use straw, but the difference was that they were to gather that material themselves.[27]

### C. *The Appeal of the Israelites* (5:15-19)

The task of meeting brick quotas along with gathering the straw and stubble for the bricks became too much for the already weary Israelites. The officers over the work gangs came and made a formal plea to Pharaoh regarding his decree (v. 15). The result of that decree was not only the denial of straw for brick making, but also greater regimentation and discipline (v. 16). The emphatic accusation was: idleness! Despondently they had to return to the children of Israel and inform them that the decree would stand and the quotas would have to be met.

### D. *Crisis in the Camp* (5:20-23)

Shortly after these events, the same officers and probably representative elders of Israel met with Moses and Aaron. Their

---

[25]See K. A. Kitchen, "Moses," *op. cit.*, p. 846.

[26]K. A. Kitchen, "Brick," *op. cit.*, p. 168.

[27]See Charles F. Nims, "Bricks without Straw," *The Biblical Archaeologist,* XIII, No. 2 (1950), pp. 22-28.

reaction was something less than cordial. They used extremely strong language in raising questions about the propriety of the words of Moses and Aaron before Pharaoh and, in fact, raised serious questions about the authority of their position. Moses did not attempt to answer the charge of those who stood before him, but in the quietness of the hours that followed we are informed that he "returned unto the Lord" and brought his case before the One who had sent him. We should not regard the response of Moses to his God as being irreverent or insubordinate, but these were words of a searching heart and of one deeply perplexed by the turn of events. What is significant about all of this is that Moses did not surrender the cause to which God had called him.

## III. Comfort from God (6:1-30)

What could God do now to encourage His servant? The use of signs was effective to strengthen a faith that had not operated (cf. 4:1-9). Now, however, something needed to be done to strengthen the faith that had been frustrated. The Lord began by identifying himself as Jehovah (v. 2). The third verse of this chapter has long been problematic to interpreters. It states that the Lord had appeared to Abraham, Isaac and Jacob by the name of *'el šadday*, but by the name *yahweh* was He not made known to them. This verse has been the basis upon which liberal critics erected their documentary hypothesis; namely, that in the early patriarchal period the tribal name of God was *'ēl šadday*, but Moses was now about to reveal for the first time the name *yahweh* as the God of Israel.[28] It is generally argued that Moses got the name *yahweh* from the Kenites and Midianites with whom he had stayed for a long period of time.

> Yahweh, therefore, is the God of the tribe to which Moses, on his flight from Egypt, joined himself by marriage; the mountain God of Horeb, who appears to him and promises him to lead his brethren out of Egypt.[29]

---

[28]John E. McFadyen, *Introduction to the Old Testament* (London: Hodder and Stoughton, 1909), p. 22.

[29]Karl Budde, *Religion of Israel to the Exile* (New York: G. P. Putnam's Sons, 1899), p. 19.

A second interpretation of the verse suggests that it is, in fact, a question – not a statement. It is argued that Exodus 6:3 should read, "And I appeared unto Abraham, unto Isaac, and unto Jacob, as God Almighty; but by my name Jehovah was I not known to them?" This view is defended by both Thomas Scott[30] and Robert Jamieson.[31] The third view of the text (and that which is generally suggested by conservative commentators) is that this represents a special revelation of the name *yahweh,* not its first introduction. This view is perhaps best expressed by Henry Cowles:

> The meaning is, not that the name Jehovah was never used by them or given of God to them: but that its special significance had not been manifested to them as He was now about to make it manifest.[32]

This viewpoint appears to be the best interpretation of the verse in the light of both the previous Pentateuchal material and the immediate context of the verse itself.[33] The divine name *'el šadday* has been traced to several roots. Some have suggested that it comes from *šad* ("breasted one") and relate it to the concept of a provider or the God who sustains. A more likely root, however, is *šāḏaḏ* which has the sense of being "strong" or "powerful."[34] The name *šadday* appears about forty-eight times in the Old Testament. The majority of these texts support the concept of power and might.

Not only did God Almighty sustain an important relationship with Abraham, Isaac and Jacob, but He had made a covenant with them which included possession of the land of Canaan (v. 4, cf. Gen. 13:14-17; 15:13-16; 28:13; 46:1-4). The following

[30]*The Holy Bible Containing the Old and New Testaments* (Boston: Samuel T. Armstrong, 1830), I, p. 202.

[31]*Critical and Experimental Commentary* (Grand Rapids: Wm. B. Eerdmans Co., 1945), I, p. 292.

[32]*Butler's Bible-Work* (New York: Funk & Wagnalls, 1877), p. 598. See also Oswald T. Allis, *The Five Books of Moses,* pp. 26 ff. and Merrill F. Unger, *Introductory Guide to the Old Testament* (Grand Rapids: Zondervan Publishing House, n.d.), pp. 251 ff.

[33]For a full discussion and defense of this view see John J. Davis, "The Patriarchs' Knowledge of Jehovah," *Grace Journal,* IV, No. 1 (1963).

[34]Gustave F. Oehler, *Theology of the Old Testament* (Grand Rapids: Zondervan Publishing House, n.d.), p. 91.

words of Jehovah are an emphatic reminder that He had not forgotten that covenant (v. 5), but fully intended to carry it out and effect the redemption of Israel (v. 6). The redemptive events to follow would be the means by which God would reveal special aspects of His covenant name hitherto not fully known (cf. vv. 3, 7).

Chapter 6 of Exodus concludes with the genealogy of Moses. In this portion we are given important information as to the Levitical background of Moses. The Amram mentioned in verse 20 as the father of Moses was probably not the same person as the Amram who was the son of Kohath (v. 18), but must have been a later descendant. It has been pointed out, if Amram the son of Kohath and the tribe father of the Amramites was the same person as Amram the father of Moses, Moses must have had 2,147 brothers and brothers' sons. This is deduced from the fact that in Moses' time the Kohathites were divided into four branches (Amramites, Izharites, Hebronites and Uzzielites) who consisted together of 8,600 men and boys. If divided equally, a fourth, or 2,150 men, would belong to the Amramites.[35] Kitchen suggests that Exodus 6:16-20 gives the tribe (Levi), clan (Kohath) and family-group (Amram by Jochebed) to which Moses and Aaron belong, and not their actual parents.[36] The name Jochebed liberally means "Jehovah is glorious," and is identified as a daughter of Levi in Exodus 2:1 and Numbers 26:59.

The thread of historical narrative broken off at verse 13 is again resumed in verse 28 and continued through 7:7; therefore, 6:28-30 provide an important introduction to the material of Chapter 7. The verses again remind the reader that the essence of Moses' message and ministry is to be found in Jehovah himself and was not the result of religious self-discovery. With the encouragement of Jehovah and the promise of success, the first major encounter was about to occur. Pharaoh challenged the God of Israel and apparently was unwilling to accept the demand of Moses as previously presented. The hardness of his heart and the hardening of his heart by Jehovah worked to provide the means by which God displayed His awesome power both to Israel and to the Egyptians.

---

[35]Keil and Delitzsch, *op. cit.*, p. 470.

[36]K. A. Kitchen, *Ancient Orient and Old Testament,* p. 54.

## Chapter 4

# *River of Blood*

(Exodus 7)

One cannot help but be awed by the splendor of ancient Egyptian temples. Even though the remains of many merely represent the fragments of past glory, the crumbling ruins are a testimony to the splendor that Egypt once enjoyed. The multitude of shrines, inscriptions and religious objects are a constant reminder that in Egypt nothing was really secular. The voices that once chanted praises to the many Egyptian deities are now silent. The trees and plants which adorned the temple areas are now absent. The beautiful barges that once glamorized the Nile no longer float but only reside in museums in crumbled condition.

> There will come a time when it will be seen that in vain have the Egyptians honored the deity with heartfelt piety and assiduous service, and all our holy worship will be found bootless and ineffectual. . . . Oh Egypt, Egypt, of thy religion nothing will remain but an empty tale, which thine own children in time to come will not believe; nothing will be left but graven words, and only the stones will tell of thy piety.[1]

The myriad of statues that have been excavated in Egypt and now adorn museums throughout the world are a grim reminder of the futility of idolatry. The emptiness and bankruptcy of the ancient Egyptian religion is not only witnessed in the crumbled temples of the past, but in the living biblical record which records for us one of the most magnificent king-vassal encounters in all of ancient history. The events recorded in Exodus 7 were indelibly impressed upon the memory of the ancient Israelites. It gave them new perspectives concerning their own God and it created new and vital hope within the breast of this long oppressed and humiliated people.

### I. The Commission Renewed (7:1-7)

A. *Moses and Pharaoh* (7:1-2)

[1]Hermes Trismegistus, quoted by Barbara Mertz, *op. cit.*, p. 251.

The early part of Chapter 7 is, in effect, God's answer to Moses' objection recorded in 6:12, 30. On two occasions Moses made mention of the fact that he doubted he would be accepted before Israel, primarily because he was one of "uncircumcised lips." This idiom reflects the idea of "slow of speech" (cf. 4:10). Similar expressions appear elsewhere in the Old Testament, such as "uncircumcised" ears (Jer. 6:10) which are ears that do not hear. Another example is also found in Jeremiah 9:26 which speaks of an uncircumcised heart; that is, a heart which is hardened and does not understand. The essence of Moses' objection was that he could not appear effectively before Pharaoh a second time in the light of Pharaoh's wrath and his own personal incapabilities. This objection, however, was not acceptable because God would provide the necessary miracles to confirm the authority of His revelation. In effect, therefore, he would be to Pharaoh as "God" (Heb. *'ᵉlōhîm*, cf. 4:16).[2] Moses' spokesman before Pharaoh was designated as his brother Aaron who would be his prophet (Heb. *nᵉḇî'eḵā*). The source of Moses' message was God himself, which is what gave that message its full authority (v. 2).

B. *God and Pharaoh* (7:3-7)

The means by which God would accomplish His purpose for His people would be to harden the heart of Pharaoh (cf. 4:21), thus leading to the exhibition of His power through "signs" (Heb. *'ōṯōṯ*, v. 3, "wonders" (Heb. *môpᵉtîm*, v. 3, cf. 11:9) and "great judgments" (Heb. *šᵉpāṭîm gᵉḏōlîm*, v. 4). By this means the Lord could bring forth His people out of the land of Egypt. In verse 4 they are spoken of as coming out as "armies." This word is used of Israel, with reference to its leaving Egypt equipped (13:18) and organized as an army according to the tribes (cf. 6:26; 12:51 with Num. 1 and 2) to contend for the cause of the Lord, and fight the battles of Jehovah.[3] The amazing feature of this account is the age of the two men who would carry Israel's cause to Pharaoh. Moses was eighty years old and Aaron eighty-

---

[2]It is possible that *'ᵉlōhîm* is here used in the sense of "judge" cf. Exod. 21:6; 22:8, 9; Ps. 82:6).

[3]Keil and Delitzsch, *op. cit.*, p. 472.

three years old (v. 7). This information is confirmed by the statement that Moses was 120 years old at the time of his death (Deut. 31:2; 34:7) which occurred forty years after the exodus (Deut. 29:5). Aaron was 123 years old at death (Num 33:38-39).

## II. Rods and Serpents (7:8-13)

It was rather apparent that Moses and Aaron could not appear before Pharaoh merely to repeat the previous request. This time their demands would be accompanied by a confirmatory sign called a "miracle" (Heb. *mōpēt*; cf. 4:21). This miracle consisted of seeing the rod which they possessed become a serpent (v. 9). Following the Lord's instructions they went to Pharaoh, presumably at a royal residence near the Delta Region, and cast down the rod as commanded. The rod suddenly became a serpent (v. 10). This miraculous sign was designed to confirm the fact that the message that Moses and Aaron brought indeed came from the living God, a God whom Pharaoh claimed not to have known – or in any case refused to obey (cf. 5:2). Pharaoh, however, was not convinced that this miracle possessed any uniqueness or was indeed anything different from what Egyptian magicians and sorcerers could duplicate; thus, wise men and sorcerers were called in to perform for Pharaoh, vindicating his suspicions (v. 11).

We know from ancient documents that magic and sorcery were not only common throughout the land of Egypt, but played a significant role in the lives of the pharaohs. From the Old Kingdom period comes a very interesting and informative tale about King Khufu and the magicians (*Papyrus Westcar* in Berlin). While the story relates to King Kheops, the builder of the great pyramid, the present papyrus manuscript dates back only to the Hyksos period. The story concerns tales told by the son of Kheops relating to the wonders which magicians had performed in the past. Later one of his sons informed him that he knew a living magician who could work miracles. This magician was brought before the king and worked miracles in the king's presence, and in addition to that predicted the future.[4] What pre-

[4]Adolf Erman, ed., "King Kheops and the Magicians," *The Ancient Egyptians* (New York: Harper and Row, 1966), pp. 36-47.

cisely do we mean when we speak of "Egyptian magic"? Included in this multifaceted subject would be

> ". . . cursing (including killing); curing; erotic magic; agricultural (including weather); divination; and resurrection. Since magic and medicine are hard to untangle, and since the Egyptians did not, as a rule, try to untangle them, we will discuss curative magic under medicine."[5]

The question that has long plagued scholars revolves around the nature of the events which followed the miracle performed by Moses and Aaron. Just precisely what did the magicians in Egypt do? The biblical text expresses the fact that they "also did in like manner with their enchantments. For they cast down every man his rod, and they became serpents . . ." (vv. 11-12). These verses have received four basic interpretations. The first is that the event was merely an optical illusion; that is:

> Moses describes the act of the sorcerers as it appeared to Pharaoh and the spectators. . . . They represent the magicians as deceiving the spectators by acting upon their imagination.[6]

Such trickery or deceit is many times attributed either to Satan himself[7] or to evil spirits.[8] This interpretation relies heavily on the Hebrew expression *b^e^lāṭêhem* (v. 22) which is variously translated as "with their enchantments" (KJV), "by their secret arts" (RSV) or "with their witchcraft" (*Jerusalem Bible*). The verb used in this passage (*lāhaṭ*) literally means to "blaze up, to flame."[9] The advocates of this viewpoint argue that the magicians produced a dazzling delusion with the use of their rods thus deceiving those present; however, since the Septuagint translates this word as *pharmakeiais* which means "sorcery, magic, or magical arts" (cf. Gal. 5:20), it may well be that the

---

[5]Barbara Mertz, *op. cit.*, pp. 207-208.

[6]F. C. Cook, ed., *The Holy Bible with an Explanatory and Critical Commentary* (New York: Charles Scribner's Sons, n.d.), I, p. 276.

[7]Matthew Poole, *Annotations Upon the Holy Bible* (New York: Robert Carter and Brothers, 1853), p. 129.

[8]Symon Patrick, *A Critical Commentary and Paraphrase on the Old and New Testaments* (Philadelphia: Frederick Scofield and Co., 1877), p. 222.

[9]Brown, Driver and Briggs, *op. cit.*, p. 529.

original root was the Hebrew *lāṭ* or *lāṭ* which means secrecy or mystery.[10]

The second interpretation offered is simply that the magicians performed an effective sleight of hand thus convincing Pharaoh that a miracle had been performed. This view would argue that actual serpents did appear but were produced by a sleight of hand rather than a mere illusion occurring with perhaps no serpents being present at all.[11] Commentators who advocate this view either argue that the magicians produced the snakes by the sleight of hand alone or that Satan actually aided in the performance of this event; in other words, the substitution of actual serpents for the rods of the magicians was accomplished by the power of Satan.

The third view which has been suggested for the meaning of this passage is best summarized by James G. Murphy:

> It is certain that the charming of serpents has long been practiced in Egypt and adjacent countries. The serpent called *hage* by the Arabs, apparently the asp, can be made to appear as dead or rigid as a stick, and of course, restored to its natural state again.[12]

K. A. Kitchen notes that this kind of conjuring was not uncommon in Egypt. The cobra (Arabic *naja haje*) could be rendered immobile if pressure was applied to the muscles at the nape of the neck.[13] It is the general viewpoint of the advocates of this position, and the ones discussed above, that men (and Satan) do not have the power to create life. It has been pointed out that the three things duplicated by the magicians – the turning of their rods into serpents (7:12), turning the water into blood (7:22), and bringing up the frogs (8:7) – did not involve the creation of life; whereas, the producing of lice from inanimate

---

[10]*Ibid.*, p. 532.

[11]See George Rawlinson, "Exodus," *Ellicott's Commentary on the Whole Bible*, Charles J. Ellicott, ed. (Grand Rapids: Zondervan Publishing House, n.d.), p. 212 and Adam Clarke, *The Holy Bible with a Commentary and Critical Notes* (New York: Eaton and Mains, n.d.), I, pp. 321-322.

[12]*Commentary on the Book of Exodus* (Andover: Warren F. Draper, 1868), p. 76.

[13]"Magic and Sorcery," *The New Bible Dictionary*, p. 769.

dust did require this (8:16-19) which the magicians could not perform and so confessed.

The final view is that the magicians actually did perform some miraculous feat, probably by evil supernaturalism. One writer argues, "it is clearly not mere jugglery nor sleight of hand."[14] It is suggested that men under the influence of demonic power can do things which would fall in the classification of miraculous; therefore, under the influence of satanic power the magicians performed real miracles, thus hardening Pharaoh's heart. It is, of course, understood that God restricts the exercise of such power, and on this particular occasion permitted the magicians to perform in such a way as to guarantee the hardening of Pharaoh's heart.

The solution to this problem is not at all easy, as indicated by the great division among conservative commentators. What is clear is that whatever the magicians did was sufficiently close to the acts of Moses and Aaron as to satisfy the heart of the wicked king. If Satan indeed does possess the power to create life (or the illusion of life), then the acts of the magicians were miraculous in nature. If, however, it can be argued effectively that evil men and evil spirits do not possess such powers, then the conclusion must necessarily be that the magicians through sleight of hand and deception were able to satisfy the desires of Pharaoh even though what they performed was not an exact duplicate of that which Moses and Aaron had done. Whatever the precise nature of their work, one thing is clear: It accomplished what God intended; namely, the hardening of Pharaoh's heart.

## III. The River of Blood (7:14-25)

### A. *Introduction to the Plagues*

There are really only three possible ways of approaching the phenomenon of the ten plagues as recorded in the Book of Exodus. One is to dismiss all of the literature of Exodus as being purely fanciful myth and having no foundation in reality whatsoever. Such a viewpoint can be quickly set aside because it

---

[14]Merrill F. Unger, *Biblical Demonology* (Wheaton: Scripture Press, 1965), p. 112.

immediately shows no concern for the historical relevancy of the biblical text. A second viewpoint would be that these were merely natural occurrences that were given theological interpretation by Moses. It is generally conceded by liberal-critical scholars who have adopted this viewpoint that the plagues were perhaps more intense than normal, but that there was nothing miraculous about their appearance or disappearance. Flinders Petrie gives the schedule for the events as follows:

> June: The Nile becomes stagnant and red, with microscopic organisms. July: Frogs abound after the inundation of the Nile. Hot summer and damp autumn months: Lice, flies, murrain and boils. January: Hail and rain. (This date fixed by the effect on the crops mentioned.) February: Appearance of locusts in early spring, over the green crops. March: Darkness from great sandstorms. April: Death of the firstborn, dated by the Passover celebration.[15]

The third approach to the plagues is that these were separate miracles. While it might be conceded that plagues analogous to these may have and probably did occur in Egypt, it must be noted that certain historical factors relating to these plagues demand that they be more than mere natural occurrences. Joseph P. Free lists five unique aspects of the plagues which set them apart as miraculous events. These are as follows: (1) Intensification. While frogs, insects, murrain and darkness were known in Egypt, these were intensified far beyond any ordinary occurrence. (2) Prediction. The fact that Moses predicted the moment of the arrival and departure sets them apart from purely natural occurrences (cf. 8:10, 23; 9:5, 18, 29; 10:4). (3) Discrimination. Certain of the plagues did not occur in the land of Goshen where Israel was living (8:22, no flies; 9:4, no murrain; 9:26, no hail). (4) Orderliness. There is a gradual severity in the nature of the plagues concluding with the death of the firstborn. (5) Moral Purpose.[16] These were not freaks of nature but were designed to teach moral precepts and lessons.

---

[15]*Egypt and Israel* (New York: E. S. Gorham, 1911), pp. 35-36.

[16]*Archaeology and Bible History* (Wheaton: Van Kampen Press, 1950), p. 95.

B. *The Purposes of the Plagues*

In view of the fact that the plagues were well ordered and their sequence demonstrated plan and design, it is obvious that they had specific purposes other than just to deliver the people of Israel. These purposes can be divided into four areas as follows:

1. The Gods of Egypt

The Egyptian religion is perhaps one of the most difficult religions (from the ancient world) to analyze.

> It is impossible to sketch a picture of a belief which is uniform and logical in all its details, and valid for the whole of Egypt, for such a uniform belief never existed. The Egyptian religion is not the creation of a single thinker, but an outcome of local, political and cultural divergencies and there was never a strong enough force in Egypt to eliminate all local beliefs or to unite them in a general theological system equally binding to Egyptians of all classes and all places.[17]

The Egyptians were just about the most polytheistic people known from the ancient world. Even to this day we are not completely sure of the total number of gods which they worshipped. Most lists include somewhere in the neighborhood of eighty gods. Studying the various deities in Egypt is a task that requires utmost patience and a complete disassociation with western theological ideas. As William Ward observes, "The many gods of Egypt acquired a variety of attributes and the many statements about them in the literature often make it impossible to describe a specific deity in logical terms."[18] This confusing situation is a product of a system known as syncretism in which one god may assume the name and attributes of two or three other gods. As time went on the associations became more complex and intertwined.

The dedication of the Egyptians to their gods is very obvious even to the casual observer as he walks the sands of Egypt. Beautiful temples and platforms with long colonnaded roadways

---

[17]Jaroslav Černý, *Ancient Egyptian Religion* (London: Hutchinson's University Library, 1952), p. 39.

[18]*The Spirit of Ancient Egypt* (Beirut: Khayats, 1965), p. 120.

are the expression of deep piety and sacrificial work. To a certain degree the gods of Egypt were quite different from deities of surrounding countries. "They lacked the nasty habits of some other deities, who thrived on incinerated babies and dripping human hearts, or required the complete annihilation of people who held other opinions on religious matters."[19] As an idolatrous system of worship, however, it was nonetheless morally and spiritually degrading. Almost all living creatures, whatever their habitat, and even inanimate objects became the embodiment of some deity. The Egyptians considered sacred the lion, the ox, the ram, the wolf, the dog, the cat, the ibis, the vulture, the falcon, the hippopotamus, the crocodile, the cobra, the dolphin, different varieties of fish, trees, and small animals including the frog, scarab, locust and other insects. In addition to these there were anthropomorphic gods; that is, men in the prime of life such as Amun, Atum, or Osiris.[20]

The New Kingdom period was one of the most interesting eras in the history of Egyptian religion because of the many changes that took place. The process of syncretism increased rapidly, assimilating Semitic deities from the north as well as adding new concepts to firmly established ones. The New Kingdom temple estate was a magnificent structure to behold consisting of four basic elements: a pylon or gateway; a court with rows of columns along one or more sides; a wide column (hypostyle) hall; and the sanctuary room itself. The pylon gateway consisted of two towers with sloping sides and flat tops. The area behind that was the colonnaded court—usually without a roof except for a small part over the columns. The next section consisted of the hypostyle hall, the best example of which is to be found at Karnak. Beyond the hypostyle hall was the shrine itself, the sanctuary of the dwelling place of the god. This was usually a rectangular room without windows. The most prominent feature of this room was a large statue of the god, or as in some cases, a god with his family. Most of the temples which survive today date from the New Kingdom period or later. All of them have one thing in common: they reflect the deep commitment of the

---

[19]Barbara Mertz, *op. cit.,* p. 251.
[20]William Ward, *op. cit.,* p. 123.

Temple of Amun at Karnak.

Egyptian to his gods and demonstrate the glory and the importance of religion in that society. It is against this background that we view and analyze the implications of the ten plagues. It is apparent from Exodus 12:12 that at least one of the plagues was directed specifically against "all the gods of Egypt." Numbers 33:4 indicates that perhaps all the plagues were directed against the deities of Egypt, "For the Egyptians buried all their firstborn, which the Lord had smitten among them: upon their gods also the Lord executed judgments" (cf. Exod. 18:11; Isa. 19:1).

2. The Egyptian Religious Functionaries

The wise men, sorcerers, magicians and priests comprised an

important professional class in Egypt and were very much a part of Egyptian bureaucracy. The priests especially held very high positions in the state organizations of Egypt. Mertz observes:

> An Egyptian official would have been baffled by the suggestion that he render unto Caesar those things which were Caesar's and unto God those things which were His. Caesar *was* God – or at least god – and there was no functional difference between church and state. At some periods a single man might hold both the vizierate and the high priesthood of Amon, the supreme civil and sacerdotal positions. This concept explains, to some extent, the apparent overlapping of functions which we find in so many official careers.[21]

The plagues surely must have pointed out to the Egyptians the inability of priests to function in such a way as to turn the tide of calamity. The prayers, the counsel and all of the wise men of Egypt were not capable of changing the disastrous situation in which Pharaoh and the people of Egypt found themselves.

### 3. The King of Egypt

Unlike other rulers in the ancient Near East, the Egyptian Pharaoh did not merely rule for the gods, but he was in a literal sense one of the gods. His birth was a divine act. He was counted specifically as the child of certain deities and thus possessed the properties of deity. As far as his physical existence was concerned, Pharaoh had been begotten by Amon-Re upon the queen mother. As regards his divine potency, he was Horus, the son of Hathor.[22] In the light of this observation it is not difficult to see why Pharaoh reacted as he did to the initial request of Moses and Aaron (Exod. 5:2). The king, as god, was to have sole rule over the people. In fact, the Egyptians' well-being was directly associated with that of the king. It was his duty to maintain justice, peace and prosperity in the land. The plagues served to demonstrate the impotency of Pharaoh, both as a ruler and as a god. He was subject to the same frustrations and

---

[21]Barbara Mertz, *op. cit.*, p. 145.

[22]Henri Frankfort, *Kingship and the Gods* (Chicago: The University of Chicago Press, 1948), p. 299.

anxieties as the average man in Egypt during the period of the plagues. The fact that he called for Moses and Aaron rather than the wise men of Egypt during times of greatest distress attests to this fact. The reaction of the people also implies a lower view of the judgment of the king on certain occasions (cf. 10:7; 12:33).

### 4. The People of Israel

The plagues brought upon the land of Egypt served not only to demonstrate the inability of the king of Egypt, his priests and the people to resist the power of God, but it also served as a visual lesson to Israel regarding the worthlessness of idolatrous forms of worship. They were used by God to demonstrate His awesome power not only in the redemption of His people from the land of Egypt, but His capability in caring for them and providing for their future needs. This should have been the lesson of all lessons and the illustration of all illustrations for Israel, but such was not the case. It is quite clear that the exercise of miraculous power is not the final answer to weak faith. It was a short two months after they had left the land of Egypt that they resorted to the very thing that God had demonstrated was useless (Exod. 32 and 33).

## C. *The Sacred Nile*

It was said long ago and very correctly so that "Egypt was the gift of the Nile." From the earliest of times to the present day the heartbeat of Egypt has been the flow of the Nile River. While overland routes were present, it is clear from ancient documents that the main means of transportation from upper to lower Egypt was the Nile River. Hardly any country in ancient or modern times has been so dependent on its waterways as ancient Egypt. This transportation led to widespread ship building and a development of ports. Sea commerce developed out of this and provided many important products for Egypt. Perhaps most important for the average Egyptian, however, was the strategic contribution of the Nile to agricultural life. Its annual rise and flooding provided new deposits of fertile soil along with much needed water in the surrounding fields. In

Egypt the Nile is at its lowest point in May. Its rise begins around June and the main flood waters reach the country in July and August, the peak occurring early in September. Were it not for this inundation Egypt would be as desolate as the deserts on either side. The Egyptians fully recognized this fact, and in thanksgiving for the blessings of the Nile, hymns were written. Not only were gods associated with the Nile, but fertility, blessing, and happiness were also associated with the faithfulness of this river. From the New Kingdom period comes a document known to us today as the "Hymn to the Nile," a composition which may have originated in the Middle Kingdom period. The words of this hymn best tell the story of the importance of the Nile River to the Egyptian.

> Hail to thee, Oh Nile, that issues from the earth and comes to keep Egypt alive! . . . He that waters the meadows which Recreated, in order to keep every kid alive. He that makes to drink the desert and the place distant from water: that is his dew coming down (from) heaven.[23]

From this hymn we learn that the very economic health of the land was dependent on the faithfulness of the Nile. Poverty and calamity accompanied the failure of the Nile River.

> If he is sluggish, then nostrils are stopped up and everybody is poor. If there be (thus) a cutting down in the food offerings of the gods, then a million men perish among mortals, covetousness is practiced. The entire land is in a fury, and great and small are on the execution block (but) people are different when he approaches. Khnum constructed him. When he rises, then the land is in jubilation, then every belly is in joy, every backbone takes on laughter, and every tooth is exposed.[24]

Not only was the economic fortune of Egypt dependent upon the river, but the psychological welfare of the people largely depended on the faithfulness of the Nile River. The Nile dominated the agriculture of Egypt; this affected the form of her calendar which was divided into three seasons (each with four

---

[23]*ANET*, "Hymn to the Nile," trans. by John A. Wilson, p. 272.
[24]*Ibid.*

thirty-day months with five "intercalary" days at the end of the year. The Nile not only provided a means of transportation for the Egyptians and irrigation for their crops, but it supplied the marshes for pasture and for hunting wild game so often depicted in Egyptian paintings. The river contained a wealth of fish, caught both by the line and the net (cf. Isa. 19:8). With this background in mind, we are now prepared to examine the plagues and their religious, economic and political implications.

D. *The Polluted Nile* (7:14-21)

Presumably there was a space of time between the hardening of Pharaoh's heart after the miracle of the rods (7:8-13) and the next encounter which took place at the Nile River or one of its branches (v. 15). It is interesting that the Pharaoh was met in the morning at the river's bank. Perhaps this meeting occurred at one of the great temple estates located along the Nile River. There were many of these and most of them were in one way or another associated with the sacredness of the Nile River. The presence of Pharaoh at the river was apparently habitual (cf. 8:20). Some have suggested that his presence there was for no other reason than for washing (cf. 2:5); however, this is doubtful and is not specifically stated in the text. More likely Pharaoh was either performing some sacred rite at the river or was perhaps worshiping. The demand was made again that the people of Israel be freed to serve the Lord in the wilderness (v. 16). For the second time Pharaoh would get an opportunity to see the rod of Moses at work. This time the warning was given that the waters would be smitten and would be turned to blood (v. 17), the result being that the fish would die and the river would stink. So loathsome would the river be that the people would not be able to use its water (v. 18). This plague was not limited to the Nile proper, but apparently included the branches of the Nile and water that had been stored (v. 19). Thus did Moses and Aaron in the sight of Pharaoh and his servants (v. 20). When the water was smitten, "all the waters that were in the river were turned to blood" (Heb. *l<sup>e</sup>ḏām*). The question as to the nature of this "blood" has been the subject of considerable debate. A popular viewpoint is that "deposits from the Abyssian lakes often colored the flood water a dark reddish-brown, especially in the upper Nile, that might well be said to look like blood."[25] In addition to the flooding of the Nile with the deposition of excessive red soil, it is suggested that:

> Such an excessive inundation could further bring down with it microcosms known as *flagellates* and associated bacteria: besides heightening the blood-red color of the water, these would create conditions so unfavorable for the fish that they would die in large numbers as recorded. Their decomposition would foul the water and cause a stench.[26]

It is very doubtful that such explanations, while seemingly attractive, are really sufficient. The problem of the timing of the event as well as its extent and devastating effect would certainly not be explained by such suggestions. Red silting of the Nile is indeed very common, but it does not bring about the widespread death of fish or create a stench that would seriously alter the life of the Egyptians. Furthermore, it is doubtful that the presence of bacteria from flooding waters could be so intense and multiply so rapidly so as to kill off fish in great numbers and bring about the results described in this chapter. One wonders, if this were purely a natural event, why Moses tried to exploit it for his own purposes. Surely this would not have any effect upon Pharaoh if it were something that was repeated annually and could be easily explained from common occurrence. The very fact that all the waters of Egypt were affected by the plague (v. 19) removes this from a purely naturalistic association. As to the nature of the blood, very little can be said. The Hebrew merely states that it changed to blood. It is not necessary to argue that the Nile River was turned into literal human or animal blood.

> The changing of the water into blood is to be interpreted in the same sense as in Joel 3:4, where the moon is said to be turned into blood; that is to say, not a chemical change into real blood, but as a change in the color, which caused it to assume the appearance of blood (II Kings 3:22).[27]

---

[25]Werner Keller, *op. cit.*, p. 112.
[26]K. A. Kitchen, "Plagues of Egypt," *op. cit.*, p. 1002.
[27]Keil and Delitzsch, *op. cit.*, p. 478.

The water, so far as can be determined, had all of the characteristics of blood as viewed by Moses. "The water appeared to be blood, as far as taste, smell, and texture go, and was taken to be blood."[28]

It was appropriate that the first of the plagues should be directed against the Nile River itself, the very lifeline of Egypt and the center of many of its religious ideas. The Nile was considered sacred by the Egyptians. Many of their gods were associated either directly or indirectly with this river and its productivity. For example, the great Khnum was considered the guardian of the Nile sources. Hapi was believed to be the "spirit of the Nile" and its "dynamic essence." One of the greatest gods revered in Egypt was the god Osiris who was the god of the underworld. The Egyptians believed that the river Nile was his bloodstream. In the light of this latter expression, it is appropriate indeed that the Lord should turn the Nile to blood! It is not only said that the fish in the river died but that the "river stank," and the Egyptians were not able to use the water of that river. That statement is especially significant in the light of the expressions which occur in the "Hymn to the Nile": "The bringer of food, rich in provisions, creator of all good, lord of majesty, sweet of fragrance."[29] With this Egyptian literature in mind, one can well imagine the horror and frustration of the people of Egypt as they looked upon that which was formerly beautiful only to find dead fish lining the shores and an ugly red characterizing what had before provided life and attraction. Crocodiles were forced to leave the Nile. One wonders what worshipers would have thought of Hapi the god of the Nile who was sometimes manifest in the crocodile. Pierre Montet relates the following significant observation:

> At Sumenu (the modern Rizzeigat) in the Thebes area, and in the central district of the Fayum, the god Sepek took the form of a crocodile. He was worshipped in his temple where his statue was erected, and venerated as a sacred animal as he splashed about in his pool. A lady of high rank would kneel down and, without the slightest trace of disgust, would drink

---

[28]Francis D. Nichol, *op. cit.*, p. 530.
[29]*ANET*, p. 272.

> from the pool in which the crocodile wallowed. Ordinary crocodiles were mummified throughout the whole of Egypt and placed in underground caverns, like the one called the Cavern of the Crocodiles in middle Egypt.[30]

Surely the pollution of the Nile would have taken on religious implications for the average Egyptian. Those who venerated Neith, the eloquent warlike goddess who took a special interest in the *lates,* the largest fish to be found in the Nile, would have had second thoughts about the power of that goddess. Hathor was supposed to have protected the *chromis,* a slightly smaller fish. Those Egyptians who depended heavily on fish and on the Nile would indeed have found great frustration in a plague of this nature.

Pharaoh, not content with the conclusion that the God of Israel had spoken and had demonstrated His power conclusively, called in the magicians to demonstrate that the gods of Egypt were equal to the challenge. Verse 22 of this chapter indicates that the magicians did the same thing with their enchantments. Apparently the magicians were able to counterfeit the miracle of Moses and Aaron to the degree that Pharaoh was satisfied. In the light of pharaonic pride it probably would not take very much to satisfy the wicked heart of this man. The question as to where the water that the magicians used came from is probably answered in verse 24. It is there noted that Egyptians digged around for fresh water since the Nile itself had been polluted. According to verse 25 this plague lasted for a period of seven days. Others have viewed this seven-day period as being the interval between the first plague and the second, but this does not appear to be the most natural reading of the text. The intervals of time between one plague and the next are not given.

The first plague brought upon Egypt eloquently revealed the power of God and the impotence of Egyptian deities. For the Egyptian who sought water for his cattle and for himself, it would have meant an exercise in deep frustration and despair. For the very religious Egyptian who faithfully sought the guid-

---

30*Op. cit.,* p. 172.

ance and protection of the various deities associated with the Nile it must have raised serious questions about the unqualified powers of such deities. To the Israelites who witnessed this event, it was a reminder of the awesome power of the God who had chosen them and had blessed them. To us who are alive today and witness the idolatry of this present generation, this miracle is a reminder of the tremendous power of a God who will not only bring blessing upon those who are faithful to Him, but will, with equal power, bring judgment and humiliation upon those who lift up their hand in rebellion.

J. J. Davis

Pylon and statues of Rameses II—Luxor.

## Chapter 5

# *The Finger of God*

(Exodus 8)

One of the fallacies of studying Egyptian history from the standpoint of political movements and developments is the dehumanization of the people who participated in that history. Far too often the rewriting of ancient history is nothing more than a drum and bugle rehearsal of militarism and political intrigue. Historians are often notorious for their lack of concern for the average man. To understand fully all of the implications of the ten plagues and the exodus which followed this, one must look at Egypt in its fullest sense. We have examined its rulers and the development of political-economic events as reflected in the Eighteenth Dynasty. It now becomes our task, as we introduce the next three plagues, to examine the people of Egypt. What would their reaction have been to such disasters? What kind of people were they? Do the paintings on their monuments reflect their character? Are these paintings accurate depictions of their dress and their behavior? We know from ancient documents that the Egyptians were a very busy people. The most delightful and rewarding way to study the ancient Egyptians is to examine their art work and their own literature. They had fields to sow and irrigate and harvest, large temples to build, enemies to fight, and tombs to repair and equip for the burial of the dead.

From the mummies that have been discovered it is possible to determine some of the essential physical characteristics of these people. On the average they were generally shorter than we are. The women were about five feet tall and the men about five feet, five inches. There were, of course, noteworthy exceptions to this, such as Amenhotep II who was six feet in height. Their skin was a light brownish color. Mummified bodies provide information concerning both the physical features and the pathology of these ancient peoples. What problems did they have? What sicknesses and illnesses plagued them the most? Mummified forms even give us some insights regarding hair styles, the use of wigs, eye paint, and other forms of adornment.

The literature of the ancient Egyptians reflects a wide variety of interests ranging from the use of music and entertainment to wisdom and occupational commitment. In spite of the apparent preoccupation with preparation for death, the average Egyptian was a practical optimist. His songs and poems reflect his general joy of life. One song is especially interesting because it is an example of the Egyptian attitude toward life, expressing the idea that he should enjoy it to the fullest:

> Be glad, that thou mayest cause thine heart to forget that men will (one day) beautify thee. Follow thy desire, so long as thou livest. Put myrrh on thine head, clothe thee in fine linen, and anoint thee with the genuine marvels of things of the god.[1]

> Spend the day merrily, oh priest! Put ungent and fine oil together to thy nostrils, and garlands and lotus flowers . . . on the body of thy sister whom thou favorest, as she sitteth beside thee. Set singing and music before thy face. Cast all evil behind thee and bethink thee of joy. . . .[2]

A great deal is also learned about the ancient Egyptians from archaeological work done on village and town sites. One such site, probably founded in the early Eighteenth Dynasty, was inhabited for about 450 years and probably typifies many of the small towns in the Egypt of Moses' day. A wall surrounded the town and a single gate led in to the main street which was only about four or five feet wide. The houses were generally built of mud brick and faced directly on the street. They were not large houses, most having only four rooms. The houses had flat roofs which many times would serve as additional living space.[3] The above description is typical of the houses of the workmen who helped construct tombs and who labored in the fields. More sophisticated and certainly more attractive were the homes of the middle class workmen and professional people such as the scribes and priests. The most impressive structures in Egypt obviously belonged to the royal class, that is, those associated with Pharaoh and his court.

Our interest in the ancient Egyptian, therefore, is not only re-

---

[1]Adolf Erman, "Songs at Banquets," *op. cit.*, p. 133.
[2]*Ibid.*, p. 252.
[3]Barbara Mertz, *op. cit.*, pp. 108-109.

lated to those with whom Moses was directly confronted in the challenges to Pharaoh, but also with the commoner who labored in the fields and worked in the stone quarries. What was their reaction? How did they interpret the catastrophic phenomena that had occurred? What did they think when they witnessed the pollution of the Nile and the humiliation of the sacred gods that dwelt in that river? With this in mind we proceed to examine the next three plagues recorded in Exodus 8.

## I. Frogs in the Land (8:1-15)

### A. *The Nature and Extent of This Plague* (8:1-6)

Following the pollution and clearing of the Nile, Moses was again commanded to appear before Pharaoh with the demand that the people of Israel be freed in order that they might serve the Lord (v. 1). If this request were refused, the Lord promised to smite the land of Egypt with frogs (v. 2). The presence of frogs in Egypt was not at all unusual. They were common to the marsh lands and to areas along the Nile River as evidenced in Egyptian paintings and inscriptions.[4] The name given to the frog was *qrr* (*krr*) which was onomatopoeic, probably vocalized *krur.*[5] The sacredness and significance of the frog to the Egyptian is demonstrated by the discovery of amulets in the form of frogs.[6] The occurrence of the term "frog" in the Bible is largely in connection with this Exodus account (cf. Ps. 78:45; 105:30). The common presence of the frog to the Egyptians was not something loathsome or to be abhorred. The frog, to a large degree, represented fruitfulness, blessing and the assurance of a harvest. This concept came about as a result of the flooding of the Nile which continued through mid-September. By the middle of December the Nile had once again returned to its normal channel. The receding water, however, left many pools and ponds over the countryside which were quickly inhabited by frogs whose chorus was often heard on balmy Egyptian evenings.

---

[4]See F. W. von Bissing, *Die Mastaba des Gem-ni-kai* (Berlin: Alexander Duncker, 1905-1911), I, pl. IV.

[5]Pierre Montet, *Egypt and the Bible* (Philadelphia: Fortress Press, 1968), p. 96.

[6]*Ibid.*

To the farmers this sound was music indeed because it indicated that the gods who controlled the Nile and made the land fertile had completed their work. The god Hapi was blessed and venerated on such occasions, for it was he who controlled the alluvial deposits and the waters that made the land fertile and guaranteed the harvest of the coming season. These associations caused the Egyptians to deify the frog and make the theophany of the goddess Heqt a frog. Heqt was the wife of the great god Khnum. She was the symbol of resurrection and the emblem of fertility. It was also believed that Heqt assisted women in childbirth.[7] Heqt was one of the eight primeval gods (ogdoad),". . . four male frog-headed gods, and four serpent-headed goddesses who personified respectively the primeval water, infinity, darkness and that which is hidden. In their time, nothing evil existed on the earth. Everywhere abundance reigned."[8] The frog was one of a number of sacred animals that might not be intentionally killed, and even their involuntary slaughter was often punished with death.[9]

This second plague was not completely unrelated to the first, for the Nile and the appearance of the frogs were very much associated. The presence of the frogs normally would have been something pleasant and desirable, but on this occasion quite the opposite was true. The frogs came out of the rivers in great abundance and moved across the land into the houses, the bedchambers, the beds, and even moved upon the people themselves (v. 3). One can only imagine the frustration brought by such a multiplication of these creatures. They were probably everywhere underfoot bringing distress to the housewives who attempted to clear the house of them only to find that they made their way into the kneading troughs and even into the beds. It must have been a unique experience indeed to come home from a long day's work, slip into bed only to find that it has already been occupied by slimy, cold frogs! Whatever popularity the goddess Heqt must have enjoyed prior to this time would have been greatly diminished with the multiplication of

---

[7]See Henri Frankfort, *op. cit.*, fig. 6, p. 15 and Pierre Montet, *Egypt and the Bible,* p. 96.

[8]Pierre Montet, *Eternal Egypt,* p. 187.

[9]George Rawlinson, *op. cit.,* p. 214.

these creatures who at this point must have tormented her devotees to no end.

> Like a blanket of filth the slimy, wet monstrosities covered the land, until men sickened at the continued squashing crunch of the ghastly pavement they were forced to walk upon. If a man's feet slipped on the greasy mass of their crushed bodies, he fell into an indescribably offensive mass of putrid uncleanness, and when he sought water to cleanse himself, the water was so solid with frogs, he got no cleansing there.[10]

Another description which has long intrigued me comes from the pen of Louis Untermeyer who describes the presence of the myriads of frogs as follows:

> Small green peepers, no larger than locusts, distended toads, the color of excretment, mottled frogs like bloated vegetation, frogs that were lumps of bronze, frogs with eyes of unblinking demons, frogs subtler than salamanders, frogs motionless, frogs that leaped into the laps of screaming children, wart-breeding frogs, frogs like droppings of mud, frogs trailing their slime after them, flying frogs that built nests in high reeds, frogs that died and bred death. Once again the sacred Nile was the source of pollution.[11]

### B. *Pharaoh's Response* (8:7-15)

Not content that the miracle performed by Moses and Aaron was a unique and valid demonstration of the power of Jehovah, Pharaoh called the magicians to appear in the royal court to demonstrate that the gods of Egypt were equal to the challenge. Verse 7 indicates that "the magicians did so with their enchantments, and brought up frogs upon the land of Egypt." The text does not describe the precise nature of their act. Did they merely produce frogs or did they create them? What is clear from the text, however, is that they were incapable of removing the plague. Their production of frogs was something less than desirable, therefore, in spite of its theological interpretation!

In frustration and to some degree in humility, Pharaoh was

---

[10]Harry Rimmer, *Dead Men Tell Tales* (Berne, Ind.: The Berne Witness Co., 1939), p. 105.

[11]*Moses* (New York: Harcourt and Brace, 1928), p. 184.

forced to call for Moses and Aaron (v. 8). His words indicate that his theological perspectives had improved considerably from the time of his intitial encounter with Moses and Aaron (5: 2). He now knew something of the power of the God of the Hebrews. He also conceded that the prayers of righteous men bring results, for he requested Moses to "intreat the Lord" that this plague would be removed, and this was followed up with the promise that the people of Israel would be permitted to leave the land and sacrifice to their God. Of special interest in this dialogue is the fact that Moses requested Pharaoh to name the time when this plague should end, a deed certainly not even attempted by the magicians (v. 9). The answer of Pharaoh is somewhat perplexing at first sight for he did not request an immediate end to the plague, but suggested that the frogs should be removed on the next day (v. 10). Why not immediately? He probably hoped that they would go away themselves, and then he should get clear of the plague without being obligated to either Moses or his God. The purpose of this provision was that Pharaoh, along with his people, might "know that there is none like unto the Lord our God" (v. 10). In answer to Moses' prayer the frogs that plagued the land died and only those that were in the river lived (v. 13; cf. v. 11). The mention of their continued existence in the river; that is, the Nile, probably indicates that the Nile at this point was no longer polluted from the previous plague. The result of the death of these thousands of frogs made the land of Egypt something less than attractive (v. 14). When Pharaoh saw "that there was respite" (Heb. *hārᵉwāḥāh* – "relief" v. 15; v. 11 Heb. text) he again hardened his heart and refused the promise which he had given to Moses. It was still too much for the arrogant Pharaoh to admit that the God of the Hebrews had surpassed the gods of Egypt in a demonstration of power. Of course, most significant for him would be the concession on his part as the ruler and a god of Egypt that he had been outdone.

## II. Dust and Gnats (8:16-19)

### A. *The Nature of the Plague* (8:16-17)

The third plague which occurred in the land of Egypt came

without warning and was the direct result of the activities of Moses and Aaron. The dust of the land was smitten and it became gnats (Heb. *kinnim* or *kinnîm* – v. 16), a species so small as to be hardly visible to the eye but with a very irritating and painful sting.[12] This Hebrew term may be derived from the Egyptians *chenemes,* "gnats" or "mosquitoes."[13] The translation "lice" is the influence of the opinions of Josephus and Talmudic writers, but has no foundation in the Hebrew text.

It is not clear against what specific deities this particular plague was directed. It is entirely possible, however, that the plague was designed to humiliate the official priesthood in the land, for it will be noted in verse 17 that these creatures irritated both man and beast, and this included "all the land of Egypt." The priests in Egypt were noted for their physical purity. Daily rites were performed by a group of priests known as the *Uab* or "pure ones." Their purity was basically physical rather than spiritual. They were circumcised, shaved the hair from their heads and bodies, washed frequently, and were dressed in beautiful linen robes.[14] In the light of this it would seem rather doubtful that the priesthood in Egypt could function very effectively having been polluted by the presence of these insects. They, like their worshipers, were inflicted with the pestilence of this occasion. Their prayers were made ineffective by their own personal impurity with the presence of gnats on their bodies.

The priests in Egypt were a group of people to be reckoned with not only religiously but economically and politically. They controlled to a large degree the minds and hearts of the people. The daily duties and functions of the official priests are now well known to us. Every morning the priest entered the Holy of Holies making sure that the door was bolted. He would then open the door and see the god who was supposed to have slept during the evening. He would wake him up and present him with his various garments – including headdresses and insignia – and then proceed to dress him. After the god had been dressed, he ate his first meal. Other meals followed this throughout the day. In

---

[12]Keil and Delitzsch, *op. cit.,* p. 483.
[13]Francis D. Nichol, *op. cit.,* p. 533.
[14]Pierre Montet, *Eternal Egypt,* p. 177.

E. Anrich

The god Horus guards the entrance to the Horus Temple at Edfu.

the evening, his insignia and garments were removed and he was put back into the shrine. While this was done, hymns had to be recited and songs sung. Much of this ceremony was accompanied by dances performed by professional dancers. This ritual was pretty much the same in all the temples with only slight variations.[15]

Small insects have always been a problem in Egypt. Fleas, aphids, lice, mosquitoes and gnats abound in great numbers in certain areas. Many devices were constructed by the ancient Egyptians in an attempt to get relief from them, such as ostrich

[15]*Ibid.*, p. 179.

plumes on the end of a stick which would be waved by servants to keep such insects away from the faces of the king and lords. Floors and walls were often washed with a solution of soda. In one medical papyrus cat grease was said to be effective against rats and fish spawn against fleas.[16]

B. *The Magicians' Response* (8:18-19)

The magicians attempted to duplicate the feat as they had done on other occasions with their special enchantments, but this time they were unable to do so (v. 18). To what shall we attribute their failure? Numerous suggestions have been offered, such as: "the magicians gave up the contest by their own choice realizing that they were unable to compete."[17] It is argued by some that mosquitos were things too delicate to be caught and manipulated and produced at a given moment by sleight of hand. This miracle was therefore impossible to counterfeit.[18] This view, however, does not appear to satisfy the obvious sense of the text. The very fact that the magicians had attempted to duplicate the miracle indicates that they fully expected to perform something that would be credible in the eyes of Pharaoh. The appropriate interpretation of this expression of failure seems to be that the Egyptian magicians were limited by the omnipotence of God who restrained the demonical powers which the magicians had used for their own purposes before.[19] The failure on the part of the magicians led to a very significant confession that the events occurring were the product of "the finger of God." This expression is used a number of times in Scripture with varying emphases (cf. Exod. 31:18; Deut. 9:10; Luke 11:20; and Ps. 8:3). The confession and the impotence of the magicians, however, did not convince Pharaoh of the need of ceasing his resistance to the plan of God.

## III. Flies in the Royal Palace (8:20-32)

A. *Announcement of the Judgment* (8:20-23)

---

[16]Pierre Montet, *Egypt and the Bible,* pp. 96-97.
[17]See Francis Nichol, *op. cit.,* p. 533.
[18]George Rawlinson, *op. cit.,* p. 18.
[19]Keil and Delitzsch, *op. cit.,* p. 483.

The time lapse between the plague of gnats and the one which was to follow is not given to us in the biblical text. The meeting between the king of Egypt and Moses for the second time takes place at the river (v. 20; cf. 7:15). This plague, unlike the previous one, came with specific warning. The Lord promised that the land would be covered with "swarms" (Heb. (*ārōb*, v. 21). The Hebrew text does not use the specific expression "flies." The word *'ārōb* is used nine times and is always related to this plague (cf. Ps. 78:45; 105:31). The idea of flies, however, is not altogether inappropriate to the text. This translation is suggested by the Septuagint rendering *kunomuia* – "dog-fly." It will be remembered that the translators of the Septuagint lived in Egypt and their observation may be important at this point. The blood-sucking gadfly or dogfly was something to be abhorred and may in part have been responsible for the great deal of blindness in the land.

It might also be noted that the Ichneuman fly, which deposits its eggs on other living things upon which its larvae can feed, was regarded as the manifestation of the god Uatchit. Perhaps other insects were likewise revered; if so, this plague takes on new dimensions.

That this catastrophe was unique and miraculous in nature is made clear by the language of verse 22 which states that the land of Goshen was set apart from the rest of Egypt in such a way that the swarms were not present in that area. Any purely naturalistic interpretation of the plague is precluded by such language, unless of course the advocate has little regard for the language of the text. This plague was not only designed to humiliate Pharaoh and the gods of Egypt, but it also pointed out clearly that it had redemptive purpose with relationship to the people of God. In verse 23 it is clearly stated that the Lord would put a "redemption" (Heb. *p^e^ḏuṯ* – AV – "division") between His people and the people of Egypt (v. 23, v. 19 Heb. text).

B. *Extent of the Plague* (8:24)

Following the warning came the plague itself, described as "a grevous swarm" (Heb. *kāḇēḏ* – "heavy"). The use of the Hebrew *kāḇēḏ* is significant here. It speaks of something oppressive or burdensome such as a yoke (I Kings 12:4, 11), famine (Gen. 12:10) or mourning (Gen. 50:11). It may also carry with it the idea of massive numbers or an abundance of things (cattle – Exod. 12:38; murrain – Exod. 9:3; and locusts – Exod. 10:14). This Hebrew expression was obviously intended to convey the sense of intensity or severity. The plague not only affected the countryside and the commoner, but reached even to the house of Pharaoh. It is appropriately recorded in the light of the above facts that the land of Egypt was "ruined" (Heb. *šāḥat*).

We know of the events in the royal court of Pharaoh during this time from the Scripture, but what about Egyptian sources? At this point there is some difficulty in attempting to ascertain "official" responses to disasters simply because very few of these were recorded.

> The Egyptians suffered from a sort of official amnesia with regard to unpleasant facts; one has the feeling that the conquest (by the Hyksos) would never have been mentioned at all if there had been a reasonable way of glorifying a king for liberating his country without referring to what he was liberating it from.[20]

In spite of this limitation, a careful study of existing documents will prove helpful in gaining some insight into royal reaction to serious problems. From the time of Rameses II we have a document recording his great battle at the site of Kadesh in the valley of the Orontes. In this story he finds himself in a very precarious position, the enemy having outwitted him and actually having placed his life in danger. His first reaction was to appeal to his favorite god. In the text we read that:

> . . . his majesty said: "What is it then, my father Amun? Hath a father indeed forgotten his son? Have I done ought without thee? Have I not gone or stood still because of thine utterance? And I never swerved from the counsels of thy mouth? How great is the great lord of Thebes, too great to suffer the foreign peoples to come nigh him."[21]

---

[20]Barbara Mertz, *Temples, Tombs and Hieroglyphs; The Story of Egyptology* (New York: Dell Publishing Co., 1965), p. 150.

[21]Adolf Erman, "The Battle of Kadesh," *op. cit.*, p. 263.

In the same document we read of another of his pleas to his god in the following words of desperation:

> I call unto thee, my father Amun. I am in the midst of foes whom I know not. All lands have joined themselves together against me, and I am all alone and none other is with me. My soldiers have forsaken me, and not one among my chariotry hath looked round about for me. If I cry unto them, not one of them hearkeneth.[22]

We might assume that the same pleas which were found on the lips of this king in times of great distress must surely have characterized the words of the commoner as he witnessed the tragic humiliation of his land and the impotence of the many gods that were about him.

C. *Pharaoh's Compromises* (8:25-29)

The faltering responses of the magicians, the impotence of the beautifully decorated deities, and the tragedies of empty temples made it clear to Pharaoh that his only hope for release from this plague was in the God of Moses and Aaron. Thus, in desperation (perhaps analogous to that of Rameses II) he called for these two aged statesmen and offered them the first of four compromises. He was willing to permit them to sacrifice to their God but only on the condition that they would do it within the borders of Egypt (v. 25). This concession, however, was not satisfactory to Moses who reminded Pharaoh that if they did this, they would be sacrificing "the abomination of the Egyptians" and in so doing would incur the wrath of these peoples upon themselves (v. 26).

A number of suggested interpretations have been offered for this expression. These have included the idea that abomination refers to the sacrifice of sheep which were presumably held more or less in detestation by the Egyptians, or it may have had reference to the sacrifice of heifers, the cow being the animal sacred to the goddess Hathor.[23] Josephus suggested that the

---

[22] *Ibid.*

[23] M. G. Kyle, "Plagues of Egypt," *The International Standard Bible Encyclopedia,* IV, p. 2404.

Egyptians were greatly scandalized when sacred animals were sacrificed or eaten.[24] Others have suggested, "The abomination would rather be this, that the Israelites would not carry out the rigid regulations observed by the Egyptians with regard to the cleanness of the sacrificial animals . . . and in fact would not observe the sacrificial rites of Egyptians at all."[25] The best explanation, however, seems to be that the abomination somehow related to the use of sheep for sacrifice. This is supported by the warning of Joseph appearing in Genesis 46:34. The first compromise of Pharaoh, therefore, was totally unacceptable and this Moses made clear. Nothing short of a long journey into the wilderness (v. 27) would be sufficient to meet the demand. Pharaoh, not willing to concede everything requested, offered a second compromise in which he would permit them to go into the wilderness, assuming that they would "not go very far away" (v. 28). In other words, he wanted the Hebrews to remain close enough to his eastern border that they could be watched and reached easily by his army. Moses did not appear to offer any objection to this suggestion. He only warned Pharaoh that he should not continue to deal deceitfully with the people of God. The promise was then given that the plague would be removed on the next day (v. 29).

D. *The Plague Ended* (8:30-32)

Moses kept his part of the agreement and, after praying, the flies were removed from the land. But this, like previous occasions, did not change the heart of this wicked and proud king. Perhaps he concluded that with four catastrophes there would be an end to any further religious calamity for his land. As on previous occasions, once freed from the humiliation of the plague, he hardened his heart and again refused to let the people of Israel go. This refusal, of course, was not accidental, but as viewed from the totality of Scripture was providential for the further expression of divine power and sovereignty.

---

[24]*Apion* I:26.
[25]Keil and Delitzsch, *op. cit.*, p. 486.

## Chapter 6

# *When the Gods Were Silent*

(Exodus 9–10)

Tragedy and pestilence in Egypt produced a number of reactions among its inhabitants. As observed in the previous chapter, one reaction would certainly have been prayer to the gods. Another reaction, clearly reflected in several Egyptian texts, was that of introspection and examination of one's manner of living before the gods. When such disasters occurred it was not uncommon to ascribe them to the wrath of the gods who perhaps were unhappy for a lack of piety and faithfulness to the daily offerings. This attitude is evident in the words of Rameses III.

> The land of Egypt was topsy-turvy. Each man being his own judge, there was no master, for many years before until other times. The land of Egypt was divided up into nobles and chieftains. Every man, rich or poor, killed his brother. Other times succeeded these, and they were barren years. Irsu, a Syrian, brought the whole land under his control, and every man killed his companion in order to rob him. They treated the gods in the same way as they treated men. No more offerings were brought to the sanctuaries. But the gods changed all this to peace and restored the country to normal.[1]

Another reaction which is suggested in Exodus 9 is that of fear and respect for the God of the Hebrews. After the warning of Moses that the land would be judged with great hail and fire, those who feared the word of Jehovah among Pharaoh's servants followed the instructions to place their cattle inside their houses where protection could be offered (9:20). It is doubtful that these servants of Pharaoh had full knowledge of the nature and character of the God of the Hebrews, but the preceding events were sufficient to convince them of His awesome power. They found it advantageous to respect this God and His servant. It may have been people from this group who joined the children

---

[1]Great Harris Papyrus I, 75. Quoted in Pierre Montet, *Eternal Egypt*, p. 193.

of Israel in their exodus from Egypt (cf. Exod. 12:38; Num. 11:4). The very realistic appraisal of the situation by Pharaoh's servants was perhaps a factor which caused Pharaoh to resist the demands of Moses, for to concede to Moses publicly would be to admit the existence of gods greater than those who historically dominated theological thinking in Egypt. Pharaoh's pride would not permit him to succumb to the demands that Moses made. Of course it should also be noted that God purposely hardened his heart in order that there might be the expression of His sovereign power.

## I. The Death of Domestic Animals (9:1-7)

### A. *Announcement of the Plague* (9:1-3)

The fifth plague, like most of the previous plagues, came with clear warning to Pharaoh. The demand was the same (v. 1). This plague was unique from the standpoint of its relationship to their personal property. Prior to this time the plagues had had the effect of irritation and pain, but not the widespread loss of personal property. Cattle and domestic animals were very precious to the Egyptians as witnessed both in their paintings and in their literature. We know from Eighteenth Dynasty inscriptions that horses were highly valued. Cattle, in addition to being practically necessary to daily life, were also very sacred to them.

According to verse 3 the hand of the Lord would be upon the cattle, horses, asses, camels, oxen and the sheep in a very grievous "plague." The Hebrew word for plague is *deḇer* which has the idea of pestilence. While the term is often used of pestilence in general (5:3; 9:15; Lev. 26:25; II Sam. 24:13, 15), it is here used in a special sense of a cattle plague (cf. Ps. 78:48). The precise nature of this plague has been difficult to determine. A common suggestion has been that it was anthrax, a disease relating to cattle; however, the text is not specific enough to be sure of this identification. Furthermore, the plague included many other domestic animals as well as cattle. What can be stated with assurance, however, is that the disease with which the animals were afflicted was highly infectious and quite clearly fatal.

Horses were common during the Eighteenth Dynasty. Their introduction for war use has been attributed to the Hyksos who dominated Egypt prior to the rise of the Eighteenth Dynasty. Notice that the animals presented to Abraham at an earlier period did not include the horse (Gen. 12:16). The mention of camels is sometimes used by critics to argue for the late date of the exodus, assuming that the camel was not domesticated prior to the thirteenth century B.C.; however, representations of camels found in Egypt, Syria, and Mesopotamia from the third and second millennia B.C. show that, at least in some places, the camel had been domesticated long before the thirteenth century.[2]

B. *Extent of the Plague* (9:4-7)

A clear separation was made between the cattle of Israel and that which belonged to the Egyptians (v. 4). Such a distinction leaves no alternative in the interpretation of the plague other than to recognize the event as essentially miraculous. It may be that the earlier plagues affected the Israelites as well as the Egyptians, for no mention is made of a clear division of the peoples (with the exception of the fourth plague, of course). Further substantiating the miraculous nature of this plague is the language of verse 5 which indicates that the Lord announced a set time for the beginning of this disaster and this time was fulfilled as announced according to verse 6. The question of the precise extent of this plague has been a matter of considerable debate simply because verse 6 indicates that all the cattle of Egypt died; however, in verse 19 it speaks of cattle needing protection from the seventh plague of hail and fire. Commentators have pointed out that this plague on domestic livestock was directed against only those animals that were "in the field" (v. 3); that is, those in open air. Animals protected by houses would not have been effected by this disaster.

> . . . All is not to be taken in an absolute sense, but according to popular usage as denoting such a quantity, that what re-

---

[2]See Joseph P. Free, "Abraham's Camels," *Journal of Near Eastern Studies* IV, No. 3 (July, 1944), pp. 187-193.

> mained was nothing in comparison; and according to verse 3 it must be entirely restricted to cattle in the field.[3]

Quite evidently Pharaoh refused to recognize the uniqueness of the event and its source; therefore, his heart was hardened and he continued to refuse the request of Moses and Aaron (v. 7).

### C. *Purpose of the Plague*

Such a plague would have had grave economic consequences in the land of Egypt. Oxen were depended upon for heavy labor in agriculture. Camels, asses and horses were used largely for transportation. Cattle not only provided milk but were very much an integral part of worship in the land of Egypt. The economic losses on this occasion must have affected Pharaoh greatly because he kept large numbers of cattle under his control (cf. Gen 47:6, 17).

The religious implications of this plague are most interesting and instructive. A large number of bulls and cows were considered sacred in Egypt. In the central area of the Delta, four provinces chose as their emblems various types of bulls and cows. A necropolis of sacred bulls was discovered near Memphis which place was known for its worship of both Ptah and a sacred Apis bull. The Apis bull was considered the sacred animal of the god Ptah; therefore, the associated worship at the site of Memphis is readily understood. There was at any one time only one sacred Apis bull. As soon as it died another was chosen to take its place, an event that attracted a great deal of attention in the area of Memphis.[4] The sacred bull was supposed to have been recognized by twenty-eight distinctive marks that identified him as deity and indicated that he was the object of worship.[5] The importance of the Apis bull is perhaps best illustrated by one of the more spectacular archaeological discoveries of the Memphis region. On November 13, 1856, Mariette

---

[3]Keil and Delitzsch, *op. cit.*, p. 487.

[4]Pierre Montet, *Eternal Egypt*, p. 172.

[5]*Archaeology and the Bible* (Westwood, N.J.: Fleming H. Revell Co., 1961), p. 181.

worked in this region, digging down to a shaft-like stairway to an underground avenue measuring 320 feet long. Later excavations indicated that the total length of the tunnel avenues reached 1,120 feet. Using only torch lights, Mariette and a few of his workmen discovered 64 large burial chambers arranged along an avenue. Near the center of each burial room was a huge red or black granite sarcophagus approximately 12 feet long, 9 feet high and 6 feet wide, each weighing about 60 tons. In each of these a sacred Apis bull had been buried. When Mariette moved through this area, it became apparent that the tombs had long ago been robbed except for one chamber which had escaped the hands of treasure hunters. The one chamber had been sealed during the reign of Rameses II. G. Frederick Owen described this discovery as follows:

> There, in the mortar was the imprint of the fingers of the mason who had set the last stone during the reign of Rameses II, and there in the dust were the footprints of those who had trod the floor more than three-thousand years ago. There also were the votive offerings dedicated by visitors who had come and gone so many centuries ago, among them an inscribed tablet of Rameses' own son, high priest of Apis and one of the chief dignitaries of the time. It is little wonder that when the great explorer stood in this tomb and saw things as they had remained inviolate for some thirty-one eventful centuries, he was overwhelmed and burst into tears.[6]

The sacred Apis bull kept in the enclosure near the temple of Ptah was fed on delicacies and given as many heifers as he wanted. Special bull fights were held in his honor.[7]

Another deity whose worship would have been affected by the impact of this plague was Hathor, the goddess of love, beauty and joy represented by the cow. The worship of this deity was centered mainly in the city of Denderah although its popularity is witnessed by representations both in upper and lower Egypt.

---

[6]*Ibid.*, p. 183. See also H. V. Hilprecht, *Explorations in Bible Lands During the Nineteenth Century* (Philadelphia: A. J. Holman & Co., 1903), pp. 634-635 and C. W. Ceram, *Gods, Graves and Scholars* (New York: Alfred A. Knopf, Inc., 1932), pp. 129-132.

[7]Pierre Montet, *Eternal Egypt,* p. 172.

This goddess is often depicted as a cow suckling the king, giving him divine nourishment. In upper Egypt the goddess appears as a woman with the head of a cow. In another town Hathor was a woman, but her head was adorned with two horns of a cow with a sun disc between them. Another deity associated with the effects of the plague would be Mnevis, a sacred bull venerated at Heliopolis and associated with the god Ra.

## II. Ashes, Dust and Boils (9:8-11)

Egyptians were constantly aware of the possibility of infectious diseases and sores. This is reflected in the fact that Sekhmet, a lion-headed goddess, was supposed to have had the power of both creating epidemics and bringing them to an end. A special priesthood was devoted to her called *Sunu.* Amulets and other objects were employed by the Egyptians to ward off evil in their lives.

The previous refusal of Pharaoh brought about the sixth plague and like the third it came unannounced. It was initiated by the symbolic casting of ashes (soot) from a furnace. This furnace may be one which was used for the melting of metal or perhaps the preparation of lime or the baking of bricks. If it were the latter, the act carried with it interesting symbolism, for the brick kilns of the Delta region represented that which was oppressive to the children of Israel. Many long hours had been spent by these peoples in the brick fields under the heavy hand of Egyptian taskmasters (1:14; 5:7-13). Symbolically, the ashes were cast toward heaven in the sight of Pharaoh. This brought about a plague of boils breaking forth with blisters or ulcers (v. 9). The Hebrew term used for boils here is *šᵉḥîn* which appears thirteen times in the Old Testament. These are related to man (II Kings 20:7; Isa. 38:21; Job 2:7) and may well have been in some cases leprous (cf. Lev. 13:18-20). Here they appeared upon both man (Heb. *'āḏām*) and beast. The intensity and severity of this plague is further reflected in the fact that the boils were breaking out in "blains" or "sores" (v. 9). These words translate the Hebrew *'ᵃḇa'bu'ōṯ* which is commonly translated blisters or boils and appears only in this context.[8] This term may

[8]Brown, Driver and Briggs, *op. cit.*, p. 101.

reflect not only severe soreness and irritation, but perhaps open and running sores. The infections here described may have been something like that which Job suffered (Job 2:7).

The magicians were probably once again called to attempt to vindicate the power of the gods of Egypt and demonstrate that the act performed by Moses and Aaron was nothing out of the ordinary. They, however, were not only unable to duplicate the miracle as had been the case with the gnats (8:18), but were apparently not even able to appear in the royal court because of the severity of this plague upon them (v. 11). The very fact that the magicians continued to be called even after their impotence had been demonstrated indicated something of the hardness of Pharaoh's heart. The impact of the magicians is not to be underestimated, however. They were a potent force in the royal court, and so impressive was their presence that their names had been retained in tradition (cf. II Tim. 3:8). This occasion, like previous ones, did not bring a noticeable change in the attitude of Pharaoh, for the simple reason that "the Lord (had) hardened the heart of Pharaoh" (v. 12). This sovereign, judicial act of God was not an isolated event. At a later time He caused Absalom to reject the good counsel of Ahithophel in order to bring judgment upon him (II Sam. 17:14). God led Rehoboam to reject the petitions of his people (I Kings 12:15). Not only was the heart of Pharaoh hardened, but also that of Sihon (Deut. 2:30) and the hearts of the Canaanites as well (Josh. 11:20). Furthermore, this should not be considered as an unjust and arbitrary act on the part of God. It must be remembered that it is the prerogative of an infinitely holy God to deal with evil men in any way He so desires. Any good that God brings to the sinner is a pure act of mercy and grace. What all sinners really deserve is death (Rom. 6:23).

This plague, like previous ones, most assuredly had theological implications for the Egyptians. While it did not bring death, it was serious and painful enough to cause many to seek relief from many of the Egyptian deities charged with the responsibility of healing. Serapis was one such deity. One is also reminded of Imhotep, the god of medicine and the guardian of healing sciences. The inability of these gods to act in behalf of the Egyptian surely must have led to deep despair and frustration.

Magicians, priests, princes, and commoners were all equally affected by the pain of this judgment, a reminder that the God of the Hebrews was a sovereign God and superior to all man-made idols.

## III. Hail and Fire (9:12-35)

### A. *A Warning from Jehovah* (9:12-21)

The seventh plague was preceded by a specific warning from Moses and Aaron and this time accompanied with significant explanation. The judgment about to occur had a two-fold purpose: (1) It was designed to indicate the uniqueness of Jehovah, the God of the Hebrews (v. 14). (2) It was also to be a demonstration of the power of this God in order that His name would be declared throughout the earth (v. 16). It might be observed that while the Egyptians left no trace of these experiences on their monuments, they were not able to prevent the spread of this story to other nations (Exod. 15:14; Josh. 2:10; 9:9; I Sam. 4:8). It is explained that Pharaoh was raised up for this very hour in order that he might be the vehicle through which the power and sovereignty of God would be demonstrated (cf. Rom. 9:17, 22). The promise was given that on the next day (v. 18) the Lord would bring about a violent storm in Egypt, bringing great hail on the land. The command was that cattle should be gathered out of the fields in order that they might be protected (v. 19). It is assumed that the cattle mentioned here are those that were not stricken by previous plagues or perhaps those cattle that had been brought from other countries. We know that:

> . . . Monarchs, in the inscriptions on their tombs, do not fail to mention the efforts that they made to improve livestock. Entire herds were brought in from the south and from Lybia. On at least two occasions, Syrian cattle were sent to Egypt.[9]

The warning issued by Moses and Aaron was followed by many of Pharaoh's servants as indicated in verse 20. This must have been somewhat distressing to the king of Egypt as he witnessed his own followers obeying the warnings of Moses and Aaron.

---

[9]Pierre Montet, *Egypt and the Bible*, p. 97.

B. *Devastation in the Fields* (9:22-26, 31, 32)

When Moses stretched his hand forth with the rod, the Lord sent thunder and hail, and fire ran along the ground (v. 23). This storm was certainly not to be considered a normal occurrence. That this was a miracle and was unique is made clear by the very language of verse 18 when it is stated that this was a storm which had no historic parallel. It is interesting that the very language of verse 18 shows that the author had considerable knowledge of Egyptian history for he speaks of their past when the lands were united and they became one nation.

The region of Cairo has but about two inches of rainfall annually, and south of this area rain is a rare occurrence. It has been noted that many times in the southern parts of Egypt no rain falls at all; therefore, it is most superficial indeed to argue that what occurs here is nothing more than an exaggerated tale of a natural event. If this were a purely natural event, then Pharaoh surely would not have responded as he did in verse 27. The thunderstorm was so violent and the lightning so great that fire raced along the ground destroying many of the crops. The miraculous aspect of this event is also supported by the notice in verse 26 that only in the land of Goshen was there no hail. One would suspect, on purely natural grounds, that if a storm were to occur anywhere it would be up in the Delta region which is near the Mediterranean Sea.

The only crops destroyed during this plague were those of the flax and the barley (v. 31) which indicates that this occurred late in January or early in February. Barley was a very important crop to the Egyptians. Flax was widely cultivated, especially since the Egyptians did not like woolen materials, which were worn by the nomads. The flax ripened about the same time as barley and was usually cut in the month of March. Wheat harvest was approximately one month later in the early part of April. Verse 32 indicates that the wheat and the "rye" (better translated "spelt") were not harmed by this plague even though they were probably growing at the time. Spelt is an inferior kind of wheat ordinarily raised in Egypt as an aftercrop.

### C. *Pharaoh's Reaction* (9:27-35)

The violent rain, hail and thunder coupled with lightning and fire forced Pharaoh to call again for Moses and Aaron (v. 27). No mention is made of wise men, magicians or priests. It was obvious to the arrogant king that only Moses and Aaron had the key to the solution of his problem. What Pharaoh did not concede to in previous events, this time he did. The theological perspectives of Pharaoh had decidedly improved. Perhaps the series of "visual aids" which preceded this judgment had had some positive effects!

Three interesting confessions are made in verse 27. The first is that he had sinned – this time. The fact that he mentions "this time" might reflect some of the arrogance and the shallowness of Pharaoh's confession. The second observation of this king is that Jehovah was righteous. This memorable statement is most significant since only a few months prior he refused to even acknowledge the existence of Jehovah (5:2). Finally, he admitted that he and his people were wicked; that is, had acted wrongly. One should not read too much into this confession, however, for Pharaoh was reacting to a situation that had forced these concessions. It is doubtful that each statement is undergirded with a high degree of sincerity. Perhaps his confession was much like that of Saul (I Sam. 15:24) or Nebuchadnezzar (Dan. 4:37). His principal concern most obviously was relief from the great storm at hand (v. 28). The intercession of Moses did not take place in the royal city (v. 29), but Moses left the city and raising his hands requested that the storm cease (v. 33). This prayer was heard, and God responded. Relief from the plague did not, however, change the heart of Pharaoh; he continued to resist as he had done on the previous occasions (vv. 34-35).

### D. *Some Theological Implications*

One cannot help but be touched with the sorrow that must have existed in the thousands of homes throughout Egypt. Those who had labored long and hard in the hot sun witnessed in a few moments the total destruction of their crops. Their desperate cries to their deities had not brought relief. We know from Egyptian documents that the loss of crops was one of the greatest disasters in this country. The economy and the life of the people were very much involved in agricultural success. Failure brought not only economic desperation but led to social disruption and great sorrow. What would the worshipers of Nut have thought when they looked skyward not to see the blessings of the sun and warmth, but the tragedy of storm and violence. Nut was the sky goddess. It was from her domain that this tragedy originated. One reflects upon the responsibilities of both Isis and Seth who also had responsibilities relating to agricultural crops. The black and burned fields of flax were a silent testimony to the impotence and incapability of wooden and stone deities. They indeed had ears but did not hear. The destruction of the crop of flax is also significant since it was flax which provided the linen for the garments of the priests throughout the land of Egypt.

## IV. Locusts from the East (10:1-20)

### A. *The Warning Issued* (10:1-11)

The locust is perhaps nature's most awesome example of the collective destructive power of a species. An adult locust weighs a maximum two grams and its combined destructive force can leave thousands of people with famine for years. Locust plagues were very much feared in ancient Egypt, so much so that the peasants were in the habit of praying to a locust god.[10]

> No one who has ever seen the locust at work accuses the Bible account of hyperbole. In 1926 and 1927, small swarms of the African migratory locusts were spotted in an area 50 by 120 miles on the plains of the river Niger near Timbuktu. The next year swarms invaded Senegal and Sierra Leone. By 1930 the whole of west Africa was flailing away at the pests with everything movable. But the locusts didn't seem to notice; swarms reached Khartoum, more than 2,000 miles to the east of Timbuktu, then turned south, spreading across Ethiopia, Kenya, the Belgian Congo, and in 1932, striking into the lush farm land of Angola and Rhodesia. Before the plague finally sputtered out fourteen years after it began, it affected five-million square

---

[10]Pierre Montet, *Eternal Egypt*, p. 39, compare also p. 169.

The Louvre

Boston Museum of Fine Arts

Hapi, god of the Nile depicted on a relief from the throne of the Pharoah Ay.

The Egyptian god Amun.

miles of Africa, an area nearly double the size of the United States.[11]

A locust is capable of eating its own weight daily. One square mile of a swarm will normally contain from 100,000,000 to 200,000,000 of the creatures. It is unusual, however, for such plagues to occupy an area of only one square mile. Swarms covering more than 400 square miles have been recorded.[12] Flying

---

[11]Daniel DaCruz, "Plague Across the Land," *Aramco World* (Nov.-Dec., 1967), p. 21.
[12]*Ibid.*

locusts have been regarded as marvels of stamina. They are able to flap their wings non-stop for seventeen hours, and may be able to fly at a cruising air speed of ten to twelve miles an hour for twenty hours or more.[13] When the young hoppers become winged adults, the bands become swarms with increased mobility and an average density of about 130,000,000 per square mile. Depending on wind condition, collective movement ranges from a few miles to more than sixty miles in one day.

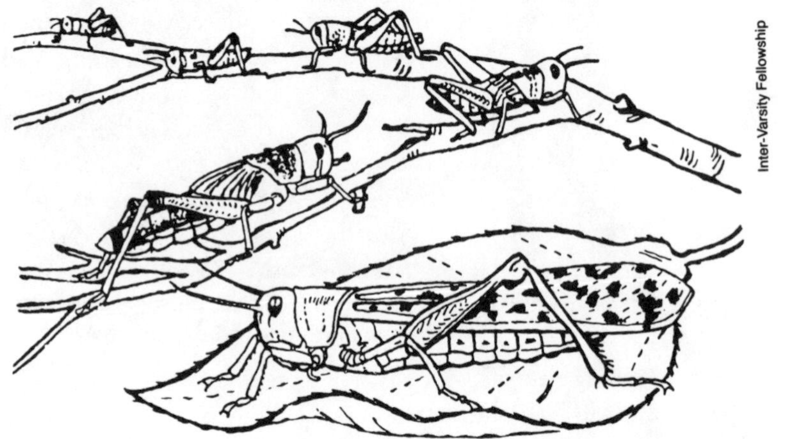


Six Stages in the Life-cycle of the Migratory or Desert Locust with the winged adult in the foreground.

Even with modern technology the locust is still a serious problem. Massive numbers of them still breed and move with devastation over parts of South Africa. Reports of such plagues appeared in the *Dallas Times Herald* of Sunday, December 8, 1963. Areas covered by the locusts include approximately 30,000 square miles, an area almost as big as the state of Maine. The Department of Agriculture in Cape Province, South Africa, pushed into service 200 spray trucks and more than 1,000 volunteers, but even that proved inadequate. The cost of fighting these small creatures ran about $30,000 a day. If fear is expressed over these plagues in areas such as South Africa where adequate rain and vegetation are present, one can only imagine the horror and despair that struck the heart of the Egyptians

---

[13] *Ibid.*, p. 23.

when the last of their crops were destroyed by millions of flying locusts. Their agricultural resources were considerably limited and had already suffered major destructions as a result of previous plagues. Their herds of cattle had been depleted, and many of the men were incapable of work due to the effects of the sicknesses brought on by the plagues.

It is against this background that we view the appearance of Moses before Pharaoh once again. In Chapter 10 we are informed of a new aspect or perhaps a new purpose for the plagues, and that is not only to humble the Egyptians and to effect the freedom of Israel, but also to be a lesson to Israel concerning the power of her God. All of these wonders were designed to reveal the redemptive power and significance of the God of Israel, Jehovah (cf. Exod. 6:3). They were performed in order that "thou mayest tell in the ears of thy son, and of thy son's son, what things I have wrought in Egypt, and my signs which I have done among them; that ye may know that I am the Lord" (v. 2).

The continued refusal of Pharaoh would be that which would guarantee the eighth plague, which was the devastation brought by locusts (v. 4). These would come in great numbers so much so that they would fill the houses both of Pharaoh's servants and of the Egyptians generally (v. 6). The patience of Pharaoh's servants was drawing to an end. While they recognized the wisdom of their god-king, they had serious questions about his reactions to the power of Moses and Aaron. Their syncretistic background made it very easy for them to include among their own gods the God of Moses. They raised a question concerning the propriety of Pharaoh's decisions in verse 7. This type of reaction publicly displayed and formally recorded is most unique. Pharaoh, not willing to appear blind and obstinate to the problems at hand, but at the same time maintaining his pride and dignity, offered to Moses and Aaron a third compromise. He was willing to allow the men (Heb. *hā'ᵃnāšîm* – "grown men") to worship, but not the little ones or their families (vv. 10-11). This condition, however, was unacceptable to Moses and with this they were driven from Pharaoh's presence.

### B. *Crisis and Confession* (10:12-19)

By means of a strong east wind which blew upon the land all day and all night, locusts were brought from Northern Arabia in large numbers. This again was a miracle of intensity and extent, for "before them there were no such locusts as they, neither after them shall be such" (v. 14). The whole land was covered, so much so that it was darkened (v. 15). This is best understood as a description of the ground itself rather than the heavens, although great clouds of locusts have the tendency to darken the skies. One of the best descriptions of a locust plague is to be found in the book of Joel where it is recorded that "A fire devoureth before them and behind them a flame burneth; the land is like the garden of Eden before them, and behind them a desolate wilderness . . ." (Joel 2:3). Not only do locusts destroy the crops but they damage trees and fruits (Joel 1:7-12). It did not take Pharaoh long to realize that he was now confronted with a crisis that was unparalleled up to this point. He called for Moses and Aaron "in haste" (v. 16). There is no mention here of magicians or counselors. His call was accompanied by a confession which is somewhat analogous to the one recorded in 9:27. He recognized the fact that he had sinned against Jehovah and against Moses and Aaron, an admission of moral liability. Not only did he recognize his sin but requested forgiveness (v. 17). Again we must be reminded of the fact that such a confession and request comes out of practical expediency. It is doubtful that his concern was one of deep spiritual conviction; rather, he was interested in an immediate deliverance from a plague that was about to destroy his land.

In spite of the fact that Pharaoh had demonstrated obstinance and dishonesty, Moses turned from the royal court and prayed for deliverance from the plague. One must admire the patience of Moses with respect to the plan of God. He did not cringe nor did he challenge God regarding this long process. The plague was ended by means of "a mighty strong west wind," more literally translated from the Hebrew, "a sea wind," probably denoting the fact that it originated from the Mediterranean to the north or northwest. While this plague was ended, the effects of this plague and the previous ones certainly meant famine for the land of Egypt, and famine meant widespread robbery and social unrest. The economic, political, social and religious implications of these disasters are very apparent both from the theological mentality of the people and from the practical expressions found in ancient documents.

## V. Darkness in the Land (10:21-29)

### A. *The Nature and Extent of the Plague* (10:21-23)

The ninth plague, like the third and the sixth, came without warning. With Moses' hand stretched toward heaven, darkness covered the land of Egypt, so thick that it could be "felt" (v. 21). This thick darkness lasted for a period of three days (v. 22). Various explanations have been offered as to the means by which this was accomplished. The usual approach is to assume that the land of Egypt was struck with a devastating sandstorm known as Khamsin. Large sandstorms, of course, are not uncommon in Egypt. These are especially common when strong, hot winds blow off the deserts to the south. It is not impossible, of course, that such may have been included in this plague, especially since it is mentioned that a man was not able to leave his house during that time (v. 23), while the Israelites had light in their dwellings. However, the entire plague cannot be ascribed merely to swirling sand in the skies over Egypt. Its miraculous nature is made clear by the fact that Israel did have light and apparently was able to continue life normally. Perhaps what we have in this instance is a combination of a violent sandstorm coupled with a supernatural darkness which made mobility impossible. The suggestion that this was brought about by an eclipse of the sun hardly deserves serious consideration in the light of the details of this context.

In the light of Egyptian theology and practice, this plague was very significant. To a large degree it struck at the very heart of Egyptian worship and humbled one of Egypt's greatest gods. The sun god Ra was considered one of the great blessings in the land of Egypt. His faithfulness in providing the warmth and light of sun day after day without fail caused them to express great joy over the faithfulness of this deity. The attitude of the Egyptians regarding the sun is perhaps best expressed in what has been called "a universalist hymn to the sun," translated by John Wilson:

> Hail to thee, beautiful Re of every day, who rises at dawn without ceasing, Khepri wearying (himself) with labor! Thy rays are in (one's) face, without one knowing it. Fine gold is not like the radiance of thee. Thou who has constructed thyself, thou didst fashion thy body, a shaper who was (himself) not shaped; unique in his nature, passing eternity, the distant one, under whose guidance are millions of ways, just as thy radiance is like the radiance of heaven and thy color glistens more than its surface.[14]

The faithful warmth and provision of the sun was something fully enjoyed by both the Egyptian statesman and the laborer who worked in the fields. They praised the sun because "thou presentest thyself daily at dawn. Steadfast is thy sailing which carries thy majesty."[15]

Of particular significance with respect to this plague was the prestige of the god Amun-Re, the chief deity of Thebes and a sun god. In the New Kingdom period this god was the Egyptian national god, part of a very important triad of deities including Amun-Re, his wife Mut, and their son Khons. Amun-Re was commonly represented by sacred animals such as the ram and the goose. A number of other deities were associated with the sun, sky and moon; for example Aten was the deified sun disc. This god was proclaimed to be the only god by Akhenaten with emphasis on a special cult centered at Amarna. Atum was also another important god in lower Egypt whose worship was centered mainly at Heliopolis. He was the god of the setting sun and was usually depicted in human form. Sacred animals associated with this god were the snake and the lion. The god Khepre, who often appeared in the shape of the beetle (*Scarabeus sacer*), was a form of the sun god Ra. Another very important sun god was Horus often symbolized by a winged sun disc. He was considered to be the son of Osiris and Isis but also the son of Ra and the brother of Seth. Harakhte, another form of Horus and identi-

---

[14] *ANET*, pp. 367-368. See also Adolf Erman, "The Hymn to the Sun from El-Amarna," *op. cit.*, pp. 288-292.

[15] *ANET*, p. 368.

Metropolitan Museum of Art

King Akhenaton, his wife Neferti, and daughter presenting offerings to the sun-god Aton.

fied with the sun, was venerated mainly at Heliopolis and was represented by the hawk.

Among the deities affected by this tragic darkness was Hathor a sky goddess and likewise the goddess of love and joy. Hathor was the tutelary deity of the Theban necropolis. She was venerated particularly at Dendera and depicted with cow horns or was a human figure which was cow-headed. The sky goddess

Nut would also have been involved in the humiliation of this plague. What of the prestige of Thoth, a moon god of Hermopolis? He was also the god of writing and of the computation of time.

This list could be greatly extended involving a number of other deities associated with the sun, stars, and light but the above are sufficient to indicate the tremendous importance of the sun and sunlight to the Egyptians. The other plagues brought about the destruction of property, personal discomfort and pain, but this plague brought about the total immobilization of the Egyptians and certainly must have resulted in great fear. The first day may have easily been explained, but by the third day the cries of the Egyptians were probably heard throughout the land. One wonders what the prestige of Pharaoh must have been at this point. Among the divine attributes of Pharaoh was the fact that he was in fact a representation of Re ". . . by whose beams one sees, he is one who illuminates the two lands more than the sun disc."[16]

B. *The Fourth Compromise* (10:24-29)

Once again in desperation Moses and Aaron were called before Pharaoh. This time in an attempt to preserve his prestige, he again offered a compromise which permitted the children of Israel to go and worship their God in the desert, but with the stipulation that their flocks and herds would be left behind (v. 24). This condition, however, was unacceptable as were the previous ones. Moses pointed out that offerings and sacrifices would have to be made and the presence of the animals was important (vv. 25-26). Pharaoh perhaps felt that this was a very reasonable concession and after all the previous negotiations may have fully expected that it would be accepted by Moses; however, such was not the case. In great rage he demanded that Moses leave the royal court and indicated that he would no longer see him (v. 28). To this Moses fully agreed. One can understand from a practical point of view the rage of Pharaoh, for the loss of these multitudes of Hebrew slaves would

[16]*ANET*, "The Divine Attributes of Pharaoh," trans. by John A. Wilson, p. 431.

J. J. Davis

Egyptian cow-goddess Hathor.

definitely have had serious economic and social implications. This last arrogant response of Pharaoh brought about the words of Moses which indicated that he would no longer voluntarily appear before the king. The speech which concludes in verse 29 is actually continued in 11:4 and following.

The great pageantry which accompanied the worship of the gods at the temples must have been greatly diminished during these months of tragedy and disaster. The political and religious prestige of Pharaoh quite certainly suffered as indicated by the frustration of Pharaoh's own servants at his inability to bring an end to the problem. The pain, death and loss suffered by the thousands of Egyptians would have ended the many songs of merriment and the hymns of praise sung to their gods, at least for the time being. Who would have expected in an age of unparalleled prosperity and military prestige, such as that which characterized the Eighteenth Dynasty, the people of Egypt would find themselves on their knees humbled before Jehovah, the God of the enslaved Hebrews? They who had beaten others were now the oppressed and the humiliated. The power of God as expressed in these plagues is a mighty witness to His sovereign intervention in the affairs of men and to the fact that His purposes will be accomplished.

Chapter 7

# *An Ordinance Forever*

(Exodus 11–12)

Pharaoh, having resisted all admonitions and warnings, continued to oppress the children of Israel. The fruit of this spiritual rebellion was one of the greatest tragedies to strike the land of Egypt. The countenance of the arrogant Pharaoh surely must have changed as he was awakened by a blood-chilling cry from his firstborn son, after which there was complete silence. What went through the mind of this man as he carried the white, limp body of his son up the hallway of his beautiful palace? What explanations could be offered in defense of the gods and himself when not only he but every family in Egypt was helpless in this tragedy? There is a sense in which we sorrow for this king and, as a matter of fact, with all sinners who have resisted the warnings of a gracious God. The exhibition of the awesome power of God is a reminder that those who reject His grace and love will ultimately be the recipients of His judgment.

The time lapse between the first plague and the last is not revealed in Scripture. In fact, there is no information connected with the first plague to indicate when it began with reference to the calendar year. It is noted, however, that the plague lasted for seven days (7:25) and probably concluded at that point because shortly thereafter frogs were able to inhabit a river which had been polluted and in which all living things had died (cf. 8:11). The seventh plague, consisting of violent storms and hail, occurred about the end of January or the early part of February, as implied by the agricultural information supplied in 9:31-32. This final plague apparently took place in the seventh month of the year. The seventh month of the year was renamed in establishing a sacred calendar for Israel. It was given the name *Abib* (Nisan) and became the first month of the religious year. Tishri was the seventh month and denoted the beginning of the civil calendar. From the sparse information found in Exodus 11–12 it is possible to conclude that all the plagues occurred within the time period of one year or perhaps less.

The literary organization of Chapters 11 and 12 is somewhat

problematic. At the conclusion of the ninth plague and Moses' conversation with Pharaoh, it is stated that Moses would not again see the face of Pharaoh (10:29). Yet in 11:4 a conversation between Moses and Pharaoh appears to be in progress. The usual approach to this problem by liberals is to designate the various portions to different sources thereby accounting for the apparent conflict in material.[1] It is difficult to take liberal observations on this material very seriously. They are generally highly subjective and are based on presuppositions which are, from a literary point of view, untenable. In addition to this, they are generally characterized by a very open anti-supernaturalism and a suspicion of the text. This attitude is reflected by the observations of Fleming James, "We must distinguish however between what we think might have happened and what Moses himself may have thought."[2] He further observes that one . . . cannot rule out entirely the possibility that miracles may happen. At the same time he regards them as highly improbable. In the story of Moses he is therefore inclined to view the recorded miracles as pure inventions or as natural events which were transformed by imagination into miracles.[3] The best solution to the problem at hand is to recognize the fact that the Exodus material, like much of the historical material in the Old Testament, is not organized after a strict chronology, but rather on a basis of certain topics. This reflects the idea of retrospect in historical narrative. In order to understand the chronology of events recorded in Chapters 10, 11, and 12 the following reorganization of material is suggested:

(1) The plague of darkness occurred (10:21-23).
(2) During the three days of darkness, God instructed Moses regarding the final plague (11:1-3) and the Passover (12:1-28).
(3) Moses' interview with Pharaoh and the hardening of Pharaoh's heart, perhaps involving an additional day (10:24-29).
(4) Moses' interview with Pharaoh continued (11:4-8).

---

[1]See Roy Honeycutt, Jr., *op. cit.*, p. 364.

[2]*Personalities of the Old Testament* (New York: Charles Scribners Sons, 1939), p. 13.

[3]*Ibid.*, p. 14.

(5) Moses' departure from the presence of Pharaoh and a summary of the plagues (11:9-10).
(6) The plague on the firstborn occurs (12:29-30).
(7) Pharaoh's call for Moses and the consequent exodus from Egypt (12:31-42).

It will be seen from the above reorganization that the conversation initiated in 10:24-29 is continued in 11:4 ff.

## I. The Last Warning (11:1-10)

### A. *Introduction to the Last Plague* (11:1-3)

As noted above, the information supplied in verses 1 to 3 was actually given to Moses prior to his appearance before Pharaoh, in all probability during the three days of darkness in Egypt. The Lord indicated that one more plague would be brought upon Pharaoh. The word for plague in verse 1 is interesting and very descriptive. It is the Hebrew word *Nega*ʿ, which describes a "stroke, plague, or mark."[4] This masculine noun is probably derived from the Hebrew verb *nāga*ʿ meaning to "touch, reach, or strike."[5]

For the first time Moses was able to see the end of the plagues. Previously God had not revealed the exact number of judgments. He merely indicated that several would be coming prior to Israel's departure (cf. 3:19; 9:14). This final plague, according to this verse, would be the means by which the deliverance of Israel would finally be accomplished. As previously revealed, before the people departed from Egypt they were to "ask" of their neighbors and they would be given "jewels of silver and jewels of gold" (v. 2; cf. 3:21-22).[6] Those receiving this jewelry were not women only, as implied by this verse, but also the men (cf. 12:35). It is well known from discoveries in Egypt that men along with women wore jewelry.

The description of Moses in verse 3 has presented a problem to some commentators and has raised a question concerning Mosaic authorship. Would Moses have described himself as

---

[4]Brown, Driver and Briggs, *op. cit.*, p. 619.
[5]*Ibid.*
[6]For a discussion of the Hebrew word *šāʾal* see p. 66.

"very great in the land of Egypt, in the sight of Pharaoh's servants, and in the sight of the people?" While critics generally point to this as evidence of late editorship, many commentators find no problem with this language in respect to Mosaic authorship. It is pointed out that such a statement was not only legitimate, based on previous experience in the royal court, but was also necessary to understanding the narrative. "He is simply explaining why the Egyptians gave so freely of their means."[7]

B. *Announcement of the Plague* (11:4-10)

1. The Time of the Plague (11:4)

The final plague was destined to occur "about midnight" (Heb. *kaḥᵃṣoṯ hallayᵉlāh* – "about the middle of the night"). The particular night was not specified, however. Perhaps this was done by design in order that Pharaoh might have time to ponder the fate that awaited him and his people. All that Pharaoh knew was that a tragedy was to strike at midnight, which, unlike some of the other announced plagues, would have left him with a fearful suspense.

2. The Nature of the Plague (11:5)

At midnight Jehovah would pass through the land of Egypt and His judgment would bring about the death of all firstborn in the land including animals as well as human beings (v. 5). This judgment was appropriate in the light of what we now know about oriental societies. The firstborn was not only an heir of a double portion of the father's inheritance, but represented special qualities of life and strength (cf. Gen. 49:3). In Egypt, the firstborn was the one who would succeed his father on the throne.

The context does not indicate that any secondary causes were employed by God to cause this death. On the contrary, as contrasted with previous judgments, it appears that secondary causes were absent and God himself struck the fatal blow. It has been the view of some commentators, however, that this, like all

---

[7]Francis Nichol, *op. cit.*, p. 546. See also George Rawlinson, *op. cit.*, p. 226.

plagues, can be explained on the basis of natural phenomena. Honeycutt suggests that in this struggle a fatal pestilence probably struck Egyptian children and in some way was related to the release of the Hebrews. Through years of transmission within Israel the memory of the event was so shaped that the end product suggested that only the firstborn were involved and that every firstborn of both man and beast was involved.[8] Such explanations are not really helpful in understanding the text. No secondary causes are indicated and no pestilence is named, as for example in II Samuel 24:15 where many people also died. It is better to regard this as a purely supernatural operation.

For many critics the death of the firstborn raises a serious moral problem with respect to the nature and character of Jehovah.

> The total witness of the Biblical revelation concerning the nature and character of God suggests that while God may utilize fatal epidemics, or other catastrophes in nature, He hardly goes about slaying children. Thus, either the nature and character of God has changed, or man's comprehension of that nature has enlarged with the fuller appropriation of God's self-revelation.[9]

The problem of judgment and the application of the *ḥerem* principle has been a problem for many scholars for years. The destruction of cities and their inhabitants on the part of Joshua and the invading armies has been regarded by many as a low view of the God of the Old Testament and certainly in conflict with the idea of God's love as revealed in the New Testament.[10] It is the view of many scholars, especially those influenced by Neo-orthodox views of Scripture, that the message contained in the Old Testament should not be taken at full, literal value, for the men who wrote in those early times were influenced by the

---

[8]Roy Honeycutt, Jr., *op. cit.*, p. 363. The same proposal was offered some years ago by Knobel; see John P. Lange, "Exodus," *op. cit.*, p. 40.

[9]Roy Honeycutt, Jr., *op. cit.*, pp. 364-365.

[10]H. H. Rowley, *The Rediscovery of the Old Testament* (Philadelphia: The Westminster Press, 1946), p. 324. For a further discussion of this and related problems see John J. Davis, *Conquest and Crisis* (Grand Rapids: Baker Book House, 1969), pp. 48-50.

theological deficiencies of that age and the language does not clearly reflect the highest view of God and His character.[11]

Such views, however, are deficient in the understanding of the origin of Scripture. If the Bible were merely the product of human genius and theological discovery, we should expect such limited revelation; however, it is clear that the Bible does not merely contain the Word of God, but is the Word of God by virtue of its divine origin and inspiration (II Tim. 3:16). In the light of the Old Testament doctrine of God's holiness and His view of sin, it is not inappropriate that He should judge the sinner by whatever means He deems necessary for that moment. This may involve the violent destruction of cities such as Sodom and Gomorrah (Gen. 18–19) or the annihilation of the inhabitants of a wicked city by invading armies (Josh. 6). The best interpretation of this whole event, therefore, is that this represents a supernatural judgment from God rather than an epidemic (which would hardly have been limited to the firstborn). Morally, God is fully vindicated in any act by virtue of His very nature. As a God of love and mercy, He will permit the sinner to live even though that sinner may resist a life-long revelation of truth. On the other hand, as a God of holiness He has the inalienable right to punish sin and the sinner at any point in his life. Theologically speaking, anything God does is right on the *a priori* grounds that He is God.

### 3. The Effects of the Plague (11:6-10)

According to the words of Moses the death of the firstborn would initiate sorrow and mourning such as never occurred in Egypt before (v. 6). The intensity with which the oriental expresses his emotions of sorrow at the time of death is well known. One can only imagine what the multitude of households must have been like with the discovery of the death of the firstborn. Even if individuals did not have children, the death of the firstborn of their animals would bring great sorrow in the light of the great value of such domestic animals. It is also possible that this "great cry" involved the reaction of the people with regard to the

---

[11]Roy Honeycutt, Jr., *op. cit.*, p. 365.

continued presence of the Israelites in their midst which obviously was now associated with the calamities which had come upon Egypt (cf. 10:7). When the time for deliverance came, no one would resist the departure of Israel. This is expressed by a proverbial saying, "A dog would not move his tongue against man or beast" (v. 7). The word which is translated "move" (Heb. *hāraṣ*) literally means "to cut into," "to sharpen," or "to bring to a point." The allusion here is to the fact that none would bring injury to Israel (cf. Josh. 10:21). Another effect of this plague would be the submission of Pharaoh's servants, a process which had already begun according to 10:7 (cf. v. 8). The continued belligerence of Pharaoh and his refusal to release Israel (cf. 10:24-29) brought about an angered reaction in Moses (v. 8). This is not a negative reflection upon Moses; in fact, the opposite would be true. He was characterized by extreme patience and faith, having been resisted numerous times in the royal court of Egypt. Pharaoh's reaction to the great wonders which had been performed in Egypt is again reviewed in verses 9 and 10 and it is pointed out that he would continue to resist to the very end. That end, of course, would be the death of his firstborn son.

## II. The Passover Lamb (12:1-13)

### A. *The Time of the Passover* (12:1-3)

The first portion of Chapter 12 has traditionally been ascribed by critical scholars to late sources (P), dating it as late as the exile. In the light of the details encountered in these chapters and the historical events with which they are related, it seems more probable to associate it with the origin of the Passover and the exodus itself. The events herein described constitute a very important time in Israel's history. In a special spiritual sense this was the "beginning of months" (v. 2). Presumably the events described in Chapter 12 occurred in the seventh month of the civil calendar. This month, however, was set aside as a special month for Israel in respect to the Passover and the exodus. From the standpoint of a religious calendar, this would be the first month (cf. Exod. 40:2, 17; Lev. 23:5). Another name for this first month of the sacred calendar is *Abib* (Exod. 13:4; 23:15; 34:18; Deut. 16:1), which literally means "ear-month" because it was at that time that the grain was in the ear. The

Israel Tourist Agency

A young son is receiving some expert instruction in the observance of the Seder, the Passover meal. Special dishes are used for the Passover. On the Seder plate is a roasted bone, a roasted egg, bitter herbs, parsley, charoses (a mixture of apples, nuts, wine, sugar, cinnamon to serve as a reminder of the mortar used during the Egyptian bondage), and three peices of matso (unleavened bread). The wine cup will be filled four times. Instructions for observing the Seder as well as the story of the Passover are in the Haggedah. Each member of the family has his own copy of the Seder book and each has a special part of the service.

month of *Abib* approximates to our month of April. After the Babylonian captivity, new calendar names were adopted and the ancient name *Abib* was changed to *Nisan* (cf. Neh. 2:1; Esth. 3:7). From this time onward two calendar reckonings were employed by the Israelites: one for sacred and the other for civil purposes, the first month of each year being in the seventh month of the other, though the numbers always ran from Nisan as the first.

### B. *Selection of the Animal* (12:4-6)

The means by which God would provide redemption for His people was the slaying of a lamb. According to the instructions given in this passage, a lamb (Heb. *śeh*) was to be taken in the tenth day of the first month (v. 3). The Hebrew term used for lamb here may refer to either sheep or goats without a particular limit to age; however, according to verse 5 an age was fixed. The translators of the Authorized Version were apparently influenced by Rabbinic interpretation which regards the regulation as meaning a year old or less, and in practice it was applied to lambs of the age of eight days to that of one year. The Hebrew, however, quite clearly means "one year old" (v. 5 – Heb. *ben šānāh* – "son of a year"). This is the same Hebrew construction as is found in Genesis 21:4 when we are told that Isaac was circumcised when he was the "son of eight days"; that is, eight days old (cf. also Lev. 27:6). This lamb was to be kept for a period of four days, from the tenth of the month to the fourteenth (vv. 3, 6). According to Hofmann the four days referred to four generations spent by the Israelites in Egypt, in which case the whole analogy would lie in the number four.[12] There is nothing in this text, however, to indicate that the number four is used symbolically.

After the animal was retained for four days, it was to be slain "in the evening" (v. 6 – Heb. *bên hā'arbāyim* – "between the evenings"). There has been a considerable difference of opinion as to the precise time meant by this expression. Two views exist on this point: (1) The period intended was that time between sunset and dark. It is argued that the first "evening" begins with the sunset and the second begins with the end of twilight. This view was held by Eben Ezra who considered that twilight lasted for approximately 1 hour and 20 minutes (i.e., from 6:00 to 7:20). This interpretation was supported by Deuteronomy 16:6, "Thou shalt sacrifice the passover at even, at the going down of the sun."[13] (2) According to Rabbinic interpreters the time when the sun began to descend from its zenith, that is, from 3:00 to 5:00, constituted the first evening, and the sunset was the second. Arguments for this view are generally based on two texts, Leviticus 23:5 and Numbers 9:3, which refer to the Passover as being on the fourteenth of the month. It is stated that if the animal were slaughtered after sunset it would then fall on

---

[12]Noted by John P. Lange, *op. cit.*, p. 36.
[13]See Keil and Delitzsch, *op. cit.*, p. 13.

the fifteenth of Nisan, not the fourteenth. According to Josephus it was the custom in his day to offer the lamb about three o'clock in the afternoon.[14] The custom during the time of Christ agreed with this latter explanation, for the passover lambs were slain in late afternoon, approximately the time when Jesus, the "Lamb of God," died for guilty men (cf. I Cor. 5:7; Matt. 27: 45-50).

Keil points out that the above arguments are based on an untenable assumption. He notes that it is obvious from Leviticus 23:32 where the feast prescribed for the day of atonement, which fell on the tenth day of the seventh month, was ordered to commence on the evening of the ninth day, "from even to even," although the Israelites reckoned the day of twenty-four hours from evening sunset to sunset, and numbering the days they followed the natural day and numbered each day according to the period between sunrise and sunset.[15] It can be concluded, therefore, that the term evening might encompass the time prior to sunset as well as sunset and the moments immediately following it. On the basis of the language of Exodus 12:6 it appears impossible to come to a final conclusion. The terminology is too ambiguous to arrive at a specific hour.

### C. *The Sacrifice of the Animal* (12:7-13)

After the lamb was slain the Israelites were to take the blood of that lamb and to strike it on the doorpost of their houses (cf. Exod. 12:22). The act of slaying the lamb and sprinkling the blood on the door, which represented the entry and the protection of the house, had great significance. It immediately pointed out the great price of redemption and symbolically it pointed toward the death of Jesus Christ (cf. I Peter 1:2; Rom. 5:8-9; Heb. 9:13-14; 13:12). Purification and cleanness apparently were associated with this symbolic act, as denoted by the use of hyssop (Exod. 12:22). Sprinkling with hyssop is normally prescribed only in connection with purification ceremonies (cf. Lev. 14:49-52; Num. 19:18-19). The door of the house symbolized not only the place of entrance, but the place of security.

---

[14]*Antiquities*, XIV:4:3.

[15]Keil and Delitzsch, *op. cit.*, pp. 12-13.

When Israel had succumbed to idolatry, she placed symbols behind the door and the doorpost (Isa. 57:8). In later periods, Arabs would many times place images on the threshhold of their homes to protect that dwelling. The idea that the lintel and doorpost were sacred and were somehow associated with evil spirits does not seem to be part of the regulation here suggested.[16]

The sprinkling of blood also eloquently speaks of a substitutionary atonement. Just as the lamb was substituted for the firstborn, thus protecting him from death, so the Lamb of God would some day die in the place of all sinners, thus providing escape from the judgment of God. After the blood had been sprinkled on the doorpost and the lintel, they were to eat the animal after it had been completely roasted with fire (v. 8). The eating of bitter herbs was also part of the meal and a very vivid reminder of the bondage of Egypt. The command not to eat the meat raw was significant because many of the surrounding pagan peoples often ate raw flesh at their sacrificial meals. In later times most sacrifices were boiled if a part was to be eaten (cf. I Sam. 2:14-15), but for the paschal lamb specific directions were given not to eat it raw nor to boil it but to roast it. This paschal meat was to be eaten with unleavened bread according to the admonition of verse 8. The command to prepare for the journey by eating the meal with the loins girded and shoes on the feet and staff in hand adds to this whole event a great air of anticipation and excitement. Of course, in later times these latter regulations were dropped, but they were most appropriate for the first Passover.[17]

This great Passover event was not only a unique revelation regarding the price of redemption from bondage for Israel, but it was a special revelation pointing to the impotence of Egyptian idolatry. It is specifically stated in verse 12 that these judgments were directed "against all the gods of Egypt," a fact easily ob-

---

[16]See E. A. Speiser, "Genesis," *The Anchor Bible*, W. F. Albright, ed. (New York: Doubleday, 1964), pp. 29, 31.

[17]For a discussion of the term *pesaḥ* – "passover," see Gustave F. Oehler, *Theology of the Old Testament* (Grand Rapids: Zondervan Publishing House, n.d.), pp. 346-347. Also see Keil and Delitzsch, *op. cit.*, II, p. 17.

served from the very nature and progression of the plagues as recorded in the Book of Exodus. Since the death of the firstborn involved both man and beast, it is quite apparent that it had far-reaching religious and theological implications. The firstborn of Pharaoh was not only his successor to the throne, but by the act of the gods was a specially-born son having divine property. Gods associated with the birth of children would certainly have been involved in a plague of this nature. These included Min, the god of procreation and reproduction, along with Isis who was the symbol of fecundity or the power to produce offspring. Since Hathor was not only a goddess of love but one of seven deities who attended the birth of children, she too would be implicated in the disaster of this plague. From excavations we already have learned of the tremendous importance of the Apis bull, a firstborn animal and one revered in a very special sense. The death of this animal and other animals of like designation would have had a tremendous theological impact on temple attendants as well as the commoners who were capable of witnessing this tragic event. The death cry which was heard throughout Egypt was not only a wail that bemoaned the loss of a son or precious animals, but also the incapability of the many gods of Egypt to respond and protect them from such tragedy.

## III. The Feast of Unleavened Bread (12:14-20)

### A. *The Origin of the Feast*

According to the biblical record the feast of unleavened bread originated within the context of Israel's exodus from Egypt as a concomitant commemoration of special redemption. Liberal scholars have generally disassociated the feast of unleavened bread from the Passover rite. It is assumed that the Passover had its origin in semi-nomadic backgrounds: whereas the feast of unleavened bread belonged to the sphere of agricultural pursuits more directly associated with the Canaanites.[18] Besides being in direct conflict with biblical statements as to the origin of this feast, there is no positive proof that the Canaanites had

---

[18]Hans-Joachim Kraus, *Worship in Israel,* trans. by Geoffrey Buswell (Richmond, Va.: John Knox Press, 1962), pp. 47-48.

| Pre-Exilic | Post-Exilic | Sacred Year | Civil Year | Festivals | Modern Equivalent | Agricultural Season |
|---|---|---|---|---|---|---|
| Abib | Nisan | 1 | 7 | 1—New Moon<br>14—Passover<br>15-21—Unleavened Bread<br>16—Firstfruits<br>21—Holy Convocation | March/April | Spring Equinox<br>Occasional Sirocco<br>Latter Rains; Flood Season<br>Beginning of Barley Season<br>Flax Harvest |
| Ziv | Iyyar | 2 | 8 | | April/May | Dry Season Begins<br>Apricots Ripen |
| | Sivan | 3 | 9 | 7—Pentecost, or Feast of Weeks | May/June | Wheat Harvest Begins<br>Dry Winds<br>Early Figs, Grapes Ripen |
| | Tammuz | 4 | 10 | | June/July | Hot, Dry Season<br>Grape Harvest |
| | Ab | 5 | 11 | | July/August | Air Still, Heat Intense<br>Olive Harvest |
| | Elul | 6 | 12 | | August/Sept. | Dates and Summer Figs |
| Ethanim | Tishri | 7 | 1 | 1—Feast of Trumpets<br>10—Day of Atonement<br>15-21—Feast of Tabernacles<br>22—Solemn Assembly | Sept./Oct. | Early (Former) Rains<br>Heavy Dews<br>Plowing, Seed Time |
| Bul | Heshvan | 8 | 2 | | Oct./Nov. | Rains, Winter Figs<br>Wheat and Barley Sown |
| | Chislev | 9 | 3 | 25—Dedication | Nov./Dec. | Winter Begins<br>Pastures Become Green |
| | Tebeth | 10 | 4 | | Dec./Jan. | Coldest Month<br>Rains (Snow on High Ground) |
| | Shebat | 11 | 5 | | Jan./Feb. | Growing Warmer<br>Almond Trees Blossom |
| | Adar | 12 | 6 | 15—Feast of Purim | Feb./March | Spring; Latter Rains Begin<br>Citrus Fruit Harvest |

**The Hebrew calendar**

a feast which was clearly analogous to the one described in Exodus 12.

## B. *The Time of the Feast* (12:14-20)

The feast of unleavened bread was to last for a period of seven days (v. 15) during which they were to eat unleavened bread. Leaven, of course, is understood to be a symbol of corruption and that which was evil (cf. Lev. 2:11 and I Cor. 5: 7-8). On the first day they were to put all the leaven out of their houses (v. 15). Violation of this standard would result in an individual being "cut off from Israel," an expression which has been interpreted by some to refer to violent death, premature death, or even eternal death; however, its simplest meaning seems to be one who would be cut off from all of the covenant rights and privileges normally afforded an Israelite.

The first day of the feast of unleavened bread also called for a public convocation or meeting during which no work could be done. The first of these seven days fell on the fifteenth of the first month (Lev. 23:6; Num. 28:17) or from the evening following the fourteenth day to the evening following the twenty-first day of that month (Exod. 12:18). The feast, therefore, included care taken with regard to personal obligations in the home, but also involved public worship with the whole nation. The seventh day was also celebrated as a day of holy convocation and worship (v. 16). The Passover (v. 14) and the feast of unleavened bread were to be perpetuated "forever" (v. 17).

## IV. Instructions for the Elders (12:21-28)

After Moses and Aaron had received full instructions regarding the Passover feast and the feast of unleavened bread, it was then their responsibility to convey this revelation to the elders and the people of Israel. Verses 21 to 28 include a record of that public declaration. Most modern critics ascribe this passage to J with final editorial work being influenced by D (Deuteronomists). This literary analysis, however, is subject to the same weaknesses as all others which have attempted to fragment the Pentateuch by means of subjective notions. The public announcement of the commemoration of the Passover and the feast of unleavened bread follows the details given in the earlier part of Chapter 12.

Emphasis is placed upon the use of hyssop which is not specifically named in verse 7. The hyssop most likely referred to was the Syrian marjoram (*Origanum maru* L.) or the Egyptian variety (O. *aegyptiacum* L.).[19] This plant is known in Palestine as *zaʿtar* which is still employed by the Samaritans at their Passover ceremonies. This plant has a rather pungent fragrant smell, a taste something like peppermint, and has masses of tiny white flowers. It is found commonly on rocks and terrace walls. Hyssop was used in connection with the purification rite for lepers (Lev. 14:4, 6), for a plague (Lev. 14:49-52) and the red heifer sacrifice (Num. 19:2-6; cf. Heb. 9:19).

Moses gave special emphasis to the perpetuation of these

---

[19]R. K. Harrison, "Plants," *New Bible Dictionary*, p. 1004.

events and pointed out their didactic necessity in verses 26 and 27. The time would come when children would ask questions regarding the annual commemoration of these ceremonies. It was very important not only to perpetuate the proper form of the ceremony, but it was incumbent upon the parents of these children to know its meaning and significance. The Church of Jesus Christ has long been plagued with those who have maintained the performance of certain rites, but the spiritual significance and symbolism of such rites have long since been lost and in most cases do not reflect personal experience. The concern which Moses showed over the meaning of an ordinance should be a warning to us that God's ordinances are to be perpetuated not only in correct form, but as representing personal experience and correct theology.

## V. Death of the Firstborn (12:29-51)

### A. *A Great Cry in Egypt* (12:29-36)

In the appointed midnight the Lord fulfilled that which He had promised; namely, a judgment upon all the firstborn in the land of Egypt. There was no respect of social or civil status in this plague. The firstborn of Pharaoh was slain as well as the firstborn of the man who was in prison. Significant is the fact that it mentions the death of the firstborn of cattle (v. 29). This, of course, takes on special significance in the light of the Egyptian view of Apis and Hathor. The death of Pharaoh's son was not a silent, painless one. It was one which brought about the awakening of Pharaoh and his servants, for the land of Egypt was characterized by wailing and tears throughout the remaining hours of the night. While Pharaoh may have found escape from the previous plagues, or perhaps provided satisfactory rationalizations of them, this one he could not escape. Its effects and implications were perfectly clear. That son whom he had cherished, the one born of the gods, now lay in his bed white, lifeless, and limp. The heart of Pharaoh and the will of Pharaoh had been broken. His spirit now changed from that of arrogance and resistance to grave concern, so much so that he called for Moses and Aaron in the night (v. 31). Without dialogue and long discussion, he simply stated that the children of Israel should leave. No qualifications, no concessions were part of his response; in fact, the departure was to take place on Moses' terms (v. 32). His concern for his own welfare is expressed in the last phrase of verse 32, "Bless me also," a most amazing request in the light of Pharaoh's assumed divinity. The God whose existence and power he had questioned in earlier times (5:2) he now asks to bless him. If Amenhotep II was the Pharaoh of the exodus, the son who died would have been his eldest son, the brother of his successor, Thutmose IV. While no Egyptian records of this event are to be found, it has been argued that the dream Stela of Thutmose IV points to the fact that he was not the eldest son and natural heir to the throne, but one who had to legitimatize that right.[20]

The fear and the frustration of the average man is also reflected in this portion of Scripture (v. 33). These events transpired with such rapidity that the dough which the Israelites had been preparing for the trip had not yet leavened (v. 34). With the urgent request of the Egyptians, the Israelites prepared to depart the land, and in the process asked the Egyptians for jewels and raiment (v. 35). From 13:18 we learn that some arms may have been taken as well, although the Hebrew text is not clear at this point. All of this, however, is small payment for over 400 years of slavery. There is no exploitation involved in these acts, nor are the Israelites robbing fear-struck Egyptians in an unwarranted manner. It is clear from verse 36 that the Lord prepared the hearts of the Egyptians in such a way that they "gave unto them such things as they required" (v. 36). This, of course, was a fulfillment of a promise given to Abraham many years earlier (Gen. 15:14).

### B. *First Steps to Freedom* (12:37-42)

Having officially been given their release, the children of Israel began their journey at the city of Rameses (v. 37). Even though the vocalization of the proper name is slightly different than that which appears in 1:11, it is apparent that the same place is meant (cf. Gen. 47:11; Num. 33:3-4). The site of Suc-

---

[20]See discussion p. 36.

coth has most recently been identified with the Egyptian word *Tjeku* mentioned as a border station in the story of Sinuhe in Papyrus Anastasi (V18:6-20:6; VI, 5:1). Some propose the idea that *Tjeku* is to be equated with Pithom[21] while others would reject this identification.[22]

The total number of Israelites participating in this exodus is not specifically given; however, the number of men over twenty years of age is listed as 600,000, a number which most critical scholars find impossible and unreal.[23] Assuming that males over twenty constitute approximately one-fourth the population, the total number of Israelites involved in the exodus would have surpassed 2,000,000 people. Scholars see a number of serious problems with accepting such numbers literally. Among them would be (1) The impossibility of that many people crossing the Red Sea in a short period of time. (2) The improbability, or perhaps even the impossibility, that the desert area of the Sinai Peninsula would be able to support that many people.[24] (3) It is argued that it would be impossible for Moses to have judged 2,000,000 people alone (cf. Exod. 18:13-17).[25] These arguments have been given careful consideration, and suggested solutions have been proposed in *Biblical Numerology*.[26] If the events accompanying the exodus are viewed in a purely naturalistic light, there is indeed a serious problem of the survival of this many people; however, Scripture makes it clear that the Lord intervened by means of supernatural provision to enable His people to survive the difficulties of desert existence. Furthermore, the number given here is in general agreement with the statistics of both Numbers 1 and 26. Many attempts have been made to reduce this number to "manageable proportions." It has been suggested that the number which appears here and in Numbers 1 and 26 was increased to make the event more

---

[21]C. deWit, "Succoth," *op. cit.*, p. 1220.

[22]Francis Nichol, *op. cit.*, p. 556.

[23]W. M. Flinders Petrie, *Researches in Sinai* (London: Hazell, Watson and Viney, Ltd., 1906), pp. 207-208.

[24]*Ibid.*

[25]R. E. D. Clark, "The Large Numbers of the Old Testament," *Journal of the Transactions of the Victoria Institute*, LXXXVII, p. 86.

[26]John J. Davis, pp. 58-86.

impressive. However, extending numbers beyond the realm of reasonable possibility would hardly make the historic narrative more credible. This would be like someone writing a story which claims that in the crash of a Volkswagen 200 people were killed traveling at a speed of 275 miles an hour. In spite of the energetic imagination of the author of the article, he would hardly have made a point in favor of the impressiveness of the event by extending the numbers beyond the realm of reasonable possibility.

A more recent attempt to bring the numbers into conformity with what is termed "realistic" figures is to reduce the number so that there would only be "2,500 fighting men and a total population of between 12,000 and 25,000 people."[27] If one is able to manipulate the numbers at will, then all historic numbers in the Old Testament must also be manipulated, otherwise ridiculous conflicts will occur. For example, the number of potential fighting men before the wanderings was 603,550. At the end of the period of wanderings there was a slight reduction in military potential to 601,730 men. Presumably if the figure suggested by Honeycutt of 2,500 fighting men represented the potential force upon leaving Egypt, this same number would represent the fighting force entering Canaan. In conflict with this are a number of specific details in the Books of Joshua and Judges which create serious problems. Joshua, for example, used 35,000 men in the defeat of Ai (Josh. 8) and the Benjamite army numbered 26,000 plus 700 of Gibeah (Judg. 20:15). Now if we accept the proposition that the Hebrew term *'elep̄* means "captain" or "family," this would then mean that Joshua used 35 "captains" or 35 "families" to attack the city of Ai (Josh. 8:3, 12), a rather small force to attack a fortified city. On top of that, at the end of this battle which is given two chapters of coverage, 12,000 people of the city died (8:25). Are we to assume that an army of 35 captains or families defeated a city numbering 12,000? Or are we to conclude that the number 12,000 ought to read 12 captains or 12 families (in which case one wonders why the city of Ai received such serious attention in such a large portion of the book of Joshua)?

---

[27]Roy Honeycutt, Jr., *op. cit.*, p. 367.

It is this type of problem that ought to warn the Bible scholar to be careful in his manipulation of numbers as they appear in the Old Testament. While it is true that some scribal errors have occurred in the transmission of numbers, these are few in number and can usually be corrected through textual studies. It is a dangerous procedure to change numbers on no grounds other than what one considers to be "reasonable" for a given period of history. (Every individual, after all, differs in what he would consider "reasonable" in any given context.) The process becomes extremely subjective and uncontrollable and the end result is a suspicion of all historical elements in the Old Testament.

Joining the Israelites was a "mixed multitude" (v. 38). This mixed multitude probably included other Semites who had settled in the Delta region, perhaps subjects of enslavement like the Israelites. It is also possible that many native Egyptians who were impressed by the power of the God of the Hebrews also joined them and perhaps in some cases even accepted the covenant faith of Israel. It is possible that some of these people were genuinely attracted to the faith of Israel, but the majority probably left Egypt for other reasons. It will be remembered that it was they who created serious problems for Moses during the years of wandering (cf. Num. 11:4). The Israelites left not only with jewels and raiment, but also with flocks, herds and a great number of cattle, all of this being literal fulfillment of the Abrahamic promise (Gen. 15:14).

Factual information concerning the number of Israelites participating in the exodus is not only given in this context, but there is also statistical information concerning the number of years involved in the actual oppression. In verse 40 this period of time is designated as 430 years. There are a number of Scriptures that relate to this period of bondage, some of which designate the time in rounded figures such as 400 years (Gen. 15:13, 16;[28] Acts 7:6). Acts 13:17-20 speaks of a 450-year period. From these passages two major views have emerged on the actual length of the Egyptian bondage. The first is that

---

[28]Gleason Archer takes the four generations as 400 years, i.e. 100 years for each generation. *Survey of Old Testament Introduction,* pp. 211-212.

the bondage consisted of only 215 years.[29] This view rests upon two basic arguments, the first of which is drawn from Galatians 3:17 and assumes that the 430 years mentioned begins with the call of Abraham and concludes with the exodus. This would mean that the Patriarchal period consisted of 215 years and the oppression in Egypt of 215 years. The other argument rests upon the Septuagint translation of Exodus 12:40 which reads, "who dwelt in the land of Egypt and the land of Canaan" rather than simply "in Egypt." This again points to the total 430-year period as including the Patriarchal age as well as the period of bondage. Harold W. Hoehner has raised five objections to this view.[30] (1) Both Genesis 15:13 and Acts 7:6 state that the sojourn would be in the land that was not theirs and they would be oppressed for 400 years. (2) Galatians 3:17 does not state that the 430 years was from the time of Abraham's call to the time of the Mosaic covenant, rather it is measured from the confirmation of the Abrahamic covenant until the Sinaitic covenant. (3) Genesis 15:13 and Acts 7:6 speak not of Abraham's sons but of his descendants being afflicted for 400 years. (4) The expression "fourth generation" (Gen. 15:16) probably refers to a 400-year period since that number is given in the same context (15:13). Generations, therefore, were calculated in this context at 100 years rather than 40. (5) The increase from one family of 70 or 75 to a nation of more than 2,000,000 would have required a residence in Egypt of more than 215 years.

The second major view of the period of oppression is that it lasted for the period of 430 years as stated in Exodus 12:40-41. Those holding this view regard the 400 years of Genesis 15:13 and Acts 7:6 as only a round number. This view assumes that the reading of the Masoretic text is to be preferred over the Septuagint. This view is held by Unger,[31] Archer[32] and others.

A third proposal has recently been offered by Harold Hoehner in which the Egyptian bondage is considered literally as a period

---

[29]See Roy Honeycutt, Jr., *op. cit.*, p. 367 and Francis Nichol, *op. cit.*, p. 557.

[30]"The Duration of the Egyptian Bondage," *Bibliotheca Sacra,* CXXV, No. 501 (1969), pp. 309-312.

[31]Merrill F. Unger, *op. cit.*, pp. 106, 150.

[32]Gleason Archer, *op. cit.*, pp. 205, 211-212.

of 400 years as stated in Genesis 15:13, 16 and Acts 7:6. The 430 years expressed in Exodus 12:40-41 and Galatians 3:17 is that period of time from the last confirmation of the Abrahamic covenant to the Mosaic Covenant.[33] This view rests on the literal meaning of Galatians 3:17 specifying the beginning of the 430-year period with the confirmation of the Abrahamic covenant. It is further argued that the specific period of *bondage* is mentioned only in Genesis 15:13, 16 and Acts 7:6. The other texts refer only to a general period of sojourn. The third supporting argument is based on the interpretation of Acts 13:19-20 which states that it was about 450 years from the commencement of the Egyptian bondage until after the conquest of Palestine. This interprets the 450 as 400 years for the Egyptian bondage, 40 years for the wilderness journey, and about seven years for the conquest of the land, making a total of 447 years or the rounded number of "about 450 years."

On the strength of the Masoretic reading of Exodus 12:40, however, it appears that the period of oppression should be regarded as 430 years, understanding, of course, that Genesis 15 and Acts 7 represent rounded approximations of these periods. The Galatians passage includes the period of time from the confirmation of the Abrahamic covenant until the exodus in 1445 B.C.[34]

## C. *Additional Instructions* (12:43-51)

When the children of Israel reached the site of Succoth, additional instructions were given concerning the Passover ordinance. These were made necessary because of the presence of many non-Israelites who had joined the Hebrews in their exodus. The provisions, therefore, deal mainly with these "strangers." No foreigner was to partake of this ordinance (v. 43). This foreigner or stranger would be one who retained his status as a foreigner by remaining uncircumcised and perhaps by not participating in other covenant practices. The man's

---

[33] *Op. cit.*, p. 313.

[34] For a complete discussion of the length of the sojourn and a defense of the 430-year view see Jack R. Riggs, "The Length of Israel's Sojourn in Egypt," *Grace Journal*, XII, No. 1 (Winter, 1971), pp. 18-35.

servant who had been circumcised would have the right to participate in this ceremony (v. 44), but those servants and foreigners who had not so subjected themselves to this ordinance of circumcision could not participate in the Passover feast.

The prohibition concerning the breaking of bones is most interesting in the light of New Testament data concerning the death of Christ (v. 46; cf. John 19:36). Details such as this make it clear that the Passover ordinance not only had symbolic value for the Israelite of the Old Testament, but clearly pointed to the coming Messiah, the Lord Jesus Christ, who would die without a broken bone for the sins of His people.

## VI. The Plagues in Perspective

Lest we lose sight of the overall purposes of the plagues, it would be well to pause for a moment of reflection. One cannot help looking at the man Moses as described in these chapters. His life was traced from childhood through boyhood, the years of desert isolation, and then through those moments of anxiety and reluctance when he received a divine call to lead the people of Israel. Whatever reluctance and anxiety Moses may have possessed prior to the exercise of God's power in the ten plagues was surely removed when he saw the hand of God at work. Moses became a very articulate statesman and a great leader who exercised unwavering faith. If God was able to take an eighty-year-old man and accomplish such significant victories, what must the potential be for the dedicated young man of twenty years? The spiritual insight and maturity of Moses will long be an example for believers in every age in every land.

Spiritual reflection also causes us to look back at the king who resisted the hand of God. His life is a pitiful record of one who ignored the clear revelation of a sovereign God. His life is also an example of what sin can do in the hardening process of the heart.

In short, therefore, what were the essential purposes of these ten plagues? First of all, they were certainly designed to free the people of God. Second, they were a punishment upon Egypt for her portion in the long oppression of the Hebrews. Third, they were designed to demonstrate the foolishness of idolatry.

They were a supreme example both for the Egyptians and for Israel. It was by these that Jehovah revealed His uniqueness in a way that had never before been revealed (6:3; cf. 10:2). Finally, the plagues clearly demonstrated the awesome, sovereign power of God. In the Book of Genesis, God is described as the Creator of the heavens and the earth and all the laws of nature. In the Book of Exodus the exercise of that creative power is revealed as it leads to the accomplishment of divine goals. God's sovereignty is not only exercised over the forces of nature, but is also revealed against evil nations and their rulers.

Reflection also causes us to search for practical considerations with regard to these chapters. What effect should the record of these miracles have on our thinking today? Two important considerations may be suggested with regard to these miracles and the God who performed them. First of all, we should always remember that the same God who humbled Pharaoh, the people of Egypt and their gods, is the same God who rules our world. Even though the nations will rage in rebellion against God with their Hitlers and Mussolinis, we are assured of the fact of God's sovereign preeminence over all the affairs of men. Second, and perhaps most significant, this same God is our Father. A personal relationship with Jesus Christ assures us of the fact that this God looks upon us not in judgment, but in mercy, a thought that should thrill the heart of every Christian. The plagues, therefore, are testimony to the power of God, His willingness to deliver, and His ability to perform that which He has promised.

## Chapter 8

# *Birth of a Nation*

(Exodus 13–16)

For the first time in over four hundred years, Israel was able to look back upon Egypt not as its master and lord, but as a defeated enemy. Events which had previously been promised and anticipated were now about to be realized. The humiliation of slavery and the discouragement of constant oppression were now things that could be left behind. The journey from Rameses to Succoth must have been a joyous and thrilling experience. The children of Israel were about to learn an important lesson, however, in addition to the fact that God's power is sovereign and not limited by the tirades of human leaders. They would learn that redemption does not guarantee complete freedom from earthly crises. The chapters before us reflect another conflict, partly a remnant of past associations with Egypt, that dealt with practical needs of this large group of people now heading for the deserts to the east.

### I. Sanctification of the Firstborn (13:1-2, 11-16)

Since the firstborn of Israel had been spared by God when the Egyptian firstborn children were destroyed, it was appropriate that these young men should be set apart for His service. It is evident from the Hebrew word used here that the command was limited to firstborn males who alone had been in danger from the previous plague. The original command regarding the sanctification of the firstborn was given on the day of the exodus (cf. 12:51). The consecration of the firstborn was closely associated with the events of the Passover and was to serve as a reminder of God's mercy to His people. This event was designed to be both positive and negative. Far too often practices of consecration have emphasized the negative whereas the biblical view of consecration is both negative and positive; that is, it involves separation *from* the world and separation *unto* God. The sanctification of the firstborn not only applied to young male children, but also to animals both clean and unclean. These were to be set apart in order that when the day of sacrifice arrived, their identity would be clear (v. 12; cf. Lev. 22:27). Since the ass was an unclean animal, that is, one which did not "part the hoof" (cf. Lev. 11:1-8; Deut. 14:3-8), it was not suitable for sacrifice. The ass is probably selected as a representative of all unclean beasts which were to be redeemed (cf. Num. 18:15). The command to set aside the firstborn of the beasts was appropriate since they too benefited from the redemption which God provided in the tenth plague. The whole purpose of this ceremony was to perpetuate the memory of the recent deliverance and to fix it in the mind of a nation which tended to forget divine blessings so easily.

The precise meaning of the term "token" (Heb. *'ôṯ*; cf. v. 9) and its implications in daily practice have been the subject of some speculation. Upon the basis of this verse and Deuteronomy 6:8 and 11:18 the Jews have concluded that this meant the wearing of literal pouches which they have designated *tephillin*, a term explained to mean prayers. The Greek designation was *phylakterion* (Matt. 23:5) from which the English word "phylactery" has been derived. The phylactery consisted of small pouches made from the skin of ceremonially clean animals, sewed to leather bands by which they were strapped to the forehead between and immediately above the eyes and to the left arms of males who had reached the age of thirteen. Inside the small pouches were strips of parchment on which were written certain passages from the Law (viz. Exod. 13:2-10; Deut. 6:4-9; 11:13-21). These passages were placed in one of the four compartments of the head phylactery. The arm phylactery had but one pocket yet contained the same four passages written on one piece of skin. It was generally tied to the inside of the left arm a little above the elbow so that the Scripture passages might be close to the heart.

Presumably this practice was in compliance with the command of Deuteronomy 6:6 that "these words, which I command thee this day, shall be in thine heart." This practice is still perpetuated today by orthodox Jews and phylacteries are worn by the pious during the daily morning prayer and by some devout men all day long. This practice, like many others, became a means of exhibiting a false piety. In Jesus' day men would make the phylacteries more conspicuous by broadening the bands, which practice was severely criticized by Christ in Matthew 23:5. Whether this practice is directly related to similar Egyptian customs is still a matter of considerable debate.[1] Many feel that the expressions found in 8:9, 16 are not to be interpreted literally but refer alone to symbolic action.[2]

## II. The Feast of Unleavened Bread (13:3-16)

The feast of unleavened bread was first made known to the children of Israel by Moses on the day of the exodus (cf. 12:15-20). This event was to be commemorated in the month of Abib (v. 4), which was the first month of the sacred calendar. One of the principal purposes of this feast was that it was to be a vivid reminder of the day when Israel was delivered from the Egyptian "house of bondage," or more literally translated "slave house." This expression is appropriate insomuch as Israel was in fact an enslaved people in Egypt (cf. 20:2; Deut. 5:6; 6:12). During the seven days when unleavened bread was eaten there would also be an air of expectancy and anticipation. The feast of unleavened bread was not only designed to bring back the memory of that great deliverance, but to remind them of the possibilities of future blessing. This is vividly portrayed in verse 5 of this chapter, for the land of promise is brought into view, a land which was then inhabited by enemies but one which would one day provide blessing and sustenance to a people who had eaten the food of slaves only.

## III. The Way of the Wilderness (13:17-22)

### A. *Forbidden Roads* (13:17)

Most traffic leaving Egypt heading eastward would take one of three roads. The most direct route to Canaan was the *Via Maris,* "the way of the sea." This road began at the frontier fortress of Sile, near modern Qantara, and reached Canaan at Raphia. This road was called by the Egyptians "the way of

---

[1]See Francis Nichol, *op. cit.,* p. 560 and George Rawlinson, *op. cit.,* p. 235.

[2]Roy Honeycutt, Jr., *op. cit.,* pp. 377-378.

Horus," but in verse 17 it is designated "the way of the land of the Philistines." According to this verse even though the road was a convenient one and the shortest to Canaan, God did not permit His people to use that route, primarily to avoid war; for this roadway was dotted with Egyptian fortresses and to pass along this way would be to encounter strong resistance and perhaps discourage the people. Another reason for avoiding this route was the fact that Moses was not to lead the people immediately into Canaan, but down to the "mountain of God" (cf. 3:12). The people were not spiritually prepared to occupy the land of Canaan as yet.

Another route that was taken by travelers heading eastward was "the way of Shur" which crossed the Sinai peninsula to southern Canaan where it connected with the important water-parting route from Jerusalem and Hebron to Beersheba in the Negeb. This route was south of the *Via Maris*. Hagar may have used this route to flee from her mistress Sarah during the Patriarchal period (Gen. 16:7). The third route, known today as "the pilgrim's way," ran across the peninsula from the head of the Gulf of Suez to Ezion-geber which was located at the head of the Gulf of Aqaba.

B. *From Succoth to Etham* (13:18-22)

The journey of the Israelites took them in the way of the "wilderness of the Red Sea" (v. 18). The exact identity of the Red Sea (Heb. *yam sûp̱* – "sea of reeds") has been the subject of very lively debate. Discussion of this problem is undertaken below.[3] The wilderness spoken of here is the desert area lying between Egypt and the Red Sea – not the wilderness of the Sinai peninsula. According to this same eighteenth verse the children of Israel left the land of Egypt "armed" (Heb. *ḥ*ª*mušîm* – from *ḥomeš* meaning variously "arrayed," "arranged" or perhaps marching "five abreast"). The use of this term in Joshua 1:14; 4:12 and Judges 7:11 has led some to suggest the meaning "armed" or perhaps "equipped for battle." Whether it is appropriate to describe the children of Israel as "armed" at this point is doubtful. They, in all probability, did secure some armor from

[3]See p. 168.

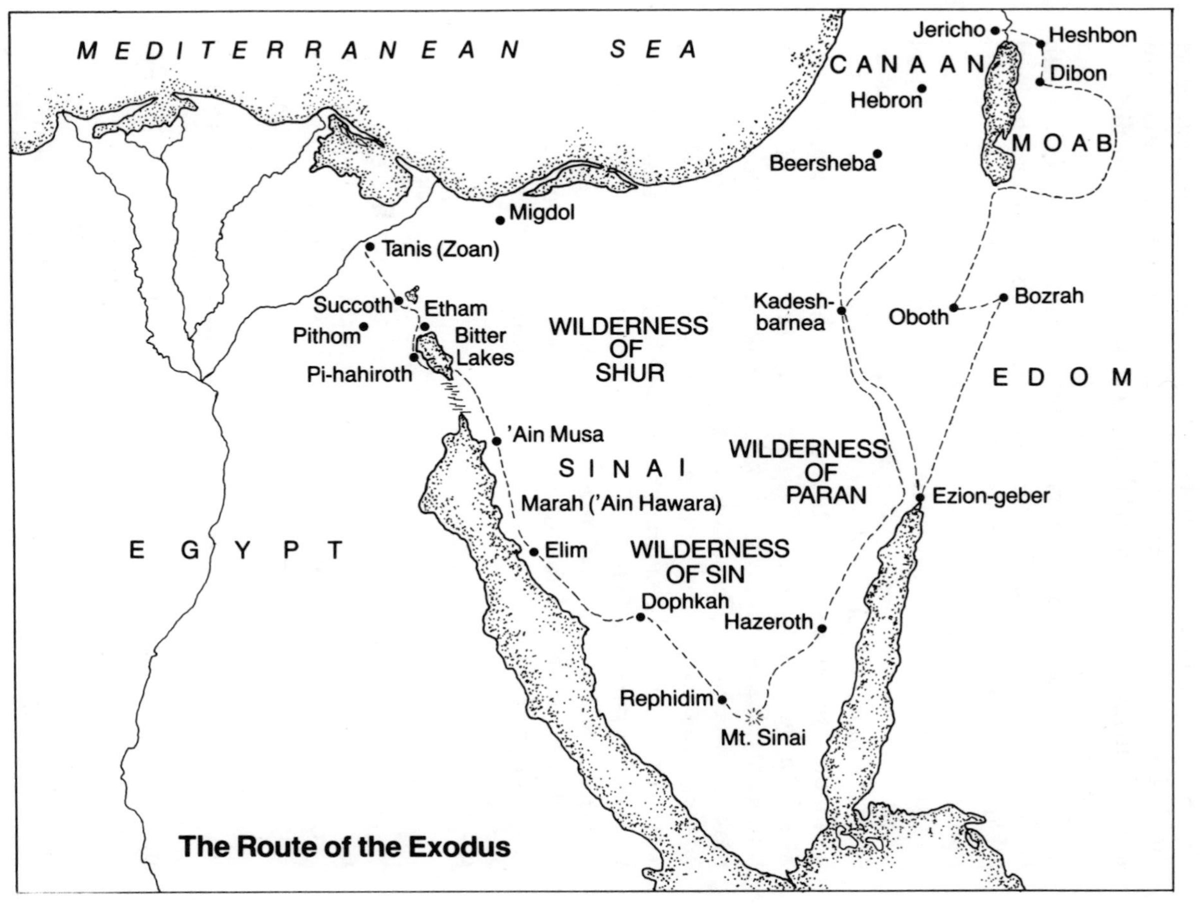

The Route of the Exodus

the Egyptians but could not at this point be described as a mobilized army. Whatever armor may have been secured was used primarily for limited defensive purposes. According to Keil and Delitzsch this term ". . . signifies equipped, as a comparison of this word as it is used in Joshua 1:14, 4:12, with *ḥ^a^lûṣîm* in Numbers 32:30, 32, Deuteronomy 3:18, places beyond all doubt; that is to say, not armed, . . . but prepared for the march, as contrasted with fleeing in disorder like fugitives."[4]

The remains of Joseph were taken with the children of Israel as previously requested (Gen. 50:24-26). No mention is made of the other sons of Jacob, but Stephen's statement before the Sanhedrin seems to imply that all the fathers were carried into Shechem (cf. Acts 7:15-16). Joseph's bones were ultimately buried at Shechem (Josh. 24:32). The journey of the Israelites took them from Succoth southward to Etham located "in the edge of the wilderness" (v. 20; cf. Num. 33:6). The Hebrew word Etham may be a transliteration of the Egyptian *khetem,* meaning fortress. Egyptian fortresses extending from the Mediterranean Sea to the Gulf of Suez are known from ancient times. These were designed to prevent the tribes of the eastern desert from entering Egypt, as well as controlling traffic between Egypt and the north.

The reason that Israel turned southward is probably due to the fact that they recognized that permission was granted them only to go into this eastern desert area – not into the Sinai peninsula. Pharaoh apparently never intended that Israel should leave Egypt completely. Presumably it was his intention that they should go to the deserts east of Egypt proper and offer the sacrifices that they had requested. The site of Succoth is usually identified with the modern *Tell el-Mashkuth* in the eastern part of Wadi Tumilat (cf. Exod. 12:37; Num. 33:5-6). This was the normal way in or out of Egypt for displaced persons. It is mentioned in the Story of Sinuhe in Papyrus Anastasi V and VI.[5]

In verse 17 it is declared that God led the people. The writer now explains the means by which this was made possible. While it was true that Moses had a general idea of what God expected

---

[4]Keil and Delitzsch, *op. cit.,* II, p. 38.
[5]C. deWit, "Succoth," *op. cit.,* p. 1220.

in this journey (3:12), specific aspects of Israel's journey had to be directed by God himself. It is clearly stated that the great pillar began to lead the children of Israel from Succoth, and it is not impossible that this cloud appeared at Rameses in order to lead them on their journey. This pillar took on the appearance of smoke by day and fire by night. There seems to have been but one pillar (Exod. 14:24), for even when shining in the dark it is still called "the pillar of the cloud" (v. 19) or simply "the cloud" (Num. 9:21). From the information supplied in verses 21 and 22 it appears that the Israelites marched some part of each day and some part of each night, which would be in accordance with modern practice. The purpose of such an arrangement is to march before the sun attains its full power and, of course, to utilize the cool of the evening. Accordingly, when it moved the people moved; when it stopped they encamped (cf. 40:36-38). From the very beginning of their journey, therefore, the glory of the Lord was among them. Later this glory was designated as *shekinah* (Exod. 16:10; 40:34). The presence of this pillar must have been a source of comfort and assurance to those who moved in anxiety, not sure of the events of the future.

## IV. Escape from Danger (14:1–15:21)

### A. *Camping by the Sea* (14:1-12)

The journey of Israel up to this point was in a southeasterly direction. If they had continued on this course, it would have carried them beyond the eastern border of Egypt and perhaps into direct conflict with Egyptian border forces. Through Moses, God ordered a change of direction which to many Israelites must have seemed strange and indeed risky, for their course was to turn in a southwesterly direction which in a short time would place great bodies of water between themselves and the Sinai peninsula to the east. The place of encampment is listed in verse 2 as Pi-hahiroth, "between Migdol and the sea, over against Baal-zephon. . . ." The exact location of these sites is at present uncertain.[6] Those who associate the crossing of the "Red Sea" with

[6]See John Bright, *A History of Israel* (Philadelphia: The Westminster Press, n.d.), p. 112.

the northern part of Egypt locate these sites somewhere near Lake Menzaleh.[7] Others have placed the sites somewhere west of the Bitter Lakes area.[8] What is of special significance in the verse, however, is the fact that geographical data are given in considerable detail, implying that the site of Pi-hahiroth was not well known. It further indicates the fact that the author of Exodus was familiar with the geographical details of this area. A writer from a later period would not have ventured to provide such detail.

The Lord again intervened in the affairs of both Egypt and Israel to renew the hardness and rebellion of Pharaoh's heart (v. 4). The purpose of this was not merely to provide additional frustration for the Israelites, but to provide an occasion by which He could demonstrate His own sovereignty to the Egyptians and illustrate the ability of God to care for His people before they embarked upon their long journey in the Sinai peninsula. When Pharaoh heard of the changed direction of the Israelites to the south and southwest he probably concluded that the Israelites had lost their way and were wandering in the deserts in complete confusion. Noting this situation and having been encouraged by his own people (v. 5) Pharaoh took six hundred of his best chariots and charioteers and began a pursuit of the children of Israel (v. 7).

It is interesting to observe the prominence given to chariot forces in this passage. The Eighteenth Dynasty was noted for its standardization of the chariot as army equipment. Fortunately for Bible students two royal chariots of the Eighteenth Dynasty have survived to the present day and we are therefore not in the dark as to their construction and size. They were open at the rear and consisted of a semicircular standing-board made of wood. This was encircled by a rim that stood approximately two and one-half feet above the standing-board. The chariots had two wheels and were drawn by two small horses. From paintings

---

[7]George E. Wright, *op. cit.*, p. 61, fig. 32. Compare also Yohanan Aharoni and Michael Avi-Yonah, *The Macmillan Bible Atlas* (New York: The Macmillan Co., 1968), p. 40, Map No. 48.

[8]See L. H. Grollenberg, *Atlas of the Bible*, trans. and ed. by Joyce Reid and H. H. Rowley (New York: Thomas Nelson and Sons, 1956), p. 44.

it is learned that they were usually manned by two men: a charioteer and a warrior. The six hundred chariots mentioned were probably of a special royal force. Other chariots were gathered from various parts of the Delta region as implied by the expression "all the chariots of Egypt" (v. 7). It should not be assumed that every chariot that existed in the land of Egypt was pressed into service.

The children of Israel left the land of Egypt with a "high hand" (v. 8). The *Revised Standard Version* translates this expression as "defiantly"; however, the Hebrew suggests a meaning of "triumphantly" or perhaps "confidently." The word horsemen which appears in verse 9 is probably not the best understanding of that word since the Egyptians did not have a cavalry unit at that time. The sense here probably refers to "riders" or "mounted men"; that is, those who drive the chariots.[9]

The Hebrews had not been encamped at Pi-hahiroth very long when word reached them of the intentions of Pharaoh. Their first reaction was to cry out unto the Lord (v. 10) but through lack of faith their anxieties soon turned to complaint and focused on Moses (v. 11). Their words took the form of bitter sarcasm and irony. Their reference to previous encounters with Moses was somewhat exaggerated as an examination of Exodus 5:21 will indicate. Their statement that it would have been better for them to have served the Egyptians than to die in the wilderness exhibits a remarkably short memory. Had they so quickly forgotten the humiliation and despair and hopelessness of the situation from which they had been delivered (cf. 2:23-24)? The reaction of the Hebrews is quite typical of those whose spiritual perspectives are those which are conditioned by the present alone. Without a historical consciousness of what God has done and a deep-rooted faith in what God will do, one is easily moved by the emotion of a given situation. The shallow responses of the Hebrews should be a warning to all of those who put all their emphasis on the present. This generation is bent on a philosophy which centers on "telling it like it is." The full responsibility of the man of God, however, in the light of revealed Scripture is not only to "tell it like it is"—

---

[9]Francis Nichol, *op. cit.*, p. 565.

thereby providing an accurate profile of contemporary man – but to tell it as it was and as it will be.

B. *Crossing on Dry Ground* (14:13-31)

The response of Moses to this potentially disastrous situation is both remarkable and exemplary. The threefold exhortation of this man indicates something of his spiritual and emotional maturity. He instructed the people first of all not to be afraid. The second command of Moses was to "stand still," which might be better translated "stand firm," reflecting a mature faith and confidence in the delivering power of Jehovah. The third imperative was to "seek the salvation of the Lord." The common verb *rā'āh,* meaning to see or behold with the eye, is used in this verse. The deliverance referred to here is, of course, physical in nature. The Hebrews were not called upon to prepare defenses or organize to fight. Moses reminded them that the Lord would fight for them and care for their safety (v. 14).

It has been objected by some that the response of the Hebrews in this portion indicates that they were very small in number. If they had 600,000 men of fighting capability, why should they be so afraid of the comparatively small military force of Pharaoh? The answer to this problem is obvious. The troops of Pharaoh, along with the highly trained and mobilized chariot force, were no match for the Israelites, who were poorly and inadequately armed and generally without any military training whatsoever.

While the situation for the average Israelite must have seemed hopeless with the sea in front of him and the Egyptian armies to his back, Moses was reminded by God that deliverance would be provided. This would be accomplished by the use of the rod (v. 16; cf. 4:17, 20) which was to be stretched over the sea and the waters would be divided (Heb. *bāqaʿ* – "to sever, cleave, break open or through"[10]). Furthermore, the children of Israel would cross through the midst of the sea on "dry ground" (v. 16). The Lord would humiliate the Egyptians by causing them to pursue Israel through the divided waters, thus bringing about their own defeat and death. The hardening of the hearts of the Egyptians is analogous to the hardening of Pharaoh's heart on

[10]Brown, Driver and Briggs, *op. cit.,* p. 131.

previous occasions (cf. 4:21). The anxiety of the Egyptians perhaps to recover lost treasures and bring upon these people a bloody revenge caused them to pursue the Israelites with abandon into the waters.

The Egyptians apparently reached the vicinity of the Hebrews' camp somewhere near the early evening. A supernatural cloud protected the Israelites during that night (v. 20). When Moses stretched out his hand over the sea, the Lord caused the sea to divide by means of a "strong east wind" which blew all that night causing the land under the waters to become dry. Again it is noted in verse 21 that the waters were "divided." The same Hebrew word is used here as was used in verse 16. According to verse 22 this special wind created a passage through the waters leaving a wall of water on the left and on the right as they traveled eastward (v. 22).

### 1. The Nature of the Crossing

The precise nature of this event has been the subject of considerable speculation and, at times, heated controversy. From the days of Josephus onward there have been critics who have denied the very historicity of this event explaining it as simply mythology.[11] Viewpoints which categorically reject the historicity of such biblical events need not be discussed at this point. Another view regards the parting of the waters as the result of the combination of a strong natural wind and the ebb tide. Rawlinson argues:

> If we imagine the Bitter Lakes joined to the Red Sea by a narrow and shallow channel, and a south-east wind blowing strongly up this channel, we can easily conceive that the water in the Bitter Lakes might be driven northward, and held there, while the natural action of the ebb tide withdrew the Red Sea water to the southward.[12]

This view is weak at two points. First of all there is no evidence that the Bitter Lakes were definitely connected with the Red Sea

---

[11]It appears that Josephus may have been reacting to such a view in *Antiquities* II:16:5.

[12]*Op. cit.*, p. 239. See also F. B. Meyer, *Exodus* (Grand Rapids: Zondervan Publishing House, 1952), I, pp. 161-162.

at this time. Furthermore, the biblical text does not speak of the ebb and flow of a tide.

Another proposal has ascribed this event to some kind of volcanic action, either in the vicinity of the sea which was crossed[13] or in the Aegean or Mediterranean areas. In an Associated Press release appearing in the *Fort Wayne Journal Gazette,* Professor Angelos Galanopoulos of Athens University is quoted as ascribing both the pollution of the Nile River and the crossing of the Israelites through the sea, to a violent volcanic eruption which occurred somewhere in the thirteenth century B.C. According to Galanopoulos, this volcanic explosion set off air waves 350 times more powerful than those of a hydrogen bomb and devastated not only the presumed continent of Atlantis, but provided associated catastrophic events such as the plagues and the separation of the Red Sea.[14] Such a proposal, however, requires too much in the way of accidental timing. Furthermore, it is very doubtful that the results described in the Bible could possibly have been achieved by such catastrophic and destructive means.

A very popular view is that the Israelites crossed in a generally shallow and marshy district which could easily have been cleared of water and laid dry by the normal action of a strong wind.[15] The difficulty with this viewpoint is that if this were merely shallow water, it is difficult to see how the Egyptians could have been drowned (cf. 14:28; 15:4-6). It is also quite unlikely that a purely natural wind could create "a wall" of water. If one should argue that the waters were indeed deep, but were still moved or parted by a natural wind, how then could the Israelites have crossed such an area? The velocity required of such a wind to move a considerable amount of water would have prohibited them from crossing such an area.

Another explanation of this problem focuses on the Hebrew

---

[13]See William Neil, *Harper's Bible Commentary* (New York: Harper & Row, Publishers, 1962), p. 79.

[14]Chris Elion, "Expedition to Seek the Lost Continent," July 10, 1966, p. 5e. See also Ronald Schiller, "The Explosion that Changed the World," *The Reader's Digest,* Nov. 1967, pp. 122-127.

[15]George Buttrick, ed., *The Interpreter's Bible* (New York: Abingdon Press, 1952), I, p. 938.

word *qādîm,* translated in the *Authorized Version* as "east." According to this viewpoint the word should be translated "previous" rather than "east" or "easterly." Jamieson argues:

> The Hebrew word *qadim,* however, rendered in our translation *east,* means, in its primary signification, *previous;* so that this verse might perhaps be rendered, "the Lord caused the sea to go back by a strong *previous* wind all that night" – a rendering which would remove the difficulty of supposing the host of Israel marched over on the sand in the teeth of a rushing column of wind strong enough to heap up waters as a wall on each side of a dry path, and give the intelligible narrative of divine interference.[16]

While it is true that this Hebrew term can have that signification, it is improbable that that is the appropriate reading at this place as evidenced by the consistent translation of this word as east in all the standard versions. Furthermore, this sense does not aid in an understanding of the passage itself, for it appears that the wind occurred only the evening that they encamped on the west side of the sea (v. 21). Had the waters been previously separated and the land dried, they could have crossed immediately upon hearing of the pursuit of the Egyptians.

This writer feels that the best interpretation of the "strong east wind" is to regard it as a supernatural wind rather than a purely natural wind. There are at least four reasons for assuming this view. First, it is doubtful that a purely natural wind would make a "wall" (v. 22). Second, if this wind came from the east (v. 21) it most likely would have walled up the water in the wrong direction; that is, north and south. Third, two walls are mentioned (v. 22) which indicates that the waters were divided by this special wind (cf. v. 16). When the people crossed there was a wall on their right hand, that is to the south; and a wall on their left hand, or to the north (v. 22). Such a walled effect would be accomplished by a special wind rather than a purely natural wind. Fourth, if this were a natural wind capable of moving enough water so as to provide a depth to drown the

---

[16]Jamieson, Fausset and Brown, *The Critical and Experimental Commentary* (Grand Rapids: Wm. B. Eerdmans Publishing Co., 1945), I, p. 327.

Egyptians, could the people have walked through such an area, assuming that a natural wind would have come through the area with tremendous velocity? The description of the waters standing up as a heap (15:8) is interesting and may shed further light on the nature of the walling up of the waters. A similar expression is used in Joshua 3:13 to describe the cutting off of the waters of the Jordan, thus providing passage for the children of Israel to cross. How wide an area was provided for the crossing is not given in the text of Exodus. It might well be that this was a considerable passageway in view of the fact that many Israelites had to cross.

If the above explanations are not to the liking of the reader, allow me to cite one other proposal which certainly ought to capture the imagination of those who grope for naturalistic explanations. According to one writer the poetic description of the crossing of the Red Sea provided in 15:8 indicates that the waters were congealed; that is, hardened or frozen. He notes:

> Over the congealed or frozen surface of the water Israel passed to safety, for the water was as hard as stone to them, as Job expressly states it: "The waters are hid as with a stone, and the face [surface] of the deep is frozen" (Job 38:30). . . . It was still Monday night, the twenty-first of Nisan, when Moses stretched out his hand over the sea and a strong east wind blew all that night. This brought about the "dry" condition of the waters: that is, the surface of the sea became frozen.[17]

While the above view is certainly imaginative, it lacks certain credibility with respect to the obvious and simple reading of the biblical text. The best expression of the means by which this event was accomplished is found in Psalm 74:13, "Thou didst divide the sea by thy strength . . ." (cf. Ps. 66:6; 78:13; 106:9; 136:13-15; Heb. 11:29). Regardless of one's view of the mechanics of this event, he must agree that the timing requires a miraculous intervention.[18]

The actual pursuit of the Egyptians took place according to

---

[17]Howard B. Rand, *Primogenesis* (Haverhill, Mass.; Destiny Publishers, 1953), pp. 166-167.

[18]Cf. Joseph P. Free, *Archaeology and Bible History* (Wheaton: Van Kampen Press, 1950), pp. 100-101.

verse 24 in the morning watch, which was the period of time from 3:00 A.M. until sunrise. According to Psalm 77:17-19 not only did the waters of the Red Sea return, but a sudden cloudburst helped to prevent the chariots from moving forward, thus preventing the successful crossing of the Egyptians and leading to great terror and frustration on their part.[19] The expression "took off" their chariot wheels (v. 25) is a translation of the Hebrew word *sûr* meaning in the Hif'il stem to "take away or to remove."[20] One suggested translation of this sentence is "and (Jehovah) made the wheels of his (the Egyptians) chariots give way, and made, that he (the Egyptian) drove in difficulty."[21] The Septuagint, on the other hand, speaks of God "clogging their chariot wheels," an idea which has been carried over into the *Revised Standard Version.* According to this approach the Egyptians would still be able to drive their chariots, but with great difficulty, thus making an immediate escape impossible.

Whatever the precise nature of the events described in verse 25 one thing is clear: they lost effective mobilization so as not to be able to retreat from the middle of the waters. The return of the waters brought an end to the Egyptian force that had committed itself to the pursuit and destruction of Israel. Verse 29 again rehearses the fact that the Israelites walked upon dry land in the middle of the sea with water on both their left hand and their right hand. It appears that the basic sense of the use of the word wall (Heb. *ḥōmāh*) is to designate a passageway between two generally perpendicular masses. On the basis of the Hebrew text alone, however, it is difficult to determine whether a literal perpendicular wall is necessarily implied. Some have suggested that the Hebrew term *hōmāh* is used figuratively, referring to defenses. According to this approach Israel was protected from attack "on their right hand and on their left."[22] In the light of the full context, however, preference certainly

---

[19]See Josephus, *Ant.* II:16:3.

[20]Brown, Driver and Briggs, *op. cit.*, p. 694.

[21]Keil and Delitzsch, *op. cit.*, II, p. 48.

[22]R. K. Harrison, "The Exodus and the Conquest of Canaan," *The Zondervan Pictorial Bible Atlas,* E. M. Blaiklock, ed. (Grand Rapids: Zondervan Publishing House, 1969), p. 63.

must be given to the former viewpoint since in crossing the Red Sea toward the east it is doubtful that they needed to be concerned with attack from the right hand or the left hand.

B. *The Place of the Crossing*

Because scholars have not been able to definitely locate Pi-hahiroth, Migdol and Baal-Zephon, the question of the exact place of the crossing continues to be the subject of very lively debate. Out of these discussions four views have emerged. The first proposal locates the crossing place in the vicinity of Lake Timsah or the southern extension of the present Lake Menzaleh. After discussing the biblical description of the body of water crossed, Philip C. Johnson concludes, ". . . the southern extension of the present Lake Menzaleh fits the description."[23] This view is based mainly on the fact that the Reed or Marsh Sea is mentioned in Egyptian writings of the thirteenth century B.C. as being near Rameses.

A second view, which also locates the body of water far to the north, has been suggested by Johanan Aharoni and Michael Avi-Yonah.[24] The crossing, according to this viewpoint, would have taken place in one of the gulfs of the northern Delta region, perhaps the Gulf of Serbonitis. Aharoni defends his view on the basis that Baal-Zephon is to be associated with a temple for mariners located on the arm of land that embraces the Gulf of Serbonitis, and Migdol was associated with the Egyptian border fortress northeast of Sile.[25]

Two difficulties arise with the above view. The first is that had they crossed this territory they would, in effect, have been going by "the way of the land of the Philistines," a road strictly forbidden by the Lord (Exod. 13:17). Furthermore, Scripture

---

[23]"Exodus," *The Wycliffe Bible Commentary,* Charles F. Pfeiffer and Everett F. Harrison, eds. (Chicago: Moody Press, 1962), p. 64. Also see G. E. Wright, *op. cit.,* p. 62.

[24]*The Macmillan Bible Atlas* (New York: The Macmillan Co., 1968), p. 40, Map No. 48.

[25]*The Land of the Bible: A Historical Geography,* trans. by A. F. Rainey (Philadelphia: The Westminster Press, 1962), p. 179.

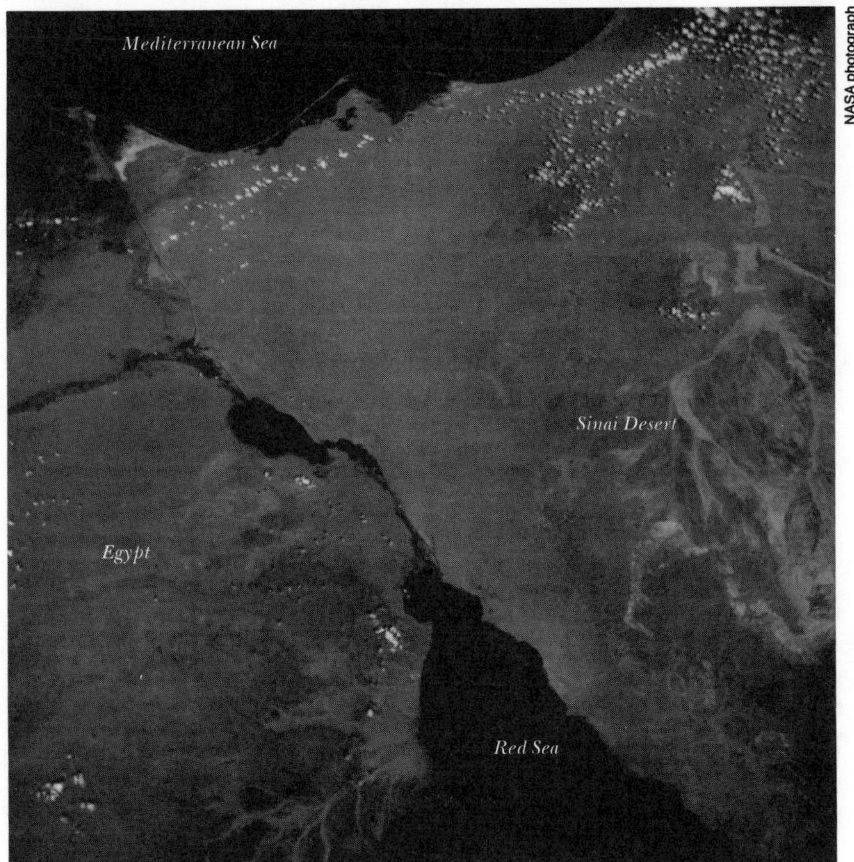


View of the Sinai Peninsula area from the Apollo 7 space craft at an altitude of 126 nautical miles.

clearly indicates that after crossing into the wilderness of Shur, the Israelites traveled for three days before coming to Marah (Exod. 15:22-23). Aharoni acknowledges that they journeyed to Marah, but makes no attempt to identify the site. If the traditional site of Marah, *'Ain-Hawarah,* is the correct one, then a three-day journey from the northernmost part of the Sinai peninsula to this site would not be possible. 'Ain-Hawarah lies on the ancient road to the Sinai copper mines, a few miles inland from the gulf and about forty-seven miles from the town of Suez.

A third view suggests that the crossing took place somewhere in the northern end of the Gulf of Suez.[26] Those who normally defend this view begin the Israelites' journey with Ra'amses, take them southward to the west side of the Bitter Lakes region with the crossing at the northern end of the Gulf of Suez. Interestingly, however, Fields suggests that the route of the exodus took Israel to the east side of the Bitter Lakes region; having gone south of the Bitter Lakes, Israel was then instructed to "turn back and encamp before Pihahairoth" (Exod. 14:2). This would then take the Hebrews to the west side of the Gulf of Suez where they crossed at its northern end. According to Fields, the Red Sea at this point would have been about four miles wide and approximately twenty feet deep.[27] This view has merit because the "Sea of Reeds" is frequently identified with the Red Sea proper elsewhere in Scripture. One difficulty with this suggestion, however, is that the children of Israel would not have entered the Wilderness of Shur from the Red Sea which is the information given in Exodus 15:22. The Wilderness of Shur is unanimously located east/northeast of the Bitter Lakes region.

John Bright objected to this view, stating that "it is unlikely that Israel crossed the tip of the Red Sea (Gulf of Suez) itself. This is so far to the south that the Egyptian cavalry would surely have caught them long before they reached it."[28] Fields, however, argues that the pursuit of the Egyptians did not come until a number of days later.

> Many people have the impression that Pharaoh began to pursue Israel almost the next day after their departure. But the Scripture nowhere states exactly how much time elapsed between Israel's departure and Pharaoh's pursuit. During that time the Egyptians embalmed and buried their first born (Num. 33:4). Surely a few days of mourning and shock followed these mass burials.[29]

---

[26]See Isidore Singer, ed., *The Jewish Encyclopedia* (New York: Funk and Wagnalls Co., 1905), p. 345 and Wilbur Fields, *Exploring Exodus, op. cit.*, pp. 33-48 and Siegfried H. Horn, "What We Don't Know About Moses and the Exodus," *The Biblical Archaeology Review*, III, No. 2 (1977), p. 29.

[27]Wilbur Fields, *op. cit.*, pp. 35-37.

[28]*Op. cit.*, p. 112.

[29]*Ibid.*, p. 43.

After crossing the Red Sea, this view proposes a southern route along the east side of the Gulf of Suez to Mount Sinai in the lower portion of the Sinai Peninsula.

A fourth view suggests that the actual place of crossing was somewhere in the Bitter Lakes. This view was first proposed in greatest detail by Father F. M. Abel, a professor at the French Dominican School of Jerusalem, who devoted his whole life to the study of biblical geography and carried out several thorough explorations of the Sinai Peninsula.[30] The results of this study are presented in Grollenberg's *Atlas of the Bible*.[31]

This view has in its favor that the Bitter Lakes region is known for its marshes and reeds and, therefore, could appropriately be called *Yam Sup* ("Sea of Reeds"). It must be conceded, however, that the presence or absence of reeds is not necessary for the expression *Yam Sup* to be applied to the Gulf of Suez, as has been done by numerous writers.[32] The word *sup* is not limited to the idea of "reeds" or papyrus plants because the same word is translated "weeds" in Jonah 2:5 and obviously refers to seaweed. Furthermore, it should be remembered that the expression *yam sup* is applied to the Gulf of Aqabah in I Kings 9:26: ". . . and king Solomon made a navy of ships in Ezion-Geber, which is beside Eloth, on the shore of the Red sea, in the land of Edom." Kitchen correctly observes:

> In the Old Testament the term *yam sup*, "Sea of Reeds" (and/or "weed"), is used to cover: (a) the Bitter Lakes region in the Egyptian delta north of Suez along the line of the present Suez Canal; and (b) the Gulf of Suez and Aqabah and possibly the Red Sea proper beyond these.[33]

In favor of the Bitter Lakes crossing is the fact that this would have led the Israelites immediately to the Wilderness of Shur after crossing *Yam Sup* (Exod. 15:22). Also, the journey from

---

30See L. H. Grollenberg, *op. cit.*, p. 48.

31p. 44.

32G. E. Wright and F. V. Filson, eds., *The Westminster Historical Atlas to the Bible* (Philadelphia: The Westminster Press, 1945), p. 38.

33"Red Sea," *op. cit.*, pp. 1077-1078.

this area to Marah would have coincided with the three days' trip mentioned in Exodus 15:22.

It should be observed at this point that the above suggestion is not that Israel crossed through a canalled area between the Gulf of Suez and the Bitter Lakes proper. This view had been suggested by some writers predicated on the idea that in antiquity the Bitter Lakes were connected to the northern section of the Gulf of Suez. In the light of archaeological evidence, it appears that this view must be abandoned. A fifteenth-century B.C. site studied by the University of California African Expedition along with William F. Albright noted that waters could not have risen in the Gulf of Suez very much above their present level.

> The edge of the site toward the sea lies only a little over a hundred meters from the sea, and less than five meters above mean Red Sea level (the hillock on which the settlement stands is only two meters above the high tide). This naturally means that the shore line has not risen more than a meter or two (if at all) during the past 3,500 years, thus confirming for the northern part of the Gulf of Suez what Nelson Glueck has found to be true of the northern part of the Gulf of Agabah. . . . .[34]

The suggestion of a crossing in the Great Bitter Lake in no way diminishes the miraculous character of the event. This proposal is not designed to find a shallow marsh area that could be conveniently crossed without divine intervention. Quite to the contrary – if the text of Exodus is to mean anything in its description of the drowning of an Egyptian army, the waters crossed would have to exhibit substantial depth. It would appear, therefore, in the light of all evidence that the best approach is to locate the crossing in some portion of the Great Bitter Lake. A crossing far to the north would prevent them from reaching Marah in three days.[35]

---

[34]"Exploring in Sinai with the University of California African Expedition," *Bulletin of the American Schools of Oriental Research,* No. 109 (1948), p. 15.

[35]For other studies on this problem see A. Lacocque, "L'idee Directrice de Exode 1 A IV," *Vestus Testamentum,* XV, No. 3, pp. 345-353, D. J. Mc-

After the Israelites crossed the Red Sea, they encamped on the other side briefly and were able to witness the miraculous power of God (Exod. 14:30-31). Josephus makes the unique (but very unlikely) observation that after the crossing of the sea a west wind set in. This wind, assisted by the current, drove the bodies of the drowned Egyptians to the eastern shore, thus providing weapons and armor for the Israelites.[36]

It would be well to observe at this point that not all scholars are agreed on the historical reality of the Red Sea crossing. There have been numerous attempts over the years to account for the origin of the story without having to resort to a literal event.

A recent proposal in this direction is the suggestion that the idea of crossing the "Red Sea" is actually a mythological motif which was common to other ancient Near Eastern literatures.

> Yam sup for the ancients had a symbolic as well as a historical meaning. Indeed, its symbolic meaning preceded its historical meaning. Symbolically it means Sea of the End, the seat at the end of the world.[37]

This writer betrays his assumptions about the nature of the biblical text in the following observation:

> The Exodus narrative should not be read as a historical account of what actually transpired in those days. Biblical writers were less interested in reporting historical data than in symbolizing for their contemporaries the salvational significance of their traditions.[38]

Such assertions, however, miss the point of prophetic admonition. If these historical events never occurred, there are no

---

Carthy, "Plagues and Sea of Reeds (Ex. 5-14)," *Journal of Biblical Literature,* LXXXV (1966), pp. 137-158. M. Copisarow, "The Ancient Egyptian, Greek and Hebrew Concept of the Red Sea," *Vetus Testamentum,* XII, No. 1 (Jan. 1962), pp. 1ff., N. H. Snaith, "*yam sup* — The Sea of Reeds: The Red Sea," *Vetus Testamentum,* XV, No. 3 (July 1965), pp. 381ff.

[36]*Antiquities* II:16:6.

[37]Bernard F. Batto, "Red Sea or Reed Sea," *Biblical Archaeology Review,* X, No. 4 (1984), p. 59.

[38]*Ibid.,* p. 63. Also see Bernard F. Batto, "The Reed Sea: Requiescat in Pace," *Journal of Biblical Literature,* 102, No. 1 (1983), pp. 27-35.

real theological or spiritual applications to be made. Joshua, for example, challenged the Hebrews to "fear the LORD and serve Him" (Josh. 24:14-15) as the logical response to God's historic faithfulness in their behalf (Josh. 24:2-13).

Even more potent is the argument of the Apostle Paul in I Corinthians 15 regarding the historic reality of the resurrection of the Lord Jesus. In essence, he argues that if Christ did not literally and historically rise from the dead, we have no theology! Faith, as presented in Scripture, is predicated upon historical realities.

The argument that historical facts are not important to Israel's theological values contradicts the plain language of the text and bankrupts the logic of prophetic preaching.

We are able to observe specific responses brought about by the great exhibition of God's power in the Red Sea deliverance. The death of the Egyptians caused the Hebrews to fear the Lord and to accept the ministry of his servant Moses (14:31). The story of the Red Sea crossing is a reminder to every believer that God is fully capable of completing His purposes and plans for those who have committed themselves to Him.

## Chapter 9

# *Pilgrimage to Sinai*

(Exodus 15–18)

The spectacular victory wrought by God over the armies of Egypt not only guaranteed freedom, but confirmed the fact that Israel had indeed been the recipient of special favor. For the first time in over four hundred years the Israelites were able to call themselves free men. Such freedom, however, was only from the slavery experienced in Egypt. With this freedom came a solemn obligation to obey the God who had delivered them.

The chapters before us are an exquisite example of godly praise and thanksgiving. The song of Moses reflects the heart and mind of a true believer as he gives due recognition to the provisions of God. These chapters also give us marvelous portraits of Joshua, Moses, Jethro and Miriam. They reveal moments of great national joy and excitement (chap. 15) as well as moments of darkness and despair (chap. 15, 17). These narratives are not merely the dry rehearsal of national events passed on by tradition and preserved out of some religious necessity. They represent an infallible record of real experiences depicted with warm emotion and dedication.

### I. In Praise of Yahweh (15:1-21)

The song of Moses is one of the most beautifully written sections of Exodus. It sets the spiritual and theological standard for all subsequent praise. The introduction to this song is contained in the words of verse 1: ". . . sing unto the Lord, for He hath triumphed gloriously: the horse and his rider hath he thrown into the sea." This expression was repeated when sung as an antistrophe by Miriam and a chorus of women (cf. vv. 20-21). Whether this occurred after every verse or at the end of the hymn cannot be determined. From a literary point of view the song is divided into three strophes or stanzas. The first is contained in verses 2 through 6, the second in verses 7 through 10, and the final in verses 11 through 18. The immediate occasion and theme for this song is, of course, the destruction of the Egyptian armies (v. 1).

The first stanza focuses upon the strength of Jehovah and His superiority over Pharaoh and his hosts. The expression, "I will prepare him an habitation" (v. 2), found in the *Authorized Version*, presents a problem. It is presumably intended to be a translation of the Hebrew expression *wᵉʾanwēhû*. This translation, however, appears to have its origin in the Aramaic targum of Onkelos where this expression has been paraphrased by the words, "I will build him a sanctuary." It is possible, of course, that this may have been one of the meanings of the word originally; however, most translators and interpreters since the time when the Septuagint was produced have preferred the idea of beauty, praise or glory. The *Revised Standard Version* suggests the translation, "I will praise him," whereas Keil and Delitzsch suggest "Whom I extol."[1] This latter suggestion is strongly supported by the fact that the last two phrases appear to be in synonymous parallelism.[2] The poetic description of Pharaoh's defeat further substantiates the concept of a crossing where the water was relatively deep. In verse 5 it speaks of the "depths" having covered the Egyptian army. The Hebrew word for depths is *tᵉhōmōt* which usually carries the sense of oceanic depths, the sea, or an abyss.[3]

The second stanza of this hymn contained in verses 7 through 10 focuses upon two major ideas: (1) The power of God over the elements, and (2) The power of God over the enemy. By means of the "breath of God" the waters were gathered together and stood upright as a heap (v. 8). The use of the Hebrew *nēḏ* ("heap") is largely restricted to this event and the crossing of the Jordan (cf. Ps. 78:13; 33:7; Josh. 3:13, 16). The last line of verse 8 is better translated, "The waves congealed in the heart of the sea," which is obviously a poetic description of the piling up of the waves as a solid mass. This stanza also gives special insight to the arrogant attitudes and the confidence of the Egyptians as they pursued the Israelites. Their desires were those of vengeance and anger. "By short clauses, following one another without connecting particles, the confidence of the

---

[1]*Op. cit.*, II, p. 51.

[2]The Targums of Jerusalem and Jonathan, the LXX and the Vulgate all support this sense.

[3]Brown, Driver and Briggs, *op. cit.*, pp. 1062-1063.

Egyptians as they pursued the Israelites, breathing vengeance, is graphically depicted."[4] The violent intentions and the deep hatred of the Egyptians did not find full expression, however, for God stepped in and the waters ended their insidious pursuit of the largely unprotected Israelites.

The third stanza of this song begins in verse 11 and continues through verse 18. It is an exquisite treatment of the transcendence of God above all the gods of the world. The eloquent question which introduces this strophe is one that rings with theological importance. It emphasizes not only the wonder-working power of God but His essential attribute; namely, holiness (v. 11). For those who are the objects of His mercy, there is redemption (v. 13). For those who rebel and challenge the power of God, there will be fear and judgment (v. 14). So great was this deliverance of Israel that chiefs and princes in Edom would hear and be afraid. The inhabitants of Canaan would "melt away" (v. 15). The prophecy was to have literal fulfillment as evidenced from Joshua 2:9-11, 24, and 5:1.

The conclusion to this song is very fitting. It speaks of the eternal reign of Jehovah (v. 18), an idea expressed elsewhere in the Bible (see Ps. 10:16; 29:10; 146:10; Rev. 11:15). Participants in this time of rejoicing not only included Moses and Aaron, but Miriam, the sister of Aaron, who also led in the choral responses of this song (v. 20). The title "prophetess" is not an unusual one as noted from its other appearances in Judges 4:4; II Kings 22:14; Isaiah 8:3; and Luke 2:36. She is the first woman, however, to be given this honor. This was no empty title, for she specifically claimed to possess the prophetic gift since God had spoken through her (cf. Num. 12:2). Micah reports the fact that the Lord delivered Israel out of Egypt by the hand of Moses, Aaron and Miriam (6:4); therefore, she played a rather important role in these events. She must have been more than ninety years of age at this time, however (cf. Exod. 2:4; 7:7).

## II. Bitter Waters (15:22-27)

Following the miraculous crossing of the Red Sea, the children of Israel entered what is designated as "the wilderness of Shur."

---

[4]Francis Nichol, *op. cit.*, p. 571.

Judean wilderness near Mt. Sinai

This is usually identified with the desert region in the northern part of the Sinai peninsula reaching from the eastern border of Egypt to the southern border of Palestine. It is mentioned several times in the narratives of the Book of Genesis (16:7; 20:1; 25:18). Later it was associated with the record of Saul's and David's victories over the Amalekites (1 Sam. 15:7; 27:8). It was probably through the center part of this desert area that the Israelites made their journey in a southeasterly direction. In Numbers 33:8 this area is designated the "wilderness of Etham."

Quite often the Sinai peninsula is illustrated by barren, desolate scenery. While much of the territory is indeed devoid of vegetation, it should not be concluded that this is an impassable desert. There are wells and springs at intervals of a day's journey all down the west coast from the Suez region to Merkhah. While vegetation is many times scarce, it can be found in significant quantities in the wadis or where there is a permanent water source. There is a rainy season lasting up to twenty days during the winter. This coupled with mist, fog, and dews helps to support some vegetation even among the rocks of this peninsula. There is some proof for the fact that in antiquity the Sinai peninsula supported a greater abundance of trees such as tamarisk and acacia. The presence of more vegetation and trees would have produced additional rain. According to Judges 5:4, the Lord provided some rain to help Israel to survive this wilderness experience.[5]

The traditional route of the journey takes the Hebrews southward along the Gulf of Suez. According to verse 23 they embarked upon a three-day journey during which time no water was available. It was not until they came to Marah that water was found and even at that it was not drinkable (v. 23; cf. Num. 33:8-9). This site is often identified with the modern 'Ain Hawarah, located several miles inland from the Gulf of Suez and about forty-seven miles from the town of Suez. Those who suggest a northern crossing of the Reed Sea prefer to identify Marah with either 'Ain Musa or an unknown spring near the Bitter Lakes area since 'Ain Hawarah is hard to reconcile with a three-day journey from the Reed Sea.[6] H. H. Rowley attempted to identify Marah with the site of Kadesh.[7] This, however, appears very unlikely in the light of the geographical details of the biblical narrative. If the identification of Marah with 'Ain Hawarah is correct, we might conclude that the sweetening of its waters was of a temporary nature, for the waters there today are quite bitter. The response of the people of Israel to this situation is somewhat amazing, for in the matter of three days they had forgotten the care and the provision of God. In spite of the fact that the cloud was there to guide them and remind them of the presence of God, they murmured. This was quite a change of attitude. Just three days earlier they were exalting their God with songs and praises. Now they had quickly forgotten and despair had set in. They had murmured once before on the

---

[5]See discussion of this verse in John J. Davis, *Biblical Numerology,* p. 61.

[6]Charles F. Pfeiffer, *Egypt and the Exodus* (Grand Rapids: Baker Book House, 1964), p. 54.

[7]*From Joseph to Joshua* (London: Oxford University Press, 1950), p. 104.

western shore of the Red ("Reed") Sea (cf. 14:11-12), and sadly enough, there would be numerous other occasions when their frustration and despair would exhibit itself in constant murmuring against God's chosen men (cf. Num. 14:2; 16:41). Appropriately Moses confronted this situation not with rebuke but with prayer. Having sought help from God, he was shown a tree which, when he had cast it into the waters, miraculously made the waters sweet (v. 25). Since there is no tree which is known to have the natural quality of changing bitter water into sweet, this act must be regarded as a miracle performed by God to demonstrate again His willingness and ability to care for His people.

The next stopping place is identified in verse 27 as Elim (Heb. *'êlim* – "terebinths" or "oaks"). The best location for this site appears to be Wadi Gharandel, located about seven miles south of 'Ain Hawarah. This place is characterized by a plentiful supply of comparatively good water with groves of palms, tamarisks, acacias and some grass. This site is used frequently today as a stopping place by the Bedouin who travel that area. The details included in the biblical account are significant and again point to Mosaic authorship. Details such as the count of the wells and the number of palm trees would hardly have been something included by a much later writer.

## III. Manna and Quails (16:1-36)

According to Numbers 33:10 the next stopping place on the journey southward was the Red Sea. The use of the term *yam sûp* obviously refers to the Gulf of Suez in this case. From here the journey continued southward and to the east to the wilderness of Sin. There are numerous opinions as to the location of this particular desert area. The encampment located in Dophkah (Num. 33:12) may be of some help in identifying this area. According to G. E. Wright the name means "smeltery" and probably refers to the Egyptian mining center at Serabit el-Khadem.[8] This would place the wilderness of Sin to the south and east of Elim. Actually four suggestions have been made in

---

[8]*Biblical Archaeology*, p. 64.

identifying the desert of Sin. (1) The dry barren coastal plain of *El-qaa,* north of the present port city of Tor, (2) the copper mine area *Wadi Magara,* (3) the plain *Debbet er-Ramleh,* north of *Jebel Musa* in the heart of the Sinai peninsula, and (4) the oasis *Feiran.*[9] The suggestion of Wright locating the site at Serabit el-Khadem appears preferable.

According to verse 1 the Hebrews arrived at Dophkah after a one-month journey. It must be assumed either that the children of Israel stayed at these sites for extended periods of time or that a number of camp sites are not named (cf. Num. 33:5-11 where seven camping places are named). The only other chronological information we have to fill in that one month is the three-day journey mentioned in Exodus 15:22.

Upon reaching the wilderness of Sin the children of Israel again murmured against Moses and Aaron (v. 2). This time their complaint centered around the fact that they lacked a sufficient quantity of food. Apparently the travels through the desert had depleted the supplies that they were able to accumulate both in Egypt and in the desert oases. They, of course, were accustomed to a rather good diet of meat, bread, fish and vegetables while living in Egypt (cf. Num. 11:5). God's answer to this problem was the provision of manna on a daily basis. The meaning of the term "mannah" has long been a puzzle to scholars. In verse 31 the term appears in the Hebrew text as *mān* but the fuller writing of the expression is probably found in verse 15 where the Hebrew reads *mān hû'*. Earlier writers suggested that the Hebrew *mān* was derived from the Egyptian word *mannu* meaning food.[10] On the basis of this etymology the expression *mān hû'* in verse 15 is translated, "It is manna." The Septuagint reading of this verse, however, appears to be preferable. It reads, *ti esti touto* – "what is this?" This reading has been followed in the *Revised Standard Version.* This interpretation is strongly supported by the following clause found in verse 15: "For they knew not what it was." One would normally expect to find the Hebrew *māh* for the interrogative rather than *mān.*

---

[9]Francis Nichol, *op. cit.,* p. 577.

[10]E. W. G. Masters, "Manna," *The International Standard Bible Encyclopedia,* III, p. 1982.

> F. M. Th. Böhl, however, has shown that the form *mān* was an old Semitic article meaning "what." It appears as *manna* in the Palestinian Amarna Letters, documents written in the 14th century B.C. We may therefore conclude that this short phrase is properly translated, "What is this?"[11]

The manna is described as having appeared in flakes or small round grains. According to Numbers 11:9 it fell with the dew and appeared when the dew left the ground (Exod. 16:14). It is described as being ". . . like coriander seed, white; and the taste of it was like wafers made with honey" (v. 31). Numbers 11:8 describes its taste "as the taste of fresh oil." The Israelites were commanded to collect an omer each for five days and double that amount on the sixth day to last them over the Sabbath (cf. vv. 16-18). This substance could not normally be kept overnight because it would decay and be filled with maggots. The extra manna which was to be kept for the Sabbath was preserved by being cooked or baked beforehand (vv. 4, 5, 16-30). In poetic portions this manna is described as "food from heaven" and "bread of the mighty" (Ps. 78:24 ff.). In Psalm 105:40 it is referred to as "bread of heaven" (cf. v. 4).

The fact that this was to be collected on six days and not on the seventh is perhaps in anticipation of the setting apart of the seventh day as a special Sabbath in Israel. Such a pattern is clearly based on the creation week (cf. Exod. 20:11). On the basis of this passage some have attempted to demonstrate that the Hebrews knew of a weekly Sabbath prior to the giving of the Law at Sinai.[12] While it is apparent that in the wilderness journey a seventh day had been set aside as a holy day to Jehovah (v. 23), it is not entirely clear that this Sabbath had been fully revealed as a national sacred day as is found in the Sinai covenant.

---

[11]Francis Nichol, *op. cit.*, p. 579. See also Martin Noth, *Exodus*, trans. by J. S. Bowden (Philadelphia: The Westminster Press, 1962), p. 135. For the use of *mannu(m)* in Akkadian as an interrogative pronoun see Wolfram Von Soden, *Grundriss der Akkadischen Grammatik* (Roma: Pontificiums Institutum Biblicum, 1952), p. 274. The early use of this form in Akkadian negates the assertion that the etymology of *man* must be traced to late Aramaic. Cf. Brown, Driver and Briggs, *op. cit.*, p. 577.

[12]*Ibid.*, p. 578.

According to verse 7 the manna made its appearance in the morning after the dew had lifted (v. 14). For all those who would rise early and collect the manna there would be adequate supply. One is reminded of the advice of Proverbs 6:9-11 where it is expressly stated that poverty and want are the reward of those who sleep late. Each man was to gather "according to his eating"; that is, according to that which could be consumed in one day. This normally amounted to an omer for each individual. An omer is considered a one-tenth part of an ephah (v. 36) which equals about two quarts. The manna had to be gathered early in the morning, for when the sun had become hot it melted (v. 21). It should not be assumed from these passages that manna constituted the only part of the diet of the Hebrews during this forty-year period. We know that the Israelites brought large flocks and herds with them out of Egypt (12:38; 17:3) and they continued to possess these not only in Sinai (34:3) but had them when they reached Edom and the country east of the Jordan (Num. 20:19; 32:1). It appears that on some occasions the Hebrews bought food and even water from the Edomites (Deut. 2:6-7). That wheat and meats were available is clearly implied in such references as Exodus 17:3; 24:5; 34:3; Leviticus 8:2, 26, 31; 9:4; 10:12; 24:5; and Numbers 7:13, 19.

Numerous attempts have been made to demonstrate that the provision of manna was nothing out of the ordinary. A widely accepted view is that the manna was identical with the lichen *Lecanora esculenta.* This lichen grows on rocks and produces pea-sized globules which are light enough to be blown about by the wind. They are well known for their sweetness and are often collected by the natives of central Asia.[13] Since such material has been absent in the region of Sinai during the last 150 years, this view has generally been abandoned. The most popular current view links the manna with tamarisk thickets in the wadis of the central Sinai mountains. Here during the month of June a granular type of sweet substance up to the size of a pea appears on the tender twigs of these bushes for a period from three to six weeks. The quantity of the manna usually

---

[13]See F. S. Bodenheimer, "The Manna of Sinai," *The Biblical Archaeologist,* X, No. 1 (Feb., 1947), p. 2.

fluctuates according to the winter rainfall. It was originally thought that this sweet substance was produced by the bark of the plant itself. It is now known, however, that insects produce this honeydew excretion on the tamarisk twigs. These drops are small, sticky, light colored and very sweet.[14] Such explanations may be appealing to those with little or no knowledge of the details of the biblical text or to those who choose to ignore them, but to the serious student of Hebrew history such explanations are decidedly inadequate.

There is no way possible that the production of this substance could satisfy the needs of the large host of Israelites who had camped in the desert. Furthermore, this food was made available to them through the full forty years until they entered the land of Canaan, at which time it ceased because it was no longer needed as a supplement. Sufficient food could then be found in the land (cf. Josh. 5:12). The tamarisk "manna" is found in the Sinai peninsula only during the months of June and July. This hardly fits the biblical requirements. Also, tamarisk manna can be kept for several days but cannot be used for baking purposes. This again points out the drastic difference between the biblical descriptions of this phenomenon and modern interpretations.

When F. S. Bodenheimer ran into difficulty with his tamarisk interpretation, he merely charged that ". . . the addition of stinking decay is a later misinterpretation and interpolation."[15] Later in the same article he remarks, "Exodus 16:21 tells us that the manna was collected early in the morning and that it 'melted when the sun grew hot.' We must regard the melting as a late and mistaken interpolation."[16] When this kind of manipulation of the biblical text is permitted it should be obvious even to the casual reader that any kind of explanation can be applied to the narrative. The very fact that so much space is devoted to this phenomenon referred to so many times in the Old Testament is an indication of its supernatural quality. Any

---

[14]A photograph of this substance appears in Werner Keller, *The Bible as History* (New York: William Morrow and Co., 1956), between pages 134 and 135.

[15]*Op. cit.*, p. 5.

[16]*Ibid.*

other explanation falls considerably short of the obvious intention and meaning of the biblical text.

The manna was not only used to help in sustaining the Israelites during the long forty-year period of wandering, but it served as a very vivid lesson to the children of Israel. According to verse 33 an omer of this material was to be gathered up and placed in a pot which would be set before the Lord. The purpose of this was to remind future generations of the faithfulness of God in providing for His people (cf. Deut. 8:3). The provision of manna on the six days alone was a very important lesson in keeping the Sabbath day properly. It was a means of teaching Israel obedience to that Law which would soon be revealed. The most significant use of the term manna, however, is when our Lord employs the term to refer to himself. Jesus Christ indeed was the manna or "the bread from heaven" (John 6:32-35). The provisions from heaven in Old Testament times were purely temporary for "your fathers did eat manna in the wilderness, and are dead" (John 6:49). But the Lord promised that the bread which He would provide – himself (John 6:51) – would provide eternal life which no man could take away. Just as manna was a refreshment and a great blessing to the hungry bodies of the ancient Israelites, so the Lord Jesus, the Bread of Life, fulfills all the hungers, desires and aspirations of the starving soul in this age.

In answer to the murmurings of the children of Israel not only was manna provided but quails as well (v. 13). The attempt on the part of some commentators to explain the word quails as meaning flying fish or locusts is decidedly inadequate and in conflict with the information provided in Psalm 78:27 which makes it clear that feathered fowls were meant. The quail referred to here is a game bird about ten inches in length (the *coturnix communis*). This species belongs to the same order as pheasants, partridges and grouse. This common quail is very abundant in the land of Syria and Arabia. In the autumn of the year this species migrates southward to central Africa and then returns in great numbers in the spring. In ancient Egyptian paintings people are shown hunting quail with hand nets thrown over the bushes where they were nesting. The Lord recognized the need for additional meat in their diet and therefore provided this bird.

The foods referred to by the Israelites and the mixed multitude (cf. Exod. 16:3; Num. 11:4, 5, 31) agree with what we know about the diet of the Egyptians from archaeology. According to biblical data the diet in Egypt included fish, cucumbers, melons, leeks, onions, garlic and meat. In a schoolboy's letter dating from the time of Rameses II the new city called House of Rameses is described.

> Its granaries are full of barley and wheat, and they reach unto the sky. Garlic and leeks for victuals (are there), and lettuce (?) of the . . . – garden; pomegranates, apples, and olives; figs from the orchard, sweet wine of Kankēme, surpassing honey; red uz-fish from the canal of . . . ; betin (?) – fish from Lake Neher; . . .[17]

In the light of this material it is easy to see why the limited desert diet would lead to frustration and bitterness, especially on the part of those who were not Hebrews.

## IV. Strife at Rephidim (17:1-7)

### A. *Source of the Problem* (17:1-3)

According to Numbers 33:12-14 two encampments were made before reaching Rephidim: Dophkah and Alush. Rephidim has been identified with two places. The first is Wadi Feiran which leads up to Mount Sinai. Others have identified it with Wadi Refayid. This latter suggestion seems desirable because the name is similar to the biblical name and it is within several hours' reach of the wilderness of Sin. The problem encountered at Rephidim was one that could be expected after a long journey in parched land. The people were without water and the welfare of their flocks was threatened (v. 3). Moses again turned to his God who had helped him in the past. This was not an

---

[17]Adolf Erman, "In Praise of the New City Called House-of-Ramesses," *The Ancient Egyptians,* p. 206. See also Barbara Mertz, *Red Land, Black Land,* p. 118.

isolated event but characterized his spiritual life (cf. Exod. 15:25; 32:30; 33:8; Num. 11:2, 11; 12:13; 14:13-19).

B. *Solution to the Problem* (17:4-7)

The people had become so dissonant and angry that they apparently were ready to stone their leader (v. 4). The leadership and competence of Moses should have been vindicated by now, but to a people easily influenced by the mixed multitude and the difficulty of the circumstances these historical facts were easily forgotten. While there is no doubt that the shortage of water reached critical proportions, nonetheless they should not have been angry with Moses, but should have turned to God who had already proven His power in the past. In answer to Moses' prayer, the Lord provided water from a rock after it had been smitten (v. 6). The location of this place is given as Horeb, which is commonly associated with the Sinai region. The only reasonable explanation for this event is that God again intervened miraculously. It is not sufficient to argue that Moses struck a rock accidently and due to the closeness of the water to the surface discovered the answer to his problem. The names given to that place were Massah and Meribah ("temptation" and "murmuring," v. 7). These terms, of course, reflect the attitudes of the Hebrews at this place. Israel was credited with "testing" the Lord; that is, they tried the patience of God, an act not limited to this occasion. The whole history of the wandering in the wilderness is a good example of the longsuffering of God with a people who constantly tempted and provoked Him (cf. Ps. 78:56; cf. 106:7, 14, 25, 29).

## V. Victory over Amalek (17:8-16)

Roaming the deserts of northern Sinai was a vicious fighting people known as the Amalekites. They were descendants of Esau's grandson after whom they had been named (Gen. 36:12). The Amalekites were undoubtedly attempting to protect their own territory as well as gaining control of the oasis area which had now been occupied by the Israelites. To meet this crisis situation, Moses called for Joshua and commanded him to organize the armies and attack the Amalekites (v. 9). This is the first mention of the man Joshua. He was about forty-five years of age at this time. His name was actually Hoshea but was later changed to Jehoshua (Num 13:16). The former name means "savior," the latter means "Jehovah is Savior." Throughout the forty years he acted as Moses' personal minister (Exod. 24:13; 32:17; 33:11; Josh. 1:1). One is immediately impressed with the faith and obedience of this young man (v. 10). Without question or objection he organized the relatively untrained and unseasoned soldiers of Israel and fought the Amalekites. It was not the military genius or the fighting skill of the Israelites that brought victory, however. It was the consistent and prevailing prayer of Moses (vv. 11-13). Following these events, the Lord commanded Moses to write these things in a book and to remind Joshua of the events (v. 14).

This is the first mention of writing as related to Scripture and official Hebrew records. We do not know exactly what script was used but presumably it was similar to the alphabetic Phoenician script or perhaps its proto-Sinaitic predecessor. The book mentioned in this verse was most likely a papyrus scroll. Papyrus was the most common Egyptian writing material and would have been well known to Moses. Moses evidently kept a diary of Israel's journey through the wilderness as implied in Numbers 33:2. In the light of the practices of Egyptian historiography it would be most unusual indeed if Moses did *not* keep such records. Such evidence strongly favors Mosaic authorship for the entire Pentateuch.

In commemoration of the great victory over the Amalekites, Moses built an altar and called the name of it Jehovah-Nissi which literally means "The Lord is my banner," a clear reference to the mighty work of God in bringing victory over His enemies. This was not the only encounter Israel had with the Amalekites, however. One year later the Amalekites joined forces with the Canaanites at Kadesh-Barnea to defeat the Israelites (Num. 14:45). They were also a problem during the Judges period (Judg. 6:33) and the time of the United Monarchy (I Sam. 14:48; 15:7; 27:8; 30:17-18; II Sam. 8:12).

## VI. The Visit of Jethro (18:1-27)

### A. *The Return of Zipporah* (18:1-6)

The visit of Jethro to the Israelite camp was no casual or accidental one. Jethro had kept close watch on the progress and fortunes of Israel since their departure from Egypt. Having heard of their victory over Amalek he decided to go visit the camp of Israel and participate in this time of festive rejoicing. There were other reasons for his presence, however, as indicated by the early verses of this chapter. Moses most likely had been separated from his wife and children for over one year. Zipporah and the two sons were evidently sent back to Jethro during the time of Moses' conflict with Pharaoh. The absence of his wife and children cause us to have an even deeper respect for his maturity and spiritual insight during Israel's most troubled moments. No hint is given in the biblical text of personal discomfort or dissatisfaction with this situation. He apparently had placed his wife and children in the hands of the Lord and concluded that in God's time they would be reunited. Therefore, for Moses this was a happy occasion not only because of Israel's victory over Amalek but because of the renewed fellowship with his wife and family.

The names which Moses gave to his two sons born to him in Midian probably reflects something of his spiritual experiences while in that land. The first son was named Gershom (v. 3). The name Gershom means "banishment" coming from the root *gāraš* ("to drive" or "to thrust away"). This name probably reflects something of the disappointment that Moses experienced in his separation from his people in the land of Egypt. The name of the second son, Eliezer, literally means "my God is help" (v. 4). This name indicates something of the gratitude which Moses had for divine protection enjoyed during his flight from Egypt. While the names of children clearly reflect personal experiences of the parents here, it should not be assumed that every name carried such significance elsewhere. It is a very precarious procedure to attempt to analyze the character or disposition of an Old Testament character on the basis of the etymology of his name alone.

B. *Jethro's Praise* (18:7-12)

The greeting of Jethro has all of the earmarks of an oriental meeting. According to verse 7 Moses went out to greet his father-in-law and did obeisance and kissed him. The admiration that Moses had for his father-in-law was not limited to family relationships alone. He respected this man for his wisdom as well as his age. The interest and concern that Jethro had for Israel is indicated by the fact that their first conversation centered about the mighty deeds that God had done on behalf of His people. The victory over the army of Egypt had undoubtedly reached the ears of Jethro and he was anxious for details concerning that event. Having heard of the goodness and the greatness of Jehovah, he rejoiced and gave praise to the God of Israel (vv. 9-10). The events of the exodus confirmed what Jethro apparently had previously believed; namely, that the Lord was greater than all the gods (v. 11). In special praise to God, Jethro, a priest, offered sacrifices to the Lord (v. 12). The idea of sacrifice, of course, was already well known as evidenced by Genesis 3:21; 4:3-4; 8:20; 12:7-8; and 22:13. Moses evidently recognized Jethro as a priest of the true God and therefore permitted the offering of a sacrifice. Perhaps in this respect Jethro was like Melchizedek (Gen. 14:18) who also was a priest of the most high God. Jethro must be considered unique, for it is clear from Scripture that the Midianites generally were idolaters (cf. Num. 25:17-18; 31:16).

C. *Jethro's Advice* (18:13-27)

Moses was not only charged with the responsibility of caring for the spiritual and military needs of the nation, but for their civil problems as well. Judging from the language of verse 13, a good deal of Moses' time was devoted to civil problems. Whether or not this type of pressure was characteristic of every day is not known. Some have speculated that the division of spoil of the Amalekites created unusual problems which demanded mediation on the part of Moses himself. As Jethro sized up the situation he rightly concluded that Moses could not exercise effective leadership if he were constantly bogged down with civil matters. His recommendation was that Moses teach the people "ordinances and laws" and then commit the implementation of the law to "able men, such as fear God, men of truth" (v. 21). On the basis of the expression "ordinances and laws" found in verse 20 some have attempted to place the visit of Jethro after the law had been given at Sinai, but this is not necessary, for the ordinances and laws mentioned here are regulations of the most general sense and not necessarily related to the special revelation given at Sinai. No doubt Moses had established basic procedures of organization and movement upon arriving in the desert. The movement of such a mass of people could not have been effectively carried out without such organization. The recommendation of Jethro was an evidence of his wisdom and perceptiveness. After men were selected, they were to be placed over the thousands, the hundreds, the fifties, and the tens (v. 21). This numerical breakdown gives some insight into the organization of the tribes into military and civil units.

Moses was fully convinced of the wisdom of Jethro's suggestion and in a short time selected men and put this system to work. The impression one gets from verses 24 and following is that Moses immediately implemented this plan; however, Deuteronomy 1:9-15 indicates that Moses did not actually arrange for the selection of these judges until after the Law had been given at Sinai. Perhaps Moses wanted to wait for divine approval of this plan before proceeding. On this basis, therefore, we must regard verses 24-27 as a later insertion. This type of historiography is not unusual in the Old Testament. On many occasions a writer deals with a subject topically rather than chronologically and thus material is inserted from later historic periods.

In times of great crises God has always provided men to lead the way to deliverance. Moses is an eloquent example of this very fact. The hand of God providentially prepared this man for this very moment. He was cognizant of Egyptian manners and was therefore able to articulate demands before the king of Egypt. Moses had been trained in military matters and was therefore capable of organizing this large mass of people for movement across the deserts. His training in Egypt had given him the ability to write and therefore provided a means by which these accounts would be recorded for eternity. Forty years of desert experience had given Moses the know-how of travel in these areas as well as the kind of preparation that would be needed to survive the desert heat. Is all this a mere accident of history? No indeed. The history before us is a supreme example of God's sovereign ability to accomplish His purposes for His people. Those who belong to Him have every reason to be confident that that which God has promised He will perform.

Charles Pfeiffer

Moses' Peak (Mt. Sinai).

## Chapter 10

# *Thunder, Clouds and Smoke*

(Exodus 19–20)

The trip south of Sinai was for Moses a return to familiar surroundings. During his days in the land of Midian he probably walked these areas many times. The arrival in the wilderness of Sinai occurred on the third month; that is, the month of Sivan, comparable to our late May or early June. The wilderness of Sinai has been located traditionally in one of two places. Some have suggested Wadi es-Sebayeh to the east of Jebel Musa. The other suggested site is the plain er-Raha, a large bush-studded plain approximately two miles long and one-half mile wide. This area would have been a very suitable place for the Hebrews to gather since it was surrounded by mountains thus forming a natural amphitheater. The events which occurred in this wilderness area represent one of the high points of Hebrew history. The exodus from Egypt constituted only the first phase of the creation of a nation. The completion of that image and the establishment of a particular religious identity took place here at Sinai. It was here that they received the law and the tabernacle. The law provided the way to life; the tabernacle demonstrated the way to worship.

### I. Arrival at Sinai (19:1-2)

After leaving Rephidim the children of Israel continued further southward reaching the desert of Sinai (v. 2). It is recorded that they arrived here "the same day" (v. 1). The Hebrew literally reads, "on this day" (*bayyôm hazzeh*). Jewish tradition placed this event on the first day of the third month of the Jewish year.[1] Similar tradition assigns the giving of the law to the fiftieth day after the Passover but this appears to be of too recent origin to be considered historical.[2] The best interpretation of this Hebrew expression is simply "at this time." This fits in

---

[1]Francis Nichol, *op. cit.,* p. 593.
[2]Keil and Delitzsch, *op. cit.,* II, p. 89.

with the context and with the verse itself.[3]

The area to which they were taken can only be characterized as majestic and inspiring. The granite mountains provide an awesome background for the events which would take place. For more than eleven months Israel remained at this place receiving the Law, ratifying the covenant and preparing the sanctuary.

## II. Preparation for the Covenant (19:3-25)

### A. *Treaty Patterns*

Thanks to the discoveries of ancient Near Eastern texts we now know quite a bit about the literary composition of covenants and treaties. Near Eastern treaties generally fall into two broad classes: The Parity Treaty and the Suzerainty Treaty. Parity treaties were, in effect, two treaties in opposite directions in which two kings of more or less equal importance bound each other to identical obligations. The Suzerainty treaties, on the other hand, were imposed by strong kings on their vassals.[4] G. E. Mendenhall has demonstrated that the literary pattern used by the Hittites in their Suzerainty treaties finds some parallels in Old Testament passages dealing with the covenant between Yahweh and Israel. Such Suzerainty treaties usually had six elements including a preamble, historical introduction, general principles for future conduct, specific stipulations, divine witnesses, and curses and blessings.[5] Both in this chapter and in Chapter 20 there appears to be a somewhat analogous arrangement of material as will be observed below.[6]

---

[3]John P. Lange, *op. cit.*, p. 69.

[4]J. A. Thompson, *The Ancient Near Eastern Treaties and the Old Testament* (London: Tyndale Press, 1964), p. 12.

[5]See *Law and Covenant in Israel and the Near East* (Pittsburgh: The Biblical Colloquium, 1955); J. Muilenburg, "The Form and Structure of the Covenantal Formulations," *Vetus Testamentum*, (1959), pp. 347-365; and K. A. Kitchen, *Ancient Orient and Old Testament* (Chicago: Inter-Varsity Press, 1966), pp. 90-98.

[6]Examples of this literary arrangement may be observed in the "Treaty between Hattusilis and Ramses II" and the "Treaty between Mursilis and Duppi-Tessub of Amurru," trans. by Albrecht Goetze, *ANET*, pp. 201-205.

B. *Challenge and Commitment* (19:3-8)

In a very general sense the material found in these verses follows the basic treaty pattern observed above. The verses could be arranged as follows: Preamble, verse 3; Historical Prologue, verse 4; Statement of General Principles, verse 5a; and the Blessings, verses 5b and 6a. The form here, of course, is shortened from that of a more lengthy Suzerainty-type treaty. The preamble found in verse 3 merely introduces the source of the legislation and challenge. Moses went up into the mountain and it was there that God instructed him as to that which he was to speak to the children of Israel. This is followed by a historical prologue in verse 4. In short, this was a reminder that their freedom from the Egyptians was brought about by God.

The expression "eagles' wings" is figurative and denotes the strong and loving care of God. The eagle, we know, watches over its young in a very careful manner. When the young eaglet leaves the nest, the mother will fly beneath it lest it should fall upon the rocks and be injured. When Israel left Egypt it was merely an eaglet, nationally speaking. Its vulnerability and its defenselessness were perfectly obvious. Without the intervention of God they would have been easily crushed and defeated. The emphasis, however, is not only upon deliverance from Egypt merely for the sake of providing liberty for the people.

The purpose of this deliverance is stated in the last clause of verse 4. God brought them unto Himself. This provides the background for the next item in this dialogue; namely, the statement of basic principles of obedience. Since God was responsible for Israel's freedom and liberty, they were therefore obligated to respond in obedience to the covenant which God was about to establish. The people were described as a "peculiar treasure" unto the Lord above all the people of the earth. The Lord wanted obedience, but not out of fear alone. He expected their obedience to be an expression of their love for Him.

According to God's plan the Israelites were to be both a royal and a priestly people. The expression "holy nation" indicates something of the moral aspects of their election. It was expected that because of the unique relationship between Israel and their God they would not be like the nations around them. They were to be characterized by holiness which is a fundamental demand for fellowship with God (cf. Matt. 5:48; I Peter 1:16). Having received these instructions Moses then called the elders of the people and challenged them with the words of the Lord (v. 7). Their response was positive, although perhaps not as fully weighed as it should have been (v. 8). In the light of all that God had done for His people the demands were reasonable and the people willingly committed themselves to them.

C. *Regulations for the Announcement of the Covenant* (19:9-25)

Before the children of Israel could approach God and receive the laws which He had for them, there had to be a period of both inward and outward preparation. The presence of God was evidenced by a "thick cloud" (v. 9). This was done in order that the people might hear the voice of God; but no man, of course, could look upon God and live (cf. Exod. 33:20; Judg. 6:23). The first thing that the people were to do in preparation for this important event was to sanctify themselves through the washing of the body and clothes (v. 10; cf. Gen 35:2) and abstinence from conjugal intercourse (v. 15) because of the defilement connected with this (cf. Lev. 15:18). The second stipulation was that bounds should be set around the mountain in order that the people might not die in wrongly approaching the presence of God (v. 12; cf. v. 23). After two days of preparation the Lord promised that on the third day He would "come down in the sight of all the people upon Mount Sinai" (v. 11). In the Bible God is often depicted as dwelling in the heavens above (I Kings 8:30, 49; John 8:23); therefore, any appearance on earth requires that He should come down (Gen. 11:5-7; 18:21; Exod. 3:8).

The people followed these instructions and, as predicted, the Lord did appear on Mount Sinai on that third day. His presence was accompanied by "thunders and lightnings, and a thick cloud upon the mount" (v. 16; cf. Deut. 4:11-12). Numerous writers have assumed these descriptions indicate violent volcanic activity.[7] On the basis of this it has been argued that Mount Sinai or Horeb must be located east of Ezion-geber where such eruptions have occurred. Such an interpretation, however, must be rejected for there is no real evidence that volcanic eruption is involved here. Would Moses under the leadership of God have brought a people to an area that would have threatened their lives by violent volcanic eruptions? The purpose of this dramatic visual presentation was to impress upon the people that majestic power of this sovereign God. It helped to highlight the tremendous importance of this occasion and call to their attention that the commitment which they had made (v. 8) was not to be taken lightly.

## III. The Ten Commandments (20:1-17)

### A. *The Nature of Biblical Law*

Ancient Near Eastern law has been classified into two categories. The first is known as casuistic formulation. This is a standardized pattern of case law. Such laws begin with the word "if" and are followed by a supposed offense framed in the third person which is followed by the action to be taken or the penalty to be enforced. This type of formulation is very characteristic of the well-known law code of Hammurabi. For example, Law 128 reads, "If a seignior acquired a wife, but did not draw up the contracts for her, that woman is no wife."[8] This type of formula is common to most of the extant Near Eastern codes which have been translated. The other type of law formulation is called apodictic and usually consists of precepts or commands in the second person. These may appear as exhortations, reminders or appeals.[9] The law as expressed in the Pentateuch utilizes both

---

[7]Denis Baly, *The Geography of the Bible* (London: Lutterworth Press, 1957), p. 23.

[8]*ANET*, "The Code of Hammurabi," trans. by Theophile J. Meek, p. 171.

[9]G. T. Manley, *The Book of the Law* (Grand Rapids: Wm. B. Eerdmans Publishing Company, 1957), p. 68. Also see Ze'ev W. Falk, *Hebrew Law in Biblical Times* (Jerusalem: Wahrmann Books, 1964), p. 16, and George E. Mendenhall, "Ancient Oriental and Biblical Law," *The Biblical Archaeologist,* XVII, No. 2 (May, 1954).

of these forms (e.g. Deut. 24:7 is casuistic, and Exod. 20:3-17, apodictic).

B. *The Purposes of the Law*

A careful study of both Old and New Testament will reveal the fact that the Law had a five-fold purpose in the plan of God. (1) It was designed to reveal man's sinfulness (Rom. 3:19-20). (2) It uncovered or illustrated the hideous nature of sin (Rom. 7:8-13). (3) It revealed the holiness of God. (4) It restrained the sinner so as to help him to come to Christ (Gal. 3:24). (5) It restrained wrong behavior so as to protect the integrity of the moral and social and religious institutions of Israel.

C. *The Source of the Law* (20:1)

Because of the obvious similarities between certain aspects of biblical law and ancient Near Eastern law (particularly the law code of Hammurabi), three theories of origin have arisen concerning the law of Moses. First there is the theory of dependence. Because of the clear similarity between certain biblical laws and laws found in the code of Hammurabi it is assumed that Moses or other writers copied or borrowed directly from this Babylonian system. A second theory has been termed the theory of intermediate transmission. According to this viewpoint the Israelites got much of their law system from the Canaanites who in turn had received their laws from the Babylonians. According to Alt the material found in Exodus 21 through 23 was adopted from Canaanite laws during the period of the judges.[10] The difficulty with such a viewpoint is that very little is known of Canaanite law due to the lack of inscriptional materials. This theory is therefore almost completely hypothetical.

The third approach to the source of biblical law may be designated the theory of independent development. P. Koschaker argues:

> Comparative law has taught us to expect an independent parallel development and to take it as the most reasonable explanation for the existence of similarities in the various legal sys-

---

[10]Ze'ev W. Falk, *op. cit.*, p. 16.

> tems. We may assume a process of reception or influence only where it can be proved or at least shown to be probable.[11]

It is further argued by the advocates of this position that due to the fact that these laws come from a common Semitic background we should expect parallels. The social and economic aspects of daily life were similar enough to have produced laws that were similar to each other. For example, one might travel to Africa and find that in a residential section the speed limit is twenty miles an hour. Upon returning home to New York City a similar residential speed limit may be encountered. It is not to be concluded that the Africans borrowed their law directly from the United States purely because they are similar. The laws of physics and motion may have played a role in restricting the speed in certain places. On the basis of pedestrian speeds and the space allotted for cars to travel, the appropriate restriction turned out to be twenty miles an hour in New York. From a purely scientific point of view the same conclusion could have been reached in Africa without the aid of American information. It is not to be assumed that all biblical law was without some Near Eastern influence, but it must be concluded that the vast majority of similarities can be attributed to common observation and economic need. Moreover the Bible student is not left in doubt as to the immediate origin of the words given in Chapter 20. Verse 1 of this chapter clearly indicates that God spoke these words. We have, therefore, a unique, unparalleled revelation. The very apodictic form of this code is in many respects unique against its ancient Near Eastern background.

### D. *The Law and the Believer*

A perplexing problem which has plagued believers in all generations is how to determine the relationship of Old Testament law to the believer of the new dispensation. Since all Scripture is God-breathed and is profitable for instruction (II Tim. 3:16), the law cannot be dismissed as unimportant and irrelevant to the believer's life. On the other hand the New Testament makes

---

[11]*Zeitschrift der deutschen morgenlandischen Gesellschaft,* LXXXIX (1935), p. 31 quoted in Ze'ev Falk, *op. cit.,* p. 33.

it very clear that the child of God living in the Age of Grace is not under law and not obligated to the Mosaic code as was the Israelite under the old economy. At least four times in the New Testament it is clearly stated that the believer is not under the law (Rom. 6:14-15; Gal. 5:18; I Cor. 9:20). The means of salvation for men in all ages has been faith. The Old Testament saint was never saved by law nor can one be saved by law in this dispensation (Rom. 3:20). The Old Testament saint was regenerated and justified by faith as is the one who receives Christ today. The difference then is not in salvation, but the means by which one's conduct is governed. In other words, in the Old Testament period fellowship with God was regulated by specific deeds and prohibitions accompanied with a series of checks and penalties. This was designed to protect Israel from the idolatry that surrounded her and provide the way for the appearance of Messiah. When Christ came He brought a new era of grace and truth (John 1:17). For the believer the law is nonetheless revealing and instructive. It gives insight into the mind of God and helps one to determine what standards of holiness He expects of those who follow Him.[12]

E. *The Content of This Law* (20:2-17)

The "words of the covenant" (34:28) were written upon two tables of stone (Deut. 4:13) and were called "the law and the commandment" in 24:12. The Bible does not indicate how these laws were organized on the two tablets. Three views have developed in this regard, one supposing that the first five commandments were placed on the one tablet and the last five on the other. On the other hand some argue that the first three laws appeared on the first tablet and the last seven on the second, distinguishing laws that related to God alone from laws which had to do with social, family and community responsibilities.[13] Finally, some have suggested that the two tablets were duplicate copies of the same law, one for each of the parties involved in the transaction. It is clear that the first group of

---

[12]For a more complete treatment of this problem see Alva J. McClain, *Law and Grace* (Chicago: Moody Press, 1954).

[13]See Keil and Delitzsch, *op. cit.*, II, p. 108.

commandments relates primarily to man's relationship to God while the latter commandments concentrate on man's relationship to the community about him.

1. The Protection of True Theology (20:2-3)

Appropriately, before giving the first law the Lord reminded the Hebrews that He had brought them out of the land of Egypt and out of the house of bondage (v. 2). The land from which they had been taken was a land characterized by idolatry and a multiplicity of deities. The Lord had drawn them apart not only to be a distinctive people, but to worship the one and only true God. The command is clear, therefore, that they were to have no other gods beside the Lord. The Hebrew expression *'al pānāy*, "before me," has been the subject of no little debate. After a rather thorough study of the use of this expression in the Old Testament, Lange comes to the conclusion that the expression must mean "over against" the Lord.

> The meaning "over against," the usual meaning of the phrase, is perfectly appropriate here. All false gods are opposed to the true God. The worship of them is incompatible with the worship of Jehovah. The command therefore is, "Thou shall have no other gods to confront me," to be set up as rival objects of service and adoration.[14]

Keil and Delitzsch reject this conclusion and suggest that the simple meaning is "in addition to me," noting that the preposition *'al* is so used in Genesis 31:50 and Deuteronomy 19:9. Both sources reject the *Authorized Version's* "before me" as inaccurate and lacking the real sense of the passage. Actually the Hebrew idiom would allow for either "in addition to me" or "in opposition to me."

The purposes for this command are obvious. In the first place there is only one true God. Furthermore, the presence of other gods would precipitate confusion among the tribes. The one thing that provided a cohesive force for the tribes of Israel was her worship of the true God. It was this truth that bound her

---

[14]John P. Lange, *op. cit.*, p. 75.

together as one people. When she departed from this basic theological principle, confusion and frustration were the immediate results (cf. Judg. 17–18). The unity and growth of the tribes of Israel depended on the perpetuation of this theological principle. It is interesting to observe that other peoples were also conscious of the unifying factor of maintaining a particular system of worship. From the town of Nuzi located near the modern Iraqian city of Kirkuk comes a legal document dating from about 1400 B.C.[15] This document contains the last will and testament of a father to his sons. In it the father commanded his sons not to make other gods because he would deposit the idols with his oldest son so that all his sons would be united through the worship of the family gods at the home of the chief heir. The text reads, "After I die, my sons shall not make gods; my gods I leave with my eldest son."[16]

2. Protection of True Worship (20:4-6)

The second command deals directly with modes of worship and forbids the production of any images or likenesses of anything either in "heaven above or earth beneath." The Hebrew word for "carved image" is *pesel* (from the root *pāsal,* meaning to carve wood or stone). A *pesel* therefore is a figure made of wood or stone – sometimes a representation of Jehovah as in Judges 17:3ff.; whereas, other times it was used for figures of heathen gods (II Kings 21:7). The word for likeness in verse 4 is *t^emûnāh* which ". . . does not signify an image made by man, but a form which is seen by him (Num. 12:8; Deut. 4:12, 15 ff.; Job 4:16; and Ps. 17:15)."[17] The expression "that which is in heaven" most likely refers to birds and stars. The following expression "that which is in the water" is a reference to fish and water animals which were commonly deified by the Egyptians and other peoples as well. Idols, according to this verse, were not only not to be worshipped, but they were not even to be made. Idolatry is, of course, foolishness because it is nothing more than

[15]Text 108, *Harvard Semitic Series* (Cambridge, Mass., 1950), XIV.
[16]Cyrus H. Gordon, "The Ten Commandments," *Christianity Today* (April 10, 1964), p. 4.
[17]Keil and Delitzsch, *op. cit.,* II, p. 115.

a product of human skill and therefore represents something inferior to man and subject to him (cf. Hos. 8:6). Such gods can be stolen or burned, thus leading to frustration. Micah's frustration should be a lesson to all who would worship gods of wood and stone (cf. 18:14-24). Regarding the psychological effects brought by the destruction of stone and wood gods, Cyrus Gordon remarks:

> . . . It is worth noting that the defeated nations, on seeing their idols dragged off or smashed, tended to become demoralized and lose their identity. Assyria, Babylonia, the Seleucids, and Rome could not destroy the Jewish religion partly because God and His people's allegiance to Him were incorporeal and therefore indestructible. The second commandment thus paved the way for the historic survival of Yahwism.[18]

The first commandment pointed to the fact that there was only one true God. It also emphasized His spiritual nature (John 4:24). It should not be concluded that this commandment prohibits the use of sculpture or painting in religion. Artistry and representations were employed in the construction of the sanctuary (Exod. 25:17-22) and in Solomon's temple (I Kings 6:23-26). There is a place for religious, illustrative material. The condemnation of imagery comes when it is intended to be a representation of a god and becomes the subject of worship. Not only was the making of images forbidden, but any form of worship of existing images was also forbidden (v. 5). The reason given is that God is a jealous God (cf. Josh. 24:19). He refuses to share His glory and majesty with wooden and stone idols (Isa. 42:8; 48:11).

The last part of verse 5 has been problematic for interpreters. Some see in this the manifestation of a vengeful spirit. It has long been recognized that under the natural course of events, iniquities of the fathers are visited upon the children. Such is the case with various diseases or among those who lack restraint and live in extravagance thus leaving the children beggars. We all inherit countless disadvantages because of the sin of our first parents. The distinction that needs to be made here is between the natural results of a sinful course of action and direct

[18]*Op. cit.*, p. 4.

punishment inflicted because of it. God does not penalize one individual for the wrongdoing of another (cf. Ezek. 18:2-24). It has been rightly observed, "The human race is a living organism, in which not only sin and wickedness are transmitted, but evil as the curse of sin and the punishment of wickedness."[19] This verse does not teach that sinning fathers are not punished, nor does it state that the sins of the father are punished in the children and grandchildren without any fault of their own. It is hardly possible that the children of wicked men could become innocent, therefore, "the children fill up the sins of their fathers" so that the sinner then suffers punishment for both his own and the sins of his forefathers (cf. Lev. 26:39; Amos 7:17; Jer. 16:11 ff.; Dan. 9:16). The positive aspect of God's love and mercy is portrayed in verse 6. He shows mercy unto thousands of those who love Him and keep His commandments.

3. Protection of the Name of God (20:7)

Commentators are divided on the specific sense of this commandment. Most scholars regard the phrase as a prohibition to false swearing only, while others include the idea of profane or vain swearing; that is, the irreverent use of the name of God. It appears from a careful examination of the text that both ideas are employed.[20] The name of God was specifically referred to as one means by which men would improve their own integrity and honesty by committing themselves to that name and all that it stood for. In Deuteronomy 6:13 we read, "Thou shalt fear the Lord thy God, and serve him, and shalt swear by his name."

> Moreover, since human witness so often contains inaccuracy and falsehood, God allowed the use of His name to attest the truth of human witness, and thus become the inspiration of a new desire and effort after truth. A man's word, given under such an oath, was to be taken so seriously that even where there was no corroborative evidence to support it, trust was placed in it (Exod. 22:10-11).[21]

---

[19]Keil and Delitzsch, *op. cit.*, II, p. 117.

[20]*Ibid.*, p. 118.

[21]Ronald S. Wallace, *The Ten Commandments* (Grand Rapids: Wm. B. Eerdmans Publishing Co., 1965), p. 54.

It was assumed that when a man made a treaty or covenant in the name of the Lord this was done in full honesty and truth (Lev. 19:12). In the new dispensation, however, the believer is encouraged not to swear by any oath (James 5:12), for the Christian is to exhibit truth on all occasions and should not need the name of God to verify that posture.

4. Protection of the Sabbath (20:8-11)

The command to "remember the Sabbath" presupposes that there was some acquaintance with a Sabbath day or a day of rest; however, this in itself is not sufficient evidence to prove that a holy Sabbath had been previously set aside as a weekly festival day for worship and praise of Jehovah. The reference here may be to the week as viewed in connection with gathering of the manna (16:23). Prior to this time no commandment had been given to man to set this day apart as a holy day. The manner by which this day would be set aside and made holy was that no work would be performed on that day (vv. 9-10). The precedent for this is found in the creation week of Genesis 1 for then the Lord created the heavens and the earth in six days but on the seventh day He rested (v. 11; cf. 31:17). This verse may reflect on the very chronological nature of the creation week, for if that week is considered analogous to the calendar week of the Hebrews, then the creation days must be regarded as normal solar days. This view, of course, does not necessitate reducing the age of the earth down to 4,000 years as some have attempted to do. Archaeology has demonstrated the presence of men on earth for at least 9,000 years. On the other hand, there is no evidence to argue conclusively that man has been present on this earth for millions of years. Such a viewpoint is demanded by the theories of biological evolution. Because of a lack of a biological mechanism, time has become the means by which evolutionary theory is supposed to take on credibility.

The observance of the Sabbath became a foundation for all the festival times and observances of the Israelites since they all culminated in a Sabbath rest. However, the Sabbath, like many other aspects of the older economy, was merely "a shadow of things to come" (Col. 2:17; cf. Heb. 10:1), to be done away when Christ had completed his work.

> But He rose again on the Sunday; and through His resurrection, which is the pledge to the world of the fruit of His redeeming work, He has made this day the *kuriake emera* (Lord's day) for His Church, to be observed by it till the Captain of its salvation shall return, and having finished the judgment upon all His foes to the very last shall lead it to the rest of that eternal Sabbath, which God prepared for the whole creation through His own resting after the completion of the heaven and the earth.[22]

The demand by some that the Christian is to observe the Sabbath is, in effect, to place him under the law of the Old Testament. Particular prohibitions associated with the Sabbath indicates that this was designed as part of God's economy for the old dispensation to teach Israel specific lessons and to prepare her for the coming of the Messiah. For example, one was forbidden to gather manna on the Sabbath (16:26) and was not permitted to light a fire on that day (35:3). It was a violation of the Sabbath to gather sticks on this day (Num. 15:35). The keeping of the Sabbath became a point of great abuse by the time of Jesus. Traditions had developed around this day so that a man found it difficult even to do good on that particular day (cf. Matt. 12:5, 11).

The Sabbath was not only designed as a special day set aside for worship of God, but it had a practical side in that it provided a needed rest for those who worked (cf. Deut. 5:13-15). It is interesting that this seventh day included rest not only for one's family and his servants, but also for the animals (v. 10). In many respects animals were considered an integral part of the community. The Sabbath was a responsibility of the total community; therefore, animals benefited from this as well as men. Note the fact that the covenant made with Noah and his sons also included the animals on the ark (Gen. 9:8-17). It will be remembered that during the final plague in Egypt the firstborn of the cattle died as well as people (Exod. 11:5). Also of in-

---

[22]Keil and Delitzsch, *op. cit.*, II, pp. 121-122.

terest is the fact that when Nineveh repented and believed God, a fast was proclaimed. Not only did men wear sackcloth, but according to Jonah 3:8 the beasts did so as well. In the light of these ideas it was therefore appropriate that animals as well as the servants and families should be included in the special day of rest.

5. Protection of Family Honor (20:12)

The fifth commandment provides the key to real social stability. To honor one's father and mother is to reverence and obey them in godly sincerity (cf. Lev. 19:3; Deut. 5:24; 18:18). Reverence and respect for parental authority is not considered something optional in Scripture (Heb. 6:1-3). Many parents have abrogated this principle in favor of better "communication." It is assumed by many modern psychologists that children and parents ought to arrange an equitable situation by which all have equal authority and are permitted to articulate self-created ideas. Such a concept is not only against biblical principles, but in the long run turns out to be impractical. All society must have norms of authority. There must be subjugation of some kind. A lack of respect for parental authority will ultimately lead to anarchism in society generally. One of the purposes of this commandment was to engender respect for all rightful authority whether that authority be in the church or in the state (cf. Rom. 13:1-7; Heb. 13:17; I Peter 2:13-18).

As society would have it today, many children are raising their parents, and the immediate product is something less than desirable. This is not only an undisciplined generation, but one bent toward the exercise of evil. Juvenile delinquency was never tolerated in the Old Testament; in fact, on some occasions it incurred the death penalty (Deut. 21:18-21). In oriental societies the handling of incorrigible and disobedient youth has always been severe discipline. Somehow the term penalty has taken on distasteful connotations and seems to be something which is evil and non-essential to a well-ordered society. In contrast to this are the many biblical admonitions to parents to exercise authority and discipline for the good of the children as well as the good of the home. We have no record of how often, if ever, this law of Deuteronomy 21 was ever applied, but one thing is sure; it gave some indication of how God feels about juvenile delinquency in its worst form.

A promise accompanies this command. If honor is given to father and mother, there would be longevity of life in the land (v. 12). The primary application of this, of course, applies to the nation and their existence in the land of Canaan, but in certain cases the Old Testament attributes long life to those who obeyed the Lord in commands such as this (cf. Deut. 6:2; 22:7). It should not be assumed, however, that parental obedience will guarantee longevity in every case, no more so than the lack of obedience would guarantee a short life for all wicked men. History and human experience mitigate against such arbitrary interpretations.

### 6. Protection of Life (20:13)

This verse literally reads, "Thou shalt not murder." The Hebrew verb used is *rāṣaḥ* which has the basic meaning of "to murder or slay."[23] Life is viewed in the Old Testament as sacred and existing "in the image of God" (Gen. 9:6). This command prohibits suicide as well as the taking of the life of a fellow man. Notice that an object is not provided in the verse. The establishment of capital punishment for those who willfully take the life of another is not predicated upon a preventive measure, but upon the fact that such an act destroys that which represents the image of God. Arguments defending the practice of capital punishment are far too often focused on its power to deter crime rather than the biblical concept of punishment. The reason for the death of a guilty murderer is made clear in Genesis 9:6. It is because he has destroyed the image of God represented in man. This image according to James 3:9 still exists in man. Capital punishment reflects God's view of human life. Apparently the Apostle Paul believed in the legitimacy of capital punishment where guilt was fully demonstrated (cf. Acts 25:11), otherwise he would have condemned the practice before Festus. It appears that Romans 13:4 and I Peter 2:13-21 imply the right of government to execute punishment where such punishment is in

[23]Brown, Driver and Briggs, *op. cit.,* p. 953.

conformity with biblical principles. In the light of this, therefore, the sixth command does not prevent the rightful exercise of capital punishment. As Lange observes:

> Hence, killing, when permitted or even commanded, is to be regarded as in principle a consequence of the duty of the preservation of life in the higher sense.[24]

7. Protection of Marriage (20:14)

Just as human life is sacred and is not to be violated by murder, so marriage is equally sacred and is not to be violated by infidelity. The Hebrew word for adultery (*nāʾap*) applies to both men and women (cf. Lev. 20:10). Infidelity within the marriage relationship was considered a very serious offense and appropriately so because God instituted marriage and blessed it as a means of filling the earth (Gen. 1). Expansion of this idea prohibits not only the act of adultery, but fornication and impurity of any kind whether in act, word or thought (Matt. 5:27-28). The penalty for infidelity in the marital relationship was death and this applied both to the man and to the woman (Lev. 20:10). Society has generally treated adultery involving the wife more severely than the husband. The commandment, however, applies with equal force to both the husband and the wife (Heb. 13:4; Rev. 21:8). This commandment, like the fifth (v. 12), was designed to protect the sanctity and the harmony of the home.

8. Protection of Property (20:15)

The right to the ownership of private property is a very important principle for the stability of any society. If this right is not respected by others, anarchy and murder are the result. This commandment forbids any act by which, directly or indirectly, we dishonestly obtain the goods of another individual. Unfortunately, in our day a philosophy based on the idea that the end justifies the means has tended to dull the moral implications of this prohibition. It is now argued that the acquisition of

---

[24]John P. Lange, *op. cit.*, p. 80.

goods is legitimate as long as one is not caught, or if the acquisition of such goods might be determined to be a greater good to the one who takes them than to the one who possesses them.

The moral aspect of the biblical code indicates something of the uniqueness of the God of Israel. All those living about Israel had no such moral prohibition. A careful study of Ugaritic epics relating to Baal and Anath reveals the fact that these deities reflected all the weaknesses and sins of man himself. Of course, gods are always reflections of their creators. Murder, adultery and stealing were as common among the gods of Canaan as they were among the men who worshipped them. It should be remembered that prohibitions against murder, adultery and stealing are not necessarily universal. In ancient Sparta, it was getting caught, not stealing, that was reprehensible. One can see how these commandments are interrelated. If you worship one of the false gods of Canaan or make idols in devotion to that God (vv. 3-5), you are likely to adopt the moral and spiritual characteristics of that deity.

9. Protection of Truth (20:16)

The ninth commandment prevents the bearing of false witness against one's neighbor. Bearing false witness or testimony against another man will ultimately lead to a complete travesty of justice and bring to an end the effectiveness of a court of law (cf. 23:1). The bearing of false testimony or witness was not only condemned in the Bible, but severe condemnation also appears in the laws of Hammurabi. In Law 1 it is recorded:

> If a seignoir accused another seignoir and brought a charge of murder against him, but has not proved it, his accuser shall be put to death.[25]

The death penalty was also applied to anyone who accused another of sorcery falsely.[26]

---

[25]*ANET*, "The Code of Hammurabi," trans. by Theophile J. Meek, p. 166.

[26]*Ibid.*, law #2.

10. Protection of the Heart (20:17)

With this command we see something of the utter uniqueness of biblical law. Not only are specific acts condemned or prohibited, but the thoughts and aspirations of an individual are also evaluated. This commandment is, in fact, supplementary to the eighth, for covetousness is the root from which theft grows. This commandment is a reminder that God looks on the heart while man merely looks on the outward appearance (cf. I Sam. 16:7; I Kings 8:39; I Chron. 28:9; Heb. 4:13). Sin usually begins with a wrong thought which when entertained develops an evil desire which ultimately gives birth to a sinful action (cf. James 1:13-15). This commandment is a staunch prohibition against all lustful desire. It serves as an effective preventative to sensuous practices. It was important that the law should not only deal with man's acts but with his thoughts and feelings which were the source of such acts. True godliness always consists of bringing "every thought into captivity to Christ" (II Cor. 10:5). Covetousness has a psychologically degrading effect upon an individual. It automatically negates any success which he may have achieved. It downgrades his interest in his own home and his family. It breaks down his respect for the possessions of others and leads to theft and adultery. Quite often covetousness leads to mental frustration, for one who develops an earnest desire to acquire something that belongs to another finds out that he is incapable of getting that thing. If we set our affection on things which are above we are not likely to get involved in the practice of covetousness for those things which are about us.

## IV. The People's Reaction (20:18-23)

The presence of God accompanied by great thunder and lightning caused the people to stand some distance from the mountain itself (v. 18). They did have a great desire to hear what God had spoken (v. 19). Moses first put the people at ease and reminded them that God was not here to destroy them but to test and prove them (v. 20). On this occasion the essence of

Moses' message was clearly faithfulness to the true God (vv. 22-23).

## V. An Altar for Worship (20:24-26)

God not only condemns inappropriate worship but in these verses establishes the means for true worship. Quite evidently burnt offerings and peace offerings already existed in Israel, for mention is made of them in verse 24. Sacrifices, of course, were begun very early in human history (cf. Gen. 4:3-4; 8:20; 12:7; 15:9; 22:7; 26:25; 31:54). Altars were already known to the Hebrews as evidenced by the fact that the patriarchs made them (Gen. 8:20; 12:7; 13:18; 22:9). The divine response to offerings, properly brought, would be blessing.

The method by which the altar was to be built was also specified. The altar was to be made of stone but that which was not hewn (v. 25). This was probably done in order to prevent the making of images in connection with the altar itself. The altar was, in fact, an expression of God's will. To take tools and to try to improve upon it would be improper and arrogant. Disobedience with respect to appropriate sacrifice was severely disciplined by God. Note for example God's reaction to Cain's rebellion (Gen. 4:3-4). It was also commanded that steps should not be constructed in connection with the altar in order that "thy nakedness be not exposed thereon" (v. 26). Perhaps the garments worn on such an occasion might lend themself to uncovering which, of course, would be in conflict with the symbolism of the sacrifice itself which provides for the covering of man's sin. On the other hand, it may be that steps could easily develop into something which would detract from the altar itself and ultimately from the whole process of sacrifice. It is felt by some writers that this regulation was merely temporary.

> When the dress of the priest had been so arranged that no exposure of the person was possible (27:42-43), this precept became unnecessary. Thus it would seem that Solomon's altar had steps (cf. II Chron. 4:1 with Ezek. 43:17).[27]

---

[27]George Rawlinson, *op. cit.*, p. 265. Note also John P. Lange, *op. cit.*, p. 83.

Since "by the law is the knowledge of sin" (Rom. 3:20), we should not only read these commandments, but study them and apply them. While we are not under law as the final rule of life in this dispensation, we are made conscious of our need for the grace of God by a knowledge of this holy law.

## Chapter 11

# *The Book of the Covenant*

(Exodus 21–24)

Prior to the year 1902 it was the consensus of most critical scholars that law codes such as are found in the Book of Exodus could not have existed prior to the first millennium B.C. This theory was predicated upon an assumed evolution of religious and civil thought in the ancient Near Eastern world. It was argued by the proponents of the Wellhausenian school of biblical criticism that the laws found in the book of Moses reflected a highly developed system of moral and theological thought which would not have been possible in the days of Moses.

This whole approach, however, had to be abandoned when the now-famous law code of Hammurabi was discovered in the Acropolis of Susa (the biblical Shushan). In December, 1901, and January, 1902, Jacques de Morgan found three large fragments of a black diorite stone. When placed together they formed a stele 7′ 4½″ high, whose base had a diameter of about 24 inches. The upper part of the stele contained a relief showing Hammurabi, the sixth king of the First Dynasty of Babylon, standing before the sun god Shamash. This stele contains almost 300 paragraphs of legal provisions dealing with the social, commercial, domestic and moral life of the Babylonians of Hammurabi's day (approximately 1728-1686 B.C.). Evidently at a time when Babylon was weak, an Elamite conqueror carried away this monument to Susa where it was discovered by Jacques de Morgan. The stele originally contained 3,624 lines, divided into 39 columns of writing. It evidently had been set up by Hammurabi in Babylon, his capital. The Elamites erased five columns of the inscription, but did not replace them with any inscriptions of their own. The pillar was broken into pieces in one of the destructions of Susa and was buried by the time of the Persian kings. The code contains a preface or prologue in which the king claims to have been commissioned by the gods to rule over the kingdom and to establish proper law. This is followed by 282 sections of the law, all of a purely civil nature. The stele concludes with an epilogue.

The publication of this code in the year of its discovery by V. Scheil caused a tremendous stir in the world of biblical scholarship. This is understood in the light of the influence of the Wellhausenian school of thought, for here was a law code that antedated Moses by three hundred years. It had already been assumed that the existence of such sophisticated law codes could not have been possible. This discovery, therefore, was the death blow to that theory. Since that discovery, other law codes have been found such as the earlier laws of Lipit-Ishtar, king of Isin in central Babylonia (about 1875 B.C.). This law code, written in Sumerian, comes from the city of Nippur and was published in 1948.[1] It was noted to be very similar to the law code of Hammurabi and in some cases having a number of laws identical with Hammurabi's code. In the year 1948 another code was published which had been discovered in Harmal near Baghdad, the code of King Bilalama of Eshnunna, who ruled about three hundred years before Hammurabi. This code is quite evidently a forerunner of the laws of Lipit-Ishtar and Hammurabi.[2] An even earlier set of laws has been discovered, which was written in Sumerian and attributed to Ur Nammu. These may go back as early as 2050 B.C.[3] Also of great importance to the Bible student are the middle Assyrian laws which are contained on clay tablets. These were discovered by German archaeologists in the course of their excavations at ancient Assur between 1903 and 1914. The tablets probably date from the time of Tiglath-Pileser I in the twelfth century B.C. The Hittite laws (about 1450 B.C.) also provide some important source material for the student of Old Testament.[5]

All the above law codes contain regulations which are chiefly

---

[1]See Francis R. Steele, *American Journal of Archaeology* LII (1948), pp. 425-450 and *ANET*, "Lipit-Ishtar Law Code," trans. by S. N. Kramer, pp. 159-161.

[2]See Albrecht Goetze, *Sumer*, IV (1948), pp. 63-102 and *ANET*, "The Laws of Eshnunna," trans. by Albrecht Goetze, pp. 161-163.

[3]See G. E. Mendenhall, "Ancient Oriental and Biblical Law," *The Biblical Archaeologist*, XVII (May, 1954), p. 23.

[4]*ANET*, "The Middle Assyrian Laws," trans. by Theophile H. Meek, pp. 180-188.

[5]*ANET*, "The Hittite Laws," trans. by Albrecht Goetze, pp. 188-197.

of the casuistic type. In this respect, therefore, we should expect to find some parallels between certain laws found in these laws and those which appear in the Bible. Far too often, however, the resemblences between biblical and ancient Near Eastern law have been greatly exaggerated, even to the point of attempting to show generic relationships. As observed in a previous chapter, such similarities may have arisen out of independent developments and not necessarily be generically related at all. As far as the Bible is concerned, it is quite clearly stated that the law code contained in the Book of Exodus came by revelation of God and was not produced by a copious method via the hand of Moses. It is often argued that the source of Moses' legal material was the code of Hammurabi. This theory, however, has been adequately disproved by a number of writers. It has been pointed out that in biblical law the divine origin is stressed nearly everywhere, giving the particular injunctions their authority. In other oriental codes, religion or theology plays only a subordinate and insignificant part. It was the king, not the god, who gave his authority to a particular code.[6]

After a very careful study of the relationships of the law of Hammurabi and the laws found in the Book of Exodus, M. David concludes, "To my mind there is even no indication whatsoever that the biblical legislator has known the code of Hammurabi and has been influenced by it in any way."[7] Noting some of the significant differences between the Old Babylonian and the Israelite law, he concludes that the foundations of the laws of these nations were in fact quite different. It was his conclusion that it is out of the question that the legislation of Israel is in any way whatsoever copied from the code of Hammurabi or that the writer of the biblical material was influenced by this code.[8] G. T. Manley has also cited a number of significant differences between the biblical law and Babylonian law. He notes that there are no real class distinctions and the whole tone of

---

[6]A. van Selms, "Law," *The New Bible Dictionary*, p. 720.

[7]"The Codex Hammurabi and Its Relation to the Provisions in Exodus," *Oudtestamentische Studiën* (Leiden: E. J. Brill, 1950), VII, p. 153.

[8]*Ibid.*, pp. 171, 178.

biblical law is religious.[9] Other differences cited deal with arrangement, form, mode of address, the community concern, and notations of time and place.[10] A great deal of the material found in the code of Hammurabi is oriented economically and culturally in such a way as to provide no parallels whatsoever with Old Testament material. For example, in the law code of Hammurabi there are statements which govern the rights and duties of soldiers, laws pertaining to travelling merchants, concerning adoption, physicians, and the responsibilities of housebuilders and boatbuilders. The law code of Hammurabi has as its moral and ethical basis necessary requirements for a smoothly operating community. Biblical law includes this, but has as its basis (1) the holiness of Yahweh (Lev. 11:44; cf. 19:2; 20:7-8), (2) the oneness of Yahweh (Deut. 6:4-5), and (3) the unchangeableness of Yahweh (Mal. 3:6; cf. Lam. 3:22-23).

Some critical scholars have argued that since much of the Mosaic law is devoted to agricultural interest, it could not have been written prior to the time of Samuel. Such an argument assumes that agricultural interests were not part of the Hebrew's heritage until the days of Samuel; however, it is too often forgotten that the Israelites at Sinai were, in fact, the heirs of four centuries of agricultural and pastoral experience in the rich and fertile region of the Nile delta.[11]

The material in Exodus that we are about to consider is commonly referred to as "the book of the covenant" based on the expression found in 24:7. The book of the covenant is considered to begin at 20:22 and to conclude with Chapter 23. These chapters contain a detailed enlargement of the principles contained in the Decalogue and are composed of various civil, social and religious laws. These regulations were quite clearly received by Moses at Mount Sinai probably after the delivery of the Ten Commandments (24:4-7).

---

[9]*The Book of the Law* (Grand Rapids: Wm. B. Eerdmans Publishing Co., 1957), p. 67.

[10]*Ibid.*, pp. 68-70.

[11]R. K. Harrison, *op. cit.*, p. 583. Also see K. A. Kitchen, *Tyndale House Bulletin*, Nos. 5-6 (1960).

## I. The Law of the Slave (21:1-11)

### A. *Rights of the Hebrew Slave* (21:1-6)

While slavery was a common phenomenon in all countries of the ancient Near East, the treatment accorded slaves differed from one land to another. In some lands (e.g., Babylonia) the demand for slaves was greater than in others. This was due, perhaps, to a lack of free laborers. In order to meet the demand for slaves, large numbers were imported to the country or were captured in warfare.[12] The economic conditions in Babylon as contrasted with Israel also had some influence on the manner in which slaves were treated. As far as Israelite law was concerned, it was unique because God was the source of law and those laws were based on unchanging moral and ethical norms, whereas other law systems were produced out of social and economic necessities.

As far as Israel was concerned an individual could become a slave a number of ways. Some were captives of war and were considered to be the property of the individual who had spared them (cf. Num. 31:26; Deut.. 20:10ff.; 21:10). Foreign slaves could also be acquired by purchase (Exod. 12:44; Lev. 22:11; 25:44-45). On occasion Hebrew children were enslaved by sale if their fathers could find no other way of meeting financial obligations (Isa. 1:1; Amos 2:6; 8:6; Neh. 5:5; Prov. 22:7). When poor people found themselves in such a condition as to be totally incapable of paying a debt, they would often sell themselves into serfdom (Lev. 25:39). One thing that is decidedly unique about the slavery situation in ancient Israel is that there was no such thing as a permanent, involuntary servitude for a Hebrew slave to a Hebrew master (Lev. 25:25-55). It appears that slavery was not a desirable aspect of social behavior in ancient Israel. Nonetheless God permitted its practice and established laws to regulate it.

The Hebrew slave sustained a rather unique relationship to his master. Treated as a member of the family, the slave was to be circumcised and the laws of the Sabbath and the festivals applied to him. There were various distinctions between certain

---

[12] M. David, *op. cit.*, p. 160.

types of slaves; for example, the Bible makes a distinction between the purchased and the house-born slave (Gen. 15:3; 17:12; Lev. 22:11). A similar distinction is also found in Babylonian documents though it apparently had no legal significance. The status of the Hebrew slave was better than that of the foreigner. Besides the limitation of service the law provided for a friendly relationship between master and servant. Since slavery was generally regarded as temporary service, he had to be treated like a hired worker and often could be the owner of property (Lev. 25:36-39, 49).

In the verses before us we have the basic regulations established for the handling of a Hebrew slave. These "ordinances" or "judgments" are the basic rules by which judicial decisions would be made. The Hebrew word used to describe them is *hammišpāṭîm*. The first regulation, found in verse 2, deals with the slave that had been purchased. An Israelite might buy his own countryman, either when he was sold by a court of justice because of theft (22:1), or when he was in debt and sold himself to cover that indebtedness (Lev. 25:35, 39). Children were at times sold in settlement of a debt (II Kings 4:1-7). In any event the maximum length of service was six years. In the seventh year he was to be freed. This seventh year does not refer to the sabbatical year (Exod. 23:11; Lev. 25:4) but to the beginning of the seventh year after the man became a slave (Deut. 15:12). When the jubilee year came, however, a Hebrew slave was to be released irrespective of how many years he had served (Lev. 25:40). This law was designed to prevent perpetual involuntary slavery. In fact, the humanitarian aspects of Hebrew slave laws are very interesting and represent a very high ethic. For example, not only was his master to grant him freedom at a specified time, but he was obligated to furnish him with provisions from the flock, the threshingfloor and the winepress (Deut. 15:12-15) in order that that man might be able to begin a new life. This type of treatment of a slave finds no real parallel among other nations of the ancient Near East.

The second regulation regarding slavery deals with a man who voluntarily puts himself in servitude. If he comes in as a slave by himself he is to be freed accordingly (v. 3). If he was married, his wife is to be released along with him. The third regulation, found in verse 4, deals with that slave who had been given a wife and had sons born of that marriage. According to this law if he is to be released the wife and children born in that marriage were to be the property of the master and were to remain as members of his household. The slave, however, could be released.

Since the conditions of slavery were not completely intolerable there apparently were occasions when the slave would find it desirable to remain with his master rather than to go out free (v. 5). In such a circumstance he had the right to declare himself a permanent slave of that man. This would be legalized by the master bringing him unto "the judges" (Heb. *hā'ᵉlōhîm;* cf. 22:8-9). Here he would make a formal declaration of the surrender of his liberty. His ear was then bored with an awl against the door or lintel of that house, and by this sign he was fastened, as it were, to that house for as long as he lived (cf. Deut. 15:17). There has been considerable debate around the translation of the Hebrew expression *hā'ᵉlōhîm.* In the *Authorized Version* it appears as "the judges." Others have suggested that a more literal translation should be taken; namely, "unto God." Lange explains,

> Not to the priest, but to the court of the assembly, which pass judgment in the name of God, and whose sentence was a divine dispensation.[13]

F. Charles Fensham sees a parallel between one of the laws of Eshnunna and this biblical law. He argues that the translation should be "unto God."

> In the laws of Eshnunna (Le) Numbers 36 and 37 we read the following. . . . "The owner of the house shall swear for him an oath in the gate of the temple of Tishpak." There is a striking similarity between Exodus 22:7 and the law code of Eshnunna in regard to the declaration of innocence of the depositee. In Exodus 22:7 he must resort to God and in the law code of Eshnunna he must take an oath which means the same thing. This comparison throws new light on the expression in Exodus 21:6 which is regarded as difficult. The door of the sanctuary

---

[13]*Op. cit.*, p. 88.

> was probably the place where the oath was taken and where, by piercing the ear of the slave, the latter takes an oath to remain a slave for the rest of his life.[14]

Others argue that the Hebrew term *hā'ᵉlōhîm* is used idiomatically to refer to "the exalted ones" or "the judges."[15] This idea is a rather old one and is found in the Targum of Onkelos.

B. *The Daughter as a Maidservant* (21:7-11)

In a patriarchal society a father had absolute control over his children, so much so that it was within the realm of the father's authority to sell his own children as slaves. Women sold in this way were able to claim their freedom at the end of six years if they so chose (Deut. 15:17). If the one who purchased this woman should refuse to make her his concubine or secondary wife he then was to look for someone to buy her from him and thus relieve him from the marriage obligation (v. 11; cf. Lev. 25: 48). She could not be sold, however, to a foreigner. No Hebrew was ever to marry a foreigner (Deut. 7:1-3). The charge of "dealing deceitfully" with her is made simply because he evidently had promised to make this girl his secondary wife and failing to do so he had violated his promise (v. 8). If, however, this young lady was purchased as a wife for his son, he is to deal with her as one of the daughters of the family (v. 9). If he should take to himself another wife she is not to be turned out nor denied her right of support (v. 10). If the above stipulations were not fulfilled she was free to return to her father and to marry again. Her father was not required to refund any part of the price that was paid for her.[16]

---

[14]"New Light on Exodus 21:6 and 22:7 from the Laws of Eshnunna," *Journal of Biblical Literature*, LXXVII (June, 1959), p. 160.

[15]George Rawlinson, *op. cit.*, p. 266. Cf. also Francis Nichol, *op. cit.*, p. 612.

[16]For additional studies on this passage see J. Hoftijzer, "Exodus 21:8," *Vetus Testamentum*, VII (1957); I. Mendelsohn, "The Conditional Sale into Slavery of Freeborn Daughters in Nuzi and the Law of Exod. 21:7-11," *Journal of the American Oriental Society*, LV (1935), Robert North, "Flesh, Covering and Response, Exodus 21:10," *Vetus Testamentum*, V (1955); and Sh. M. Paul, "Exod. 21:10 a Threefold Maintenance Clause." *Journal of Near Eastern Studies*, XXVIII (1969).

## II. Laws Relating to Personal Injury (21:12-36)

### A. *Acts of Homicide* (21:12-14)

The Bible is very clear on the matter of intentional murder. In no way was such a man to be pardoned or freed. Life, in essence, is the property of God; the possession of it is leased to human beings for a number of years. This lease can be extended or contracted in accordance with God's will.[17] When a man arrogates to himself the right of ownership in the life of human beings and interferes with the right of enjoyment of life by taking it away – that is, killing it – he has violated one of the essential laws of God and therefore forfeits his own right to the possession of life. In this regard Hayim S. Nahmani makes the following interesting observation:

> . . . in the case of homicide, in the harm that was caused by the *actus reus,* three parties are involved, God as the owner, the dead man as represented by his kinsman, and the murderer, i.e., the killing has violated God's right of ownership and also violated the dead man's right to life that was leased to him by God and also the rights of the dead man's kinsman by depriving him of his services. This attitude is reflected in the manner of punishment. In the case where there is a challenge to God's authority only, the whole community, as agents of God, inflicts the death penalty usually by stoning (Deut. 17:2-7; Lev. 24:10-16; Num. 15:35-36) and in the case of homicide it is the duty of the kinsman to inflict the death penalty. He is called the "avenger of blood" (Num. 35:19-25; Deut. 19:12).[18]

Cases of homicide fall into two distinct categories: (1) incidents where the killing was without premeditation, and (2) where a murder was committed with malice and forethought. The law described in verse 12 is in agreement with the one given to Noah (Gen. 9:6). If an enemy of a man should be delivered into his hands by God, then that act of slaying was not considered premeditated murder. It would have been regarded as manslaughter or justifiable homicide. For this there was no specific legal penalty; however, in order to prevent his own life

---

[17]Cf. I Kings 21:27-29; II Kings 20:1-6; Job 1:12-19.

[18]*Human Rights in the Old Testament* (Tel Aviv: Joshua Chachik Publishing House, Ltd., 1964), p. 53.

being taken by the "avenger of blood" (i.e., a near kinsman), he would be permitted to flee to a place of asylum, which in the days of Joshua consisted of six cities, three on the east side of the Jordan and three on the west side (Josh. 20). If, however, a man slew his neighbor with presumption, he was to receive no mercy, even at the altar (v. 14). The altar was evidently a place of safety. If a man had been charged with premeditated murder and was not guilty of that crime, it perhaps provided a means by which he could receive a hearing before the judges; however, if the man was quite clearly guilty of intentional murder, even if he took refuge at the altar he would be punished (cf. I Kings 2:28-34). In other words, for the man who was not guilty of premeditated murder there was a place of mercy, and provisions were made for a fair trial. On the other hand, where premeditated murder was clearly established, it was the responsibility of the *gōʾēl haddām* ("redeemer of blood") to avenge the death of that member of his family.

### B. *Inflictions of Physical Injury* (21:15-36)

#### 1. Violence to Parents (21:15, 17)

Mistreatment of a father or mother through striking (v. 15) or cursing (v. 17; cf. Lev. 20:9) were all to be placed on the par with murder and were punished in the same way. The smiting of one's parents does not refer to killing them, but beating them violently. It implies a deliberate and persistent opposition to parental authority. Far more is involved here than a single act of disrespect or irreverence. In the law code of Hammurabi it is stated that "if a son has struck his father, they shall cut off his hand."[19] It will be noticed that in this instance Babylonian law is less severe, but nonetheless conveys the tremendous importance of parental authority and respect for that authority.

#### 2. Kidnapping or Stealing Men (21:16)

It was not an uncommon practice for men to kidnap others and sell them into slavery, as illustrated in the Joseph story (Gen. 37:

---

[19]*ANET*, "The Code of Hammurabi," trans. by Theophile J. Meek, p. 175, law #195.

25-28). Normally those stolen were foreigners, and legal offenses were not connected with that. If the one kidnapped, however, was a fellow countryman, the punishment was severe (cf. Deut. 24:7). The death penalty is established for the practice because it was a crime against the dignity of that man and a violation of the image of God. In the code of Hammurabi if one stole the younger son of another that man was to be put to death.[20]

### 3. Quarrels Leading to Injuries (21:18-19)

If two men fought together and the one smote another with a stone or with his fist and that individual did not die, the man was not guilty of a capital crime and, therefore, as a punishment needed only to compensate for that man's loss of time. If, on the other hand, the injured man did die, it is assumed that the penalty of verse 12 would have been enforced. It is at this point that we see some striking differences between the penalties found in the Mosaic law and those which are recorded in the law code of Hammurabi. In Hammurabi's code there are careful class distinctions which are the means by which penalties are determined; for example, if two men of equal rank fight and an injury is inflicted on one of them, the other man should swear, "I did not strike him deliberately" and he would only have to pay for the services of a physician.[21] If the injured man died because of that quarrel, however, he was again required to swear as was required in law 206 and if it was a member of the aristocracy he was required to pay one-half mina of silver.[22] If the man injured was only a member of the "commonality," he had to pay only one-third mina of silver.[23] It will be noted that in the Bible such class distinctions are not apparent. All men are treated equally with respect either to guilt or to innocence in the crime with which they were charged.

---

[20]*Ibid.*, p. 166, law #14.
[21]*Ibid.*, p. 175, law #206.
[22]*Ibid.*, law #207.
[23]*Ibid.*, law #208.

4. Injuries to Servants (21:20-21, 26-27)

The punishment or chastisement of slaves was considered the right of the owner (Prov. 10:13; 13:24), but this right did not involve the unjustified outbreak of violent beatings. If he should so unjustly beat his servant or maid with the rod and that individual died, he was to be punished (v. 20). The precise nature of the punishment is not prescribed. In all probability such a man would be brought before an official body of judges and they would determine the nature of guilt and prescribe the punishment accordingly. If the slave, however, lived several days after the beating the owner was not held for the punishment insomuch as the master had paid a sum of money for the slave (v. 21). This loss of the slave was considered punishment enough for the master. Perhaps the continued existence of that slave for a day or two made it clear to the judges that it was not the intention of the master to kill his servant; in other words, there was no premeditated murder involved for which a severe penalty would be required. It is apparent from biblical notices that the slaves were carefully protected and the master did not have unlimited or uncontrolled power over them.

On the other hand, in ancient Babylon slaves were considered as mere working material and owners appeared to have unrestricted power over them. In the law code of Hammurabi the principal interest with regard to the slave-master relationship was the protection of the financial investment of the master. Consequently, if one killed another man's slave or did any harm to him, that was judged in the light of the financial loss brought to the master who consequently had to be indemnified.[24] Furthermore, the person who either assisted a slave in fleeing his master or who hid him in his house was punished with death.[25] If a man removed the distinctive mark of a slave without the consent of that slave's master he was to have his hand cut off.[26] For those who captured runaway slaves there was a reward.[27] Another important distinction between Babylonian

[24]*Ibid.*, pp. 170-175, laws #116, 199, 213 and 214.
[25]*Ibid.*, pp. 166-167, laws #15, 16 and p. 176, law #227.
[26]*Ibid.*, p. 176, law #226.
[27]*Ibid.*, p. 167, law #17.

and Hebrew practices is the fact that in Babylon when one fell into slavery for debts he had to serve for three years without any compensation[28]; whereas, the Hebrew served for a longer period of time but was compensated for his service at the end of his term.[29]

If a master smote his servant or maid thereby bringing about the injury of an eye or a tooth that slave was to be freed (vv. 26-27). The eye was considered the most severe injury and the tooth the lesser injury, but the punishment nonetheless was the same.

5. Injuries to Pregnant Women (21:22-25)

If a pregnant woman should be injured as, for example, in the process of attempting to stop an argument, and "no mischief follows," i.e., there was no death (cf. Gen. 42:4, 38; 44:29), the woman's husband would determine the nature of the punishment and the judges would make a final disposition of the matter (v. 22). The judges are included in the penalty aspect in order to prevent excessive sums being extracted from the guilty man. If, on the other hand, death did follow, then the death penalty was applied (v. 23). According to the law code of Hammurabi the punishment was slightly different. In law 209 we read, "If a seignior struck another seignior's daughter and has caused her to have a miscarriage, he shall pay ten shekels of silver for her fetus."[30] If, however, that woman died, they took the daughter of the offender and put her to death.[31] If a similar blow was struck, causing miscarriage to a commoner's daughter, the penalty was considerably less.[32] The same was true if the crime had been committed against a slave. The penalty in this case was minimal.[33]

The rationale behind the severe punishment of the man who brings about the death of the woman (v. 23) is stated in verses

---

28*Ibid.*, p. 170, law #117.
29Cf. Deut 15:12-14.
30*ANET*, p. 175.
31*Ibid.*, law #210.
32*Ibid.*, laws #211, 212.
33*Ibid.*, cf. laws #213, 214.

24 and 25. The principle of *lex taliones* is a well-known one in the ancient Near East. It is designed to bring about equitable punishment in relationship to the nature of a particular crime. Many have regarded such an operational principle in law barbaric and lacking social sophistication. Theoretically, of course, such retaliation is the most exact and strict type of judgment, but in practice difficulties arise; for example, how is the force of a blow to be accurately measured? How are certain burns or wounds to be inflicted as to be equitable? Is the literal principle of an eye for an eye to be followed when the offender only has one to begin with? Shall he pay the price of blindness for his misdeed? On the other hand, there is a certain sense in which the punishment is perhaps the fairest treatment of a particular crime. In any event, the intention of the passage is to establish appropriate justice in the light of the nature of particular crimes, a principle which has influenced all jurisprudence since this time. This law was applied in ancient Babylon only if the two parties involved were of equal rank.[34]

6. Injuries Caused by Animals (21:28-32)

If an ox should gore a man or woman to death that ox should be stoned and the flesh could not be eaten. The owner of the ox, however, would not be punished (v. 28). If, on the other hand, the ox was known to be a wild and uncontrolled beast and had injured others in the past, then if death is caused by that animal because of the negligence of his owner both the animal and the owner are put to death (v. 29). In reality, however, the crime committed by that man was one of negligence and not an intentional crime; therefore, he would normally be allowed to redeem his life by a payment of money (v. 30). The amount of money apparently would be determined by the judge. This same principle was followed when the victim was a son or daughter (v. 31). If a slave or maid was slain by such a wild animal, compensation was made to the amount of thirty shekels of silver and the ox was to be killed (v. 32). The thirty shekels of silver was apparently the redemption price for a slave. Provisions dealing

[34]*Ibid.*, laws #195-214.

with the goring of an ox are also found in the law code of Hammurabi.[35]

### 7. Injuries Caused by Negligence (21:33-36)

The remaining part of this chapter is concerned mainly with injuries to the property of Hebrews. It is focused mainly on cattle and flocks which were the most prized possessions of the Hebrews. Pits and cisterns were very common to Palestine because of the lack of rain water. These were necessary for the storage of water during the dry season. They were usually covered by a flat stone and it was the duty of the one who owned that cistern (or the one who used it regularly) to be sure that it was covered over so that animals should not fall into it. In such cases when the animal died the owner of the cistern had to compensate the loss of that animal and he in turn would receive the carcass. Another situation which apparently was not uncommon would be when one man's ox would hurt another's so that it would die. In this situation the live ox would be sold and the money would be divided. The dead ox was also divided between the two parties. If however, the ox that brought about the death of the other was known to be a violent one and was not properly restrained by his owner then the owner was responsible to pay the full price of the ox that had been slain (v. 36).

## III. Laws Concerning Theft (22:1-4)

The first fifteen verses of Chapter 22 continue the theme of honesty and responsibility in the treatment of personal property. The first four verses focus on the theft of livestock. If a man should steal an ox or sheep and kill it or dispose of it, he was given a severe fine which included the restoration of five oxen for the one ox and four sheep for the one sheep stolen (v. 1). On the other hand, if the thief was caught with the animals still in his possession and alive he was required only to restore double (v. 4).

Verses 2 and 3 focus upon the treatment of the thief himself. If he was caught breaking in in the night and was killed, no

[35]*Ibid.*, p. 176, laws #250-251.

retribution should be taken on the owner of the house. The last clause literally reads "there shall be no blood to him." The idea of blood literally means blood guiltiness indicating that the avenger of blood was not permitted to pursue the slayer (Num. 35:27). However, if this unlawful or forcible entry into the house occurred in daylight and the thief was slain, the slayer of the thief was held guilty of that blood and could be slain by the next of kin. The reason for the difference between the two aspects of this law is that one who enters the house by night is judged as having uncertain motives. In other words, his entrance may have a purely murderous intent or at least the intent to commit murder if the occasion should arise. On the other hand, one who enters by day fully exposes himself and the weapons he carries. Presumably he is not planning murder and therefore was not to be killed. The biblical regulations are quite similar to the law of Hammurabi. In Babylon "if a seignior made a breach in a house, they shall put him to death in front of that breach and wall him in."[36] It should be noted that in this instance the penalty for robbery was death with the stipulation that he would be buried at the place where the robbery was attempted. Observe also that in this law it does not state that he even successfully completed the theft, but merely that he had broken into the enclosure. Law 22, on the other hand, speaks specifically to the point and indicates that if one committed robbery and was caught, he was to be put to death.

## IV. Laws Concerning Property Damage (22:5-6)

The destruction of personal property in ancient Israel was considered a serious offense. Even if the damage was caused accidentally, appropriate restitution had to be made. The language of verse 5 seems to be describing the wilful or intentional destruction of another man's property by releasing his animals in that man's property to feed.[37] For such destruction that man was to make full restitution out of the best of his own

---

[36]*Ibid.*, p. 167, law #21.

[37]Keil and Delitzsch, *op. cit.*, II, pp. 138, 167, understand this as "injury done from carelessness." But this view does not seem to fit the language of the text.

fields and vineyards. Verse 6 describes the accidental destruction of another man's property. It was not uncommon in the ancient world to clear land with the use of fire. Such a practice, of course, had its risks, for with an increase of wind the fire may get out of control and spread to another man's property thereby destroying the grain in that field. When this occurred the man who started the fire was required to make full restitution.

### V. Laws Concerning Dishonesty (22:7-15)

The practice of leaving or depositing personal property with another was not unusual in ancient times. There were very few professional bankers or keepers of warehouses in ancient Palestine. When one had to leave his country for purposes of business it was common for him to deposit his goods with another to care for them. The laws included in verses 7 to 13 deal with the responsibility of the man who accepted such deposits especially in the light of possible theft or destruction of that property. If, for example, that material was stolen and the thief was caught the thief was required to pay double (v. 7). If, however, the thief was not caught, then the master of that house was to be brought "unto God" (Heb. *hā'ᵉlōhîm;* cf. v. 9; 21:6). The master of the house was then required to swear that he has not taken the goods or that he has disposed of them wrongly. The Septuagint evidently supports this interpretation of the verse. It reads, " . . . the master of the house shall come forward before God, and shall swear that he has not wrought wickedly in regard of any part of his neighbor's deposit."

In other matters of a breach of trust the two parties were to come before "God" ("the judges," AV). It is understood that by coming before God they stood before duly appointed judges who would settle the matter and establish the penalty. If the guilt of the one man was established, he was required to pay double to his neighbor v. 9). Verses 10 through 13 contain laws dealing with this particular problem and in each case where guilt has been established, restitution was to be made to the owner of the lost or stolen property.[38] Verses 14 and 15 are concerned

[38]*ANET*, "The Code of Hammurabi," trans. by Theophile J. Meek, p. 171, law #124 and p. 176, laws #244-245.

with the practice of borrowing which is appropriately included with these laws because it designates a deposit of one man's property into the hands of another. It will be noted from the biblical text that the borrower must take all the risks unless the owner of the property remains with the object that is borrowed.

## VI. Laws Concerning Immorality (22:16-17, 19)

The seduction of a young lady was regarded very seriously in ancient Near Eastern society. According to the biblical law found in verse 16 if a man should entice a maid that is not betrothed, he was required to pay the dowry of that girl and to take her as his wife.[39] If, on the other hand, her father refused to give her to him as a wife he was still required to pay the dowry of virgins (v. 17). The seduction of a girl who was betrothed was punished much more severely (cf. Deut. 22:23-24). The code of Hammurabi devotes a great deal of space to marital problems and the legal ramifications of the paying of a dowry and the implementation of divorce.[40]

Included in the regulations against immorality is a law which prohibits one from lying with an animal (v. 19). This evidently was a practice common to the peoples of Canaan (cf. Lev. 18:23-24). Because of the obvious unnaturalness and degrading effect of such an act the penalty for this was very severe (cf. Lev. 20:15-16; Deut. 27:21). This practice was evidently also common among the Hittites. In the laws of the Hittites it was permissible for a man to cohabit with certain animals for which there would be no punishment.[41]

## VII. Laws Relating to Civil and Religious Obligations (22:18—23:9)

The presence of "witches" was strictly forbidden by Hebrew law. The word translated "witches" here is more accurately

---

[39]Cf. also Gen. 34:12.

[40]*ANET*, "The Code of Hammurabi," trans. by Theophile J. Meek, pp. 170-175, laws #128-184.

[41]*ANET*, "The Hittite Laws," trans. by Albrecht Goetze, p. 197, law #200 (A). Note, however, the regulations regarding pigs, law #199.

rendered "sorcerers" (cf. 7:11). This word is used to describe one who claimed supernatural knowledge or power which was used to influence the gods or to cast magic spells. It has often been defined as "one who mutters charms." The fact that women are the ones designated here rather than men might suggest that the female sex was more addicted to this kind of practice.

Sacrificing to false deities was also considered a crime of the gravest sort in the economy of ancient Israel. It represented open rebellion to the true God and was punished by death (v. 20; cf. Deut. 13:1-16). The expression translated "he shall be utterly destroyed" in the Hebrew text is *yāḥᵒrām.* This term carries the sense of devoting something or someone to complete destruction.[42] This provides another example of the fact that any form of idolatry or worship of false deities was strictly forbidden and carried with it the greatest of penalties.

Great sympathy and love was to be shown for a stranger. The prohibition against oppressing a foreigner is most significant because such laws apparently did not exist among other nations. The Israelite was commanded to love strangers (Lev. 19:34) and was strictly forbidden to mistreat them (Lev. 19:33). The prime reason for this was the fact that they themselves were once strangers in the land of Egypt and knew well the hardships of being oppressed (Deut. 10:19).

The Bible, like other ancient Near Eastern law codes, shows a great deal of interest and mercy toward the widows and orphans who, like strangers, were defenseless and thus objects of special divine care (vv. 21-24). The penalty for afflicting widows and fatherless children was very severe (v. 24). Many additional laws and provisions were enacted in order to alleviate the pressures and the difficulties of widows (cf. Exod. 23:11; Lev. 19:9, 10; Deut. 14:29; 16:11, 14; 24:19-21; 26:12, 13). In times of apostasy the nation forgot many of these regulations and did indeed exploit the widows and orphans (Ps. 94:6; Isa. 1:23; 10:2; Jer. 7:5-7; 23:3; Zech. 7:10; Mal. 3:5; Matt. 23:14).

The poor among the Hebrews not only had the dangers of fall-

---

[42]See discussion of the term *ḥerem* in John J. Davis, *Conquest and Crisis*, pp. 45-46.

ing into slavery because of poverty, but could also be easily exploited by the rich. The laws of verses 25 to 28 are designed to prevent the exploitation of the poor by the charging of exorbitant rates of interest upon loans. In fact, the prohibition against any interest seems to be apparent in the Mosaic law. It will be noted that this law was designed specifically to protect the "poor" (cf. Lev. 25:25, 35, 39, 47). Whenever possible, it was the duty of the brother of that poor man to make the necessary loan and that without interest (Deut. 15:7-11). It should not be concluded from this that the charging of interest is immoral or wrong. It appears that Christ approved of the principle of profit which, of course, includes interest on loans under normal conditions (cf. Matt. 25:27; Luke 19:23). These laws were designed to prevent the poor from being taken into perpetual slavery.

Verse 28 focuses upon proper respect for constituted civil and religious authority. In the original text the word *'ᵉlohîm* has been variously translated "gods," "judges," or "God." The word "gods" should definitely be ruled out since the Hebrews held false gods in contempt and obviously then would not be expected to respect false deities. It is possible that the word should be translated "judges" here as it has been in other passages (cf. 21:6; 22: 8-9). However, on the basis of Leviticus 24:15-16 it appears that the translation "God" is preferable.[43] What was true of God was also true of the rulers of the people who in the early period consisted of the heads of the families (Num. 3:24, 30, 35) and the heads of tribes (Num. 7:10, 18, 24). This principle is carried in the New Testament in Romans 13:1-7; Hebrews 13:17; and I Peter 2:13-18.

The concluding three verses of this chapter deal with the subject of consecration. The offering of the firstfruits of the land was required of all the people. Every firstborn son was to be given to the Lord and redemption money was to be paid for him (Exod. 13:13; Num. 3:46-48). Everything else that was considered firstborn was to be offered in sacrifice. The consecration of every individual was of great importance in the economy of the Old Testament. If one was to be holy, it was mandatory that he not eat the flesh of an animal which had been "torn" be-

---

[43]See Keil and Delitzsch, *op. cit.*, II, p. 143.

cause (1) it had come in contact with an unclean carnivorous beast, and (2) the blood had not been properly drained from it. Such meat was to be cast to the dogs who were known scavengers and would eat anything (including Jezebel, II Kings 9:30-37!).

The miscellaneous laws of 23:1-9 included a variety of subjects. In verse 1 the concern is with false reports. This law is really an expansion of the ninth commandment which forbade slander and false witness. The next prohibition is a significant one in that it deals with influences within a society. It was commanded that one not follow a multitude to do evil or be influenced by a multitude in the implementation of justice. It has always been characteristic of human behavior to want to be accepted by the masses and to be part of a large movement. The rampant growth of evil can be attributed to a large degree to this kind of human interest and reaction. Of course, such practices are strictly forbidden as evidenced not only here, but in the New Testament (cf. Matt. 7:13-14).

The subject of the perversion of justice is continued in verse 3 where it is commanded that one should not "countenance a poor man in his cause"; that is, justice should be equitably applied to both the rich and the poor. To favor a poor man because he was poor was to violate the principle of true justice just as it was to rule in favor of a rich man because he was rich. It was the guilt or innocence of the party that was the crucial point of real justice (cf. Lev. 19:15). True godly behavior would always produce proper attitudes and actions with respect to a man's possessions (vv. 4-5) and with respect to true justice for the poor man (v. 6).

The godly man was warned not to be a part of a "false matter" or false accusation. The innocent and the righteous were not to be slain for the warning was given that God would not "justify the wicked." A truly godly man also would not be part of bribery in a court of justice. The problem of bribery with respect to legal cases was very common in the ancient Near East and often carried with it the death penalty. The Mosaic code, however, did not appear to fix any specific penalty for this evil (cf. Deut. 16:18-20). In spite of this warning, the acceptance of bribes all too often became common practice in ancient Israel (cf. I Sam. 8:3; note also Ps. 26:10; Prov. 17:23; Isa. 1:23; Mic. 3:9-11). This section of miscellaneous laws concludes with another warning not to oppress a stranger or foreigner. This is a repetition of the injunction given in 22:21 but here it probably has specific references to courts of law as opposed to private reaction in the previous passage.

## VIII. Ceremonial Laws (23:10-19)

### A. *The Sabbatical Year* (23:10-13)

After six years of active agricultural pursuits (v. 10) the Israelite was required to allow that land to rest completely in the seventh year (v. 11). The seventh year seems to have been unique with Israel. After six years of sowing, pruning and gathering the land was to lie fallow for one year. The purpose of this practice was to permit the poor to glean from those fields whatever remains could be eaten by the beasts (v. 11; Deut. 15: 2-18). There was, of course, anxiety among the Israelites with regard to the ability of the land to produce enough in that sixth year for them to survive. It was promised, however, by the Lord that the sixth year would provide enough for three years (Lev. 24:20 ff.). As Israel indulged more and more in apostasy and embraced the practices of the Canaanites the sabbatical year was abandoned. The seventy-year captivity was intended to make up for the failure to observe these sabbatical years (II Chron. 36:17-21). To fail to observe the year was to incur the displeasure of God as indicated in Leviticus 26:34-43; II Chronicles 36:21; Jeremiah 34:14-22. The culmination of the sabatical years was reached each fiftieth year, known as the year of jubilee. The law of the sabbatical year is intricately tied in with the weekly Sabbath institution. The latter, of course, is grounded in God's creative activity (cf. Exod. 20:11). All Sabbaths were reminders of the sovereignty of God in His exercise of power in creative acts. Furthermore, the Sabbath year was a reminder that the land belonged to God and man merely possessed it in a trust under God (Lev. 25:23).

This section appropriately concludes with a reminder to avoid all aspects of idolatry even to the point of not mentioning the name of other deities (v. 13). It might be pointed out here that the prohibition not to mention the names of other gods was not only a protection against idolatry, but served as a prohibition against intermarriage with other nations. It is well known that in the marriage contract recognition had to be given to the gods of the various parties involved. To permit such false worship to be perpetuated and to allow the names of false deities to be widely circulated served as an endorsement of that false religion. All altars and idols were to be obliterated according to the law (cf. Deut. 12:3; Josh. 23:7).

B. *The Three Feasts* (23:14-19)

Having twelve tribes as the foundation of the nation created great concern when it came to the matter of national unity and identity. The one thing that provided the cohesion necessary for national unity was Israel's God and her religion. The maintainance of national, spiritual and social unity was provided for in three major feasts. It was required that all males should appear before the Lord during these three feast seasons (v. 17). The practical effect of this would be a continued uniting at a central place: namely, the tabernacle.

The first feast to be attended was the feast of unleavened bread (v. 15) which came in the early spring at the beginning of the barley harvest in the month of Abib (Nisan). It began with the Passover and a holy convocation and lasted for seven days. At the end of the seven days another holy convocation was held (cf. Lev. 23:5-8). During this seven-day period unleavened bread was to be eaten in commemoration of the hasty exodus from Egypt (Exod. 12:33, 34, 39). This feast had many spiritual lessons to teach the children of Israel. Foremost was the fact that God constantly wanted sin to be put away from their midst. It implied complete separation from that which is evil. Leaven is, of course, always a symbol of sin and error in Scripture (cf. Matt. 16:6, 11-12; I Cor. 5:6, 8). The practice of putting away leaven was to be a reminder of God's great concern for purity of life. On the other hand, from a positive point of view, it pointed to the fact that God desired men to receive that which was good. In the ultimate sense, this pointed to Jesus Christ who is the perfect bread of life (John 6:35, 48, 51).

The second feast to be commemorated by all the males was

the feast of harvest (v. 16) or, as it is called in the New Testament period, the feast of pentecost. In 34:22 it is called the "feast of weeks" because, according to Leviticus 23:15-16 and Deuteronomy 16:9, it was to be kept seven weeks after the feast of unleavened bread. This feast was always a joyful occasion (Deut. 16:9-11) simply because it was an expression of gratitude for all that God had provided for them. To give expression to such thankfulness for the grain which God had provided, two loaves were baked with leaven and presented before God (Lev. 23:17).

The final feast to be attended by all the males was the feast of ingathering, called "the feast of tabernacles" elsewhere in Scripture. The latter title was given because the people were commanded to make for themselves small booths in which to dwell during this feast (Lev. 23:33-36; Deut. 16:13-15; 31:10; John 7:2). This festival began on the fifteenth day of Tishri, which came late in October or early in the month of November. The feast itself lasted for eight days. It was marked by holy convocation at the beginning and at the end. This feast, like the previous one, was a time of great gladness and thanksgiving for the final harvest which God had provided. These three feasts provided a very opportune time for all Israelites to gather together and to renew friendships and fellowships. It was an important means of spreading information and offering opportunities for families to be reunited. Such occasions, when commemorated properly, provided a skillful means of maintaining national and spiritual unity.

The prohibition not to "boil a kid in his mother's milk" (v. 19) appears to be strange to us, but significant light has been shed on this prohibition by means of the excavations at Ras Shamra, the ancient city of Ugarit. We now know that boiling sacrificial kids in their mother's milk was a common ritual practice of the Canaanites. One Ugaritic text read,

> Over the fire seven times the sacrificers cook a kid in milk (?) (and) mint (?) in butter and over the cauldron seven times fresh water (?) is poured.[44]

---

[44]"Shachar and Shalim," 1:14 in G. R. Driver, *Canaanite Myths and Legends* (Edinburgh: T. & T. Clark, 1956), p. 121.

On the basis of v. 19, Exodus 34:26 and Deuteronomy 14:21, the Jewish dietary law forbidding milk to be consumed at any meal in which meat is eaten, was built. Orthodox Jews even keep separate kitchen equipment to be provided for the preparation of milk and meat dishes.

## IX. Laws Relating to Conquest (23:20-33)

In anticipation of their eventual conquest of the land of Canaan, certain regulations were established concerning their travel to the land of Canaan and the confrontation with the enemies of that land. Four basic ideas emerge in the remaining verses of this chapter. *First,* there is emphasis upon obedience to divine leadership (vv. 20-23). The angel mentioned in verse 20 has been identified three different ways. Some consider Moses to have been that angel while others see it as one of the created angelic beings. More popular, however, is the view that this angel was indeed the angel of Jehovah or the second person of the trinity.[45] In the light of the context and other evidence the last view appears to be preferable. Since this is Jehovah himself who leads, He demands absolute obedience (v. 21). Those who disobeyed were regarded as enemies and treated as such (v. 22). This angel would also lead them in the land as they confronted the major enemies and it would be He who would provide the key to victory (v. 23).

The *second* important theme of this section deals with the worship of the true God (vv. 24-26). True worship involved complete separation from idolatry as well as in a positive sense doing that which God desires.

The *third* theme centers around the provisions that God would make for their victory while fighting in the land of Canaan (vv. 27-31). The means by which He would dishearten the enemy, thus making successful battles possible for Israel, would be to send His "fear" before them. This same thought is expressed in verse 28 in symbolic terminology when He states, "I will send hornets before thee." Some have taken this as a reference to literal hor-

---

[45]See George Rawlinson, *op. cit.*, p. 276 and Keil and Delitzsch, *op. cit.*, II, p. 152.

nets. John Garstang, however, understood it as a veiled reference to the Egyptian armies that defeated the Hyksos and other peoples in Palestine shortly before the conquest. He supported his contention by noting that a bee (or hornet) was considered as a sacred symbol of the pharaohs.[46] A final and perhaps preferable viewpoint is that the expression "hornet" is really figurative, referring to the panic-producing power of God which aided in overcoming both Sihon and Og. This suggestion is supported by the proximity of verse 28 to verse 27. There is a sense in which they appear in a synonomous parallelism (cf. Deut. 2:25; 7:20). That fear and panic played a strategic role in the victories both in Transjordan and Canaan is clear from Numbers 22:3; Joshua 2:9, 11; 5:1; 9:24.[47]

It was also promised in verses 29 and 30 that the peoples of the land of Canaan would not be driven out immediately; this would prevent the land from becoming desolate and keep wild beasts from multiplying. The process of occupation and colonization was to be a progressive one in order that they might maintain complete control over that land. The problem of roaming wild dogs and lions was not uncommon in places where the population was small (cf. II Kings 17:24-25). Other delays in the colonization of the land were due to the fact that God wanted to "prove" Israel to see whether they would obey His ways (Judg. 2:21-23). The bounds that God set for their occupation (v. 31) were not fully realized until the time of David and Solomon.

The *fourth* section of Chapter 23 concludes with the warning that no covenant was to be made with the peoples of Canaan or with their gods (v. 32). The procedure for conquest and colonization involved driving the enemy completely out of those territories in order that the temptation of idolatry would be removed (v. 33). The prohibition relating to covenant-making in these verses relates to those peoples "in the land" alone. Israel was permitted to make peace with those cities that were far off, according to Deuteronomy 7:1-2; 20:10-15.

---

[46]*Joshua-Judges*, p. 259.
[47]John J. Davis, *Conquest and Crisis*, pp. 88-89.

## X. Ratification of the Covenant (24:1-8)

After covenantal law had been given to Moses he was commanded to write down all these words and put them in a book (vv. 4, 7). This book became known as "the book of the covenant" and was to be read in the hearing of all the people in order that they might respond to the challenges of Jehovah. The process of completing the book of the covenant included times of special worship and involved Aaron, Nadab and Abihu (v. 1). Nadab and Abihu, of course, were the two oldest sons of Aaron (6:23) and would have been the father's natural successors to the priesthood. Their sin, offering "a strange fire," prevented this from occurring, however (Lev. 10:1-2).[48] Seventy elders also participated in this time of worship and were probably official representatives of the twelve tribes. Burnt offerings and sacrifices were given to the Lord on this momentous occasion (v. 5). The blood of the sacrifices, which was then sprinkled on the people, became an official sign of the covenant treaty (v. 8). Sealing a covenant with blood was not an uncommon custom (cf. Gen. 15:9-13, 17).

## XI. The Glory of the Lord (24:9-18)

This occasion of worship was a splendid one indeed. The people had been impressed by the greatness of the revelation which Moses had received. They willingly accepted the provisions of that covenant and the evidence of that acceptance came in the form of proper sacrifice and blood-sprinkling. The elders, along with Aaron, Nadab and Abihu, actually were able to "see" the God of Israel. The precise nature of that which they saw is not known to us, but it was almost beyond description. Keil and Delitzsch appropriately warn,

> We must not go beyond the limits drawn in 33:20-23 in our conceptions of what constituted the sight . . . of God; at the same time we must regard it as a vision of God in some form of manifestation which rendered a divine nature discernible to

---

[48]This act was clearly an idolatrous form of worship. The Hebrew *zr* is frequently used in connection with the worship of strange gods (cf. Deut. 32:16; Isa. 17:10; 43:12; Jer. 2:25; 3:13; Ps. 44:21; 81:10).

> the human eye. Nothing is said as to the form in which God manifested himself.[49]

Some have suggested that the vision they saw was of the Son of God, the second person of the Godhead.[50] Whatever the precise nature of the vision, it was majestic and served to illustrate the power of the God who had given the revelation.

Following this event Moses was commanded to return to the top of the mountain. Making the trip part way up was Moses' servant Joshua (v. 13). The elders were not permitted to ascend near the top. They were commanded to wait for the return of Moses and Joshua. In their absence Moses appointed Aaron and Hur as national leaders and whatever problems should arise were to be brought to them (v. 14). Moses then ascended alone to the summit of the mountain where a cloud covered the area. This cloud is again identified with the glory of the Lord (v. 16). For six days Moses remained up in that area awaiting the voice of God. On the seventh day a voice was heard. The glory of this occasion was also visible to the Israelites who had settled in the valley just near this great mountain. For forty days and forty nights Moses remained in the top of that mountain in communion and fellowship with the God of Israel (v. 18). During this entire time he was without food (Deut. 9:9). The whole purpose of this long time of fellowship was to receive the tables of stone on which the law would be written (v. 12; cf. Deut. 9:9).

The believer has an equally glorious opportunity in this age for we are able to come nigh to the very presence of God in the holy of holies because of the blood of Christ (Heb. 10:19). We no longer have to wait at the bottom of the mountain for revelation. That has been given to us in the Holy Scriptures. Our responsibility now is to read and obey.

---

[49]*Op. cit.*, II, p. 159.

[50]Francis Nichol, *op. cit.*, p. 632.

Chapter 12

# God's Dwelling-Place

(Exodus 25–27, 30–31, 35–40)

For most Israelites the trip southward from the wilderness of Shur to Sinai must have appeared unnecessary and extremely disconcerting. This was not the way to the occupation of a fruitful land or settlement in that territory promised to their father Abraham. However, as one studies the pages of the Book of Exodus he is made aware of the wisdom of God as He prepared His people for that occupation. They had received a system of law which would provide for a balanced and functioning society. It would prevent the exploitation of the poor which was common in the land of Canaan. It would set up safeguards against polytheism and idolatry which was the dominant factor in Canaanitic religion. Now the final phase of that divine preparation is focused in a tent – the dwelling-place of God. The tabernacle was to be the focal point of Israelite worship and spiritual encounter. From this time until the days of Saul it would be the focal point of national life. It would serve as a rallying and unifying point among the twelve tribes scattered throughout the land of Canaan.

Up until the modern era of archaeological discovery, critical opinion was dominated by the view of Wellhausen regarding the origin of the tabernacle. In his *Prolegomena* he argued that the wilderness tabernacle was nothing more than an idealized view of the temple. From this it was concluded that the narratives describing the tabernacle were no more than historical fiction and the work of a post-exilic priestly compiler. About 1919 another view was proposed which raised questions concerning the simple idealism of the Wellhausenian view and suggested that perhaps the tabernacle concept found its origin in late Arabic sources. H. Lammens discovered the presence of a *qubbah* in old Arabic sources which pointed to the existence of some kind of palladium or tent shrine.[1] J. Morgenstern followed this clue

[1]*Bulletin de l'Institut Francais d'Archeologie Orientale*, XVII (1919), pp. 39 ff.

and developed it, demonstrating that images and related objects of a particular tribal deity were kept in small tents normally made of red leather which were even at times carried into battle.[2] The term *qubbah* appeared in an Aramaic inscription

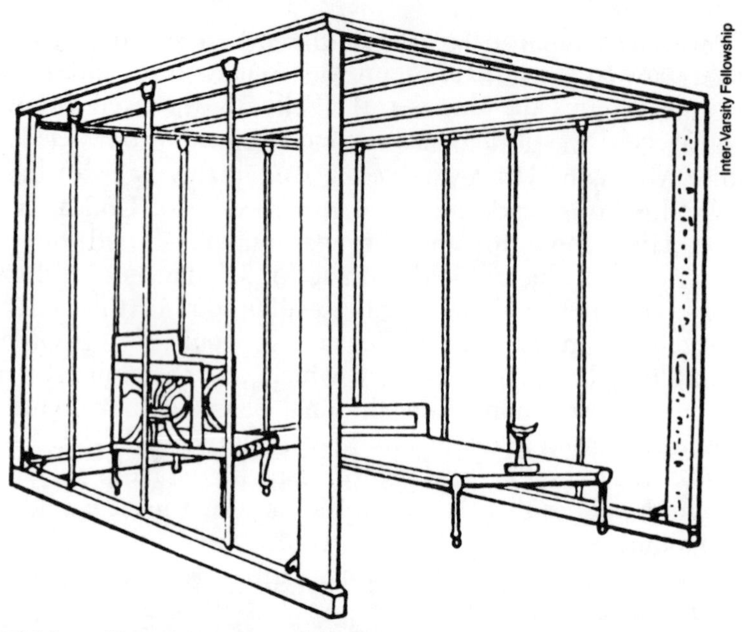


**The portable pavilion of Hetep-heres shown without its coverings but with chair, bed and head-rest placed within. From Giza, Egypt, c. 2600 B.C.**

from Palmyra and apparently designated some kind of sacred tent. Bas-reliefs and terra cottas from that area depicted what seemed to be portable tent shrines which were carried by camels.[3] More recent studies have pointed to the fact that at Ugarit the Canaanite deity El may have had some such portable shrine as a regular feature of his cult in the Amarna age.[4] K. A.

[2]*Hebrew Union College Annual*, V (1928), pp. 81 ff.; XVII (1942-1943), pp. 153 ff.; XVIII (1943-1944), pp. 1 ff. See also Frank M. Cross, Jr., "The Tabernacle," *The Biblical Archaeologist*, X (Sept., 1947), pp. 59 ff.

[3]See R. K. Harrison, *op. cit.*, p. 403.

[4]W. F. Albright, "The Furniture of El in Canaanite Mythology," *Bulletin of the American Schools of Oriental Research*, No. 91 (1943), pp. 39 ff, No. 93 (1944), pp. 23 ff.

Kitchen has shed an interesting light on the concept of movable shrines in noting that prefabricated structures existed in Egypt and, of course, were designed to be moved about.[5] While all these studies are interesting and informative they nonetheless do not provide a legitimate origin for the biblical tabernacle. The existence of portable shrines in Egypt is, of course, a devastating blow to the critical theories of Wellhausen. Even without these discoveries the theories of Wellhausen lacked careful notice of certain biblical details which immediately raised questions concerning the validity of that theory. R. K. Harrison rightly observes,

> The tabernacle, which was confidently assigned to a post-exilic date and held to have been based upon late Temple practice, can hardly have been later than the monarchy, since it lacked such important features of pre- and post-exilic worship as singers, a point that Wellhausen apparently failed to notice.[6]

He further observes, "In particular, the fact that there are no specific references or allusions to Jerusalem in the Pentateuch would be unthinkable in any alleged source emmanating from the southern kingdom in the 9th century B.C."[7]

The only really adequate explanation for the magnificent tabernacle structure is that it originated not in the fertile mind of Moses, but as a revelation from God. The simplicity and rich symbolism of this structure and its furniture were definitely beyond the capacity of a finite mind. Furthermore, Scripture makes it perfectly clear that the origin of the tabernacle was found in God and given to Moses by special revelation (Exod. 25:9, 40; 26:30; cf. Heb. 8:5; 9:23-24).

The remaining chapters of the Book of Exodus will be treated somewhat differently than the pattern followed previously in this book. Since there is duplication of the material concerning the structure and description of the tabernacle, Chapters 25 to 31 and Chapters 35 to 38 will be combined. The sad account of the time of apostasy during Moses' stay in the mountains (32–34)

---

[5]See *The Tyndale House Bulletin*, Nos. 5-6 (1960), pp. 8 ff.
[6]*Op. cit.*, p. 527.
[7]*Ibid.*

will be treated separately as will the priesthood also described in the Book of Exodus. Wherever possible the outline of this chapter will follow the sequence of material as presented in the Scripture.

## I. Names Given to the Tabernacle

There are five different names or titles given to the tabernacle in the Pentateuch. Each one sheds some interesting light on either the nature of that structure or its function. The first one used is the Hebrew word *miqdāš* (Exod. 25:8). This is the word that is translated "sanctuary" and denotes a place which is sacred.[8] This word is derived from the Hebrew *qādaš* denoting that which is holy or separate. A second term used is *miskān,* translated "the tabernacle" in Exodus 25:9. This masculine noun is derived from the Hebrew verb *šākan* meaning to "settle down, abide, or dwell."[9] This term, of course, speaks of one of the functions of the tabernacle: namely, to be a residing place for God among His people. The third term is the very common Hebrew word *'ōhel,* translated "tent" in Exodus 26:36. This is the word that is commonly used for a temporary or collapsible dwelling. The fourth expression used to describe this tabernacle is the Hebrew *'ōhel mô'ēḏ.* This expression occurs in Exodus 29:42 but is poorly translated in the *Authorized Version* by the expression "the tabernacle of the congregation." The term *mô'ēḏ* is derived from the Hebrew verb *yā'aḏ* meaning "to meet at an appointed place."[10] A preferable translation would be "the tent of meeting" (RSV). The fifth expression occurs in Exodus 38:21 and is the Hebrew *miskan hā'ēḏuṯ,* translated "the tabernacle of the testimony" (cf. Num. 17:7). A variation of the same name appears in Numbers 17:23 as *'ōhel hā'ēḏûṯ* ("tent of the testimony"). The tabernacle received these designations from the law of the two tables, which were placed in the ark which stood in the innermost sanctuary. A common name for these tables was "the testimony" and the ark which contained them was therefore designated "the ark of the testimony" (cf. Exod. 25:21-22;

[8]Brown, Driver and Briggs, *op. cit.*, p. 874.
[9]*Ibid.*, p. 1014.
[10]*Ibid.*, pp. 416-417.

31:18). It was therefore appropriate that the whole tabernacle should be called the tabernacle or tent of the testimony.

## II. Purposes of the Tabernacle

From the standpoint of Israel's immediate needs the tabernacle served as a dwelling place for God and a meeting place for the people (cf. Exod. 25:8; 29:43-46; 40:34-37). It should not be concluded that the Israelites had conceived of their God as a localized deity. Far from that. The tabernacle merely served as a meeting place between God and His people. This is not to say that God could not be encountered elsewhere; but from a standpoint of national interest and necessity in worship practices a *place* of worship was not only desirable but necessary. Places of worship have always been part of godly exercise and are not condemned by Scripture. It is when such places supplant or exchange the true worship for false that they are condemned. The most sacred part of the tabernacle, of course, was the ark of the covenant and the area between the cherubim. It was here that God actually dwelt in a special way (cf. Num. 7:89; I Sam. 4:4; II Sam. 6:2). In the Targums this special presence of God came to be known as *šᵉkinah*. This expression does not appear in the Old Testament, but correctly denotes that which dwells in a certain place (cf. I Kings 6:13). Furthermore, the sanctuary provided a visible center for the worship of the one true God and thus provided a bulwark against the worship of the many gods of the heathen. This, like the law, was a protection against idolatry (Exod. 29:43, 45; Num. 35:34).

The tabernacle also provided a prophetic prefigurement of the redemptive program of God as focused in Jesus Christ. It is clear from the Book of Hebrews that the earthly tabernacle was not only a pattern of the heavenly, but was designed to point to the ministry and the deity of our Lord. Though it is true that God "dwelleth not in temples made with hands" (Acts 7:48) the miracle of the virgin birth made it possible for the Lord Jesus to dwell among men (John 1:14). It is not accidental that the word "dwelt" in this text is literally translated "tabernacled." The dwelling place of Christ now is in the heavenly sanctuary where He makes intercession for the saints. The tabernacle of

Moses' day was a remarkable picture of both the high priestly work of Christ here on earth and His eternal work in the heavens.

## III. Problems in Interpreting the Biblical Data

There are several difficulties with which one is confronted as he considers the multitude of details relative to the construction and function of the tabernacle. The first is the interpretation of the Hebrew word *'ammāh,* translated "cubit." The cubit was normally recognized to be the distance from the elbow to the fingertip. This "natural" cubit is referred to as the "cubit of a man" (Deut. 3:11). Such a measurement was often used to indicate the general size of a person (for cubits, the height of a man, cf. I Sam. 17:4; I Chron. 11:23). The standard Hebrew cubit was 17.5 inches which was slightly shorter than the common Egyptian cubit of 17.6 inches. There was also what has been called a long or "royal" cubit which was a hand breadth (palm) longer than a standard cubit of six palms (Exod. 40:5): that is, 20.4 inches. The Babylonian cubit was 19.8 inches and the royal Egyptian cubit was 20.65 inches. The question that now arises is, Which cubit was used in the measurements of the tabernacle? Some have argued that since Moses had been educated in the royal court in Egypt and the Hebrew slaves had been employed on various royal construction projects it should be assumed that the royal Egyptian cubit was the one used by Moses in the construction of the tabernacle.[11] Others, however, have preferred the smaller cubit of either 17.5 (Hebrew) or 17.6 (Egyptian).[12] The final differences between the structure calculated both ways are not really significantly different; however, it is confusing to students to encounter different statistics in the various commentaries. In designating the approximate sizes of the various objects in the tabernacle we shall be using the shorter cubit as the standard measurement.

A second major problem deals with filling in the multitude of details which have been omitted in the Exodus account. Those

---

[11]Francis Nichol, *op. cit.*, p. 636.

[12]T. Whitelaw, "Tabernacle," *The International Standard Bible Encyclopedia,* V, p. 2891.

who have felt an obligation to reconstruct every single detail of the tabernacle have found themselves greatly frustrated by the absence of certain numerical data. Of course, there is probably a good reason why many details are omitted. From a revelational point of view they are not necessary to our appreciation of the fundamental significance and function of that tabernacle. The Bible was written not merely to satisfy our curiosity about details in the past, but to serve as a complete revelation of God's person and program for men.

It is unfortunate that many writers have gone to extremes in extending typology to every portion of the tabernacle. It is quite apparent that some of the parts in the tabernacle were there for only one reason: to give it structural support; they were not intended to convey some mystical typological meaning.

Equally disconcerting is the constant emphasis on numbers on the part of some writers. It is assumed by them that all biblical numbers have symbolic or typological value and thus it is the responsibility of the Bible student to discover these "hidden meanings" by arranging mathematical formulas. The whole system of mystical numerology as applied to Scripture has been recently evaluated and criticized. There is serious doubt that the numerological patterns of Scripture are, after all, intended to convey theological or even practical concepts.[13] It is true, of course, that the tabernacle contains some basic symbolism. This is apparent from the many references to the tabernacle in the Book of Hebrews. However, it is extremely dangerous to extend this typology beyond the bounds of the information given in the Book of Hebrews or similar information elsewhere in the New Testament.

A third major problem with the interpretation of the tabernacle centers around the exact shape of this structure. The traditional viewpoint is that the tabernacle proper was an oblong flat-roofed structure with the coverings over the top and hanging down on either side and the back. This interpretation is defended in some detail by A. R. S. Kennedy[14] and followed by a

---

[13]For a detailed discussion on this matter see John J. Davis, *Biblical Numerology*, pp. 103-149.

[14]"Tabernacle," *A Dictionary of the Bible,"* James Hastings, ed., (New York: Charles Scribners Sons, 1902), pp. 658-662.

The Tabernacle as envisioned by A. R. S. Kennedy

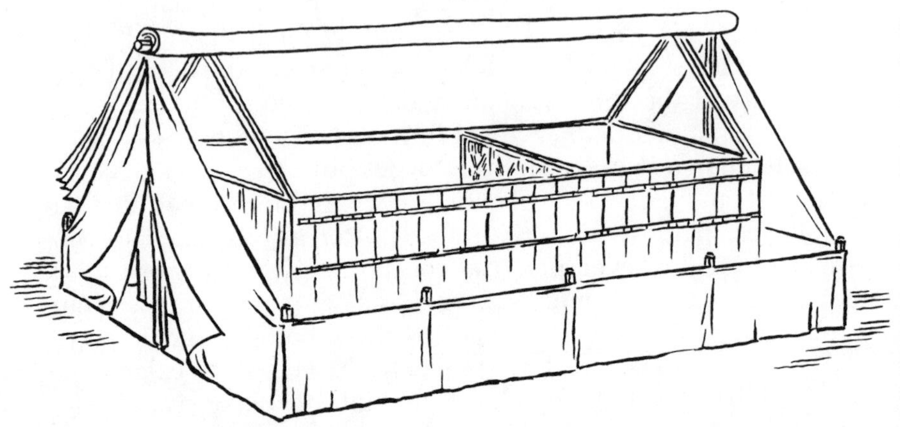

Model of the Tabernacle as proposed by Dr. Shick. Note the gable construction.

number of others.[15] James Fergusson found great difficulty in aligning this with the biblical term "tent" and therefore developed a structure that was more like the traditional form of a tent with ridge pole, sloping roof and other apparatuses of such an erection.[16] In a modified form this approach has been fol-

[15]D. W. Gooding, "Tabernacle," *New Bible Dictionary*, p. 1232 and Francis Nichol, *op. cit.*, pp. 641-642.

[16]"Temple," *Dictionary of the Bible*, William Smith, ed., (New York: Hurd and Houghton, 1870), pp. 3193-3197.

lowed by T. Whitelaw[17] and R. H. Mount.[18] Those holding the latter view argue that the traditional approach does not really represent a tent. Furthermore, it is argued that if the inner or ornamental curtain was so used, only about one-third of it would be seen; nine cubits on each side would be entirely hidden between the walls of the tabernacle and the goats' hair curtain,[19] but Kennedy has adequately answered this argument by demonstrating that the walls were not made of solid planks but were frames composed of two uprights joined by cross rails somewhat like a ladder.[20]

Another argument commonly presented related to the problem of stress under rainy conditions. Fergusson argued,

> . . . every drop of rain that fell on the tabernacle would fall through; for, however tightly the curtains might be stretched, the water could never run over the edge, and the sheep-skins would only make the matter worse, as when wetted their weight would depress the center, and probably tear any curtain that could be made, while snow lying on such a roof would certainly tear the curtains to pieces.[21]

While to a certain degree this is a valid argument, and one must admit the possibility of extended and frequent rainstorms in the Sinai Peninsula, it hardly presents a long range problem. However, one might assume that even though not specifically stated in the text provisions were made for this particular problem. The Israelites were surely not unaware of the possibility of rain and the difficulties of stress on a completely flat roof. The skins were, therefore, probably prepared appropriately to provide some run-off on the roof. The fourth argument presented in favor of a gabled construction is that only one cubit of goats' hair curtain was to hang down on each side; whereas, the traditional view makes ten cubits hang down on each side of the tabernacle

---

[17]"Tabernacle," *op. cit.*, V, pp. 2887-2891.
[18]*The Law Prophesied* (Published by the author, 1963), pp. 49-61.
[19]James Fergusson, *op. cit.*, p. 3195.
[20]*Op. cit.*, p. 660.
[21]*Op. cit.*, p. 3195.

(Exod. 26:9, 12, 13).[22] D. W. Gooding replies that this argument

> . . . springs from failure to observe that the term "tabernacle" means the linen curtains, not the framework. Similarly, the claim that at the western end there was an overhanging awning called a *miskan,* as distinct from the *'ohel* (= the whole structure) is based on a misunderstanding of these technical terms.[23]

The traditional viewpoint of a flat roof is supported by a number of writers and this appears to be preferable in the light of all the biblical data that we presently have at hand. The outside curtains (26:8) were to be thirty cubits long, the exact length required to provide a flat roof and to extend down on either side, thereby covering the gold-plated framework in the walls. On the other hand, a gabled roof would increase the length of the covering required for the top part of the tabernacle proper and thereby expose the gold-plated boards which appears to be in conflict with one of the purposes of such a covering. Gold was otherwise reserved for the interior of the structure. It might be noted further that the fact that the inner curtain was two cubits shorter than the outer three which covered it probably implies that the outer curtains were designed to protect it and that they probably reached to the ground.[24]

In the second place the most serious difficulty faced with the gabled-roof view is that no ridge pole is mentioned in the text nor is the existence of one even implied. Third, there is nothing to indicate that the five "pillars" varied in length so as to provide for a gabled roof. Fergusson claims that the "middle bar" of Exodus 26:28 was a ridge pole; however, it appears that the better interpretation is that the "middle bar" was one of the five bars mentioned in the previous verse.[25] It is more natural to regard the middle bar of Exodus 26:28 as one of the five bars mentioned in verse 27 of that chapter. Gooding further observes,

---

[22]*Ibid.*
[23]*Op. cit.*, p. 1232.
[24]Francis Nichol, *op. cit.*, p. 641.
[25]*Op. cit.*, p. 3196.

> Again, a ridge-pole would require that one of the door pillars and one of the veil pillars should be higher than the others to support the pole and there would have to be a pillar at the back of similar height. None of these things is mentioned in the directions.[26]

Another problem with the view of a gabled roof and one which is solved by a flat-roof concept is that the gabled roof would probably leave the ends open. Furthermore the curtain which separated the holy place from the most holy did not extend to the top of the building so that the light from the Shekinah might be partially visible above it from the first section of the sanctuary. Moreover, the innermost parts of the sanctuary theoretically could have been visible from the outside of the court itself with this arrangement.[27] With all facts in view, therefore, the traditional flat-roof concept appears to be the best.

## IV. Materials for the Building (25:1-9)

### A. *Nature of the Materials*

In preparation for the construction of the tabernacle Moses was commanded to challenge the people to bring willingly gifts for the structure (vv. 1-2). God desired only those gifts that were given from a joyful heart and not merely out of religious obligation. Grudging gifts are not particularly desirable or useful to God (cf. II Cor. 8:4-5; 9:7). The people, according to 35:21-29 and 36:3-7, did respond out of a joyful heart, so much so that they had to be "restrained from bringing." A similar spirit was witnessed in David's time when preparations for construction of the Temple were undertaken (cf. I Chron. 29:1-9).

The basic metals for the structure are listed in verse 3 and include gold, silver and bronze. The word "brass" in the King James Version should be changed to the word "bronze." The material used was an alloy of copper and tin, not the later material known as brass which was an alloy of copper and zinc. The gold and silver probably came into Israelite possession when

---

[26]*Op. cit.*, p. 1232.

[27]Cf. Francis Nichol, *op. cit.*, p. 642.

they left Egypt and "borrowed" from the Egyptians (cf. 3:22; 12:35-36). The various types of cloth and goats' hair (v. 4) that were required could easily have been acquired from the Egyptians or perhaps by trade with the desert peoples. Also required were rams' skins dyed red and "badgers' skins" (v. 5). The term badger is probably a poor translation for the Hebrew *taḥaš*. This word is closely related to the Arabic *tukhash* or *duksash*, a name for a marine animal resembling the seal, more particularly the dugong or sea cow. Since the Arabic term applies not only to this one species but also to seals, dolphins, sharks and dogfish, perhaps the Hebrew term is equally flexible. The best single candidate for this identification, however, would be the dugong or sea cow. This herbivorous animal grows to about ten to twelve

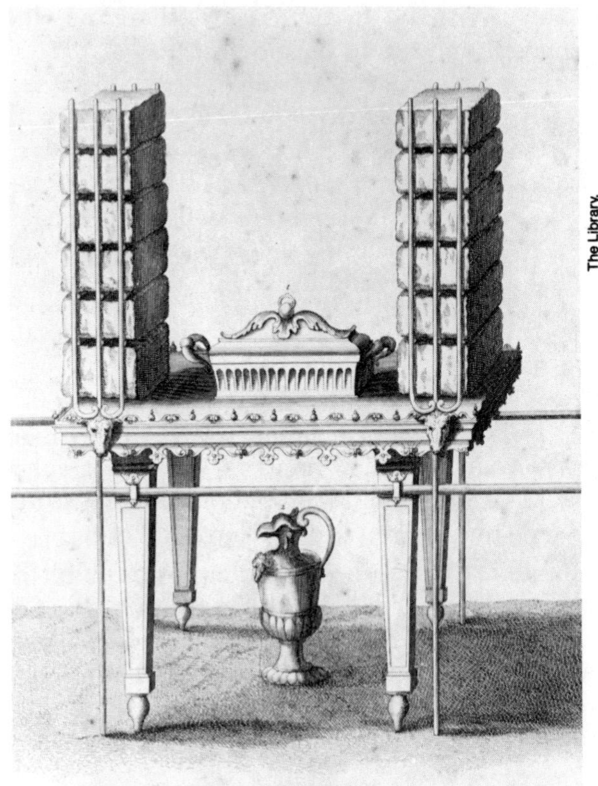

The Library, Jewish Theological Seminary of America

Table of shewbread.

feet long, and has a round head and a divided tail. It is often found among the coral rocks of the Red Sea. The term shittim wood (v. 5) is better translated Acacia, of which two species grow in the deserts of Sinai, and et-Tih and around the Dead Sea. The one is *Acacia Seyal*, Del., and A. *Tortilis*, Hayne. It is a hard, durable, close-grained wood. It is very heavy and indestructible by insects. These characteristics made it very suitable for the construction of the framework and furniture of the tabernacle. This tree is remarkably luxuriant in dry places, sometimes attaining to a height of twenty feet. It is adorned with yellow flowers and was used commonly for tanning wood, making fuel and even for parts of mummy cases.[28] The oil of verse 6 is undoubtedly olive oil (27:20).

### B. *The Source of the Materials*

The primary source for the materials required was, of course, Egypt. As noted above the Israelites were able to take with them a great deal of valuable material from Egypt at the time of the exodus (cf. 3:22; 12:35-36; 35:23; 38:8). Additional material was probably also acquired when they defeated the Amalekites in Rephidim (17:8-16). Whatever materials were needed in addition could have been acquired by trade with caravans which passed through the Sinai Peninsula.

## V. The Ark of the Covenant (25:10-22; 37:1-9)

The only object in that part of the tabernacle proper called the holy of holies was the ark of the covenant. This object is also called "ark of the Lord," "ark of God," "ark of the covenant of the Lord" (Deut. 10:8) and the "ark of testimony." The Hebrew term for the ark is *'ªrôn*. This word refers to a chest or coffer of small dimensions, used to contain money or other valuables (II Kings 12:9-10; II Chron. 15:8-11). The word is probably related to Akkadian *aranu,* meaning box. According to verse 10 this chest was to be made of acacia wood measuring 2½ x 1½ x 1½ cubits. Assuming that the cubit was about 18 inches (to

---

[28]Merrill F. Unger, "Shittah Tree, Shittim Wood," *Unger's Bible Dictionary*, pp. 1143-1144.

round off 17.6), the dimensions would be 3′ 9″ long and 2′ 3″ deep. The whole ark was to be covered with gold and carried on poles inserted through rings at the four lower corners (vv. 11-15). The ark served as the repository for the two tables of the law (vv. 16, 21; 40:20; Deut. 10:1-5). A pot of manna and Aaron's rod were also added to this collection (Heb. 9:4-5).

The lid of this chest was known as the "mercy seat" and was made of solid gold (v. 17). On the top and on either end stood two cherubim of gold with outstretched wings (vv. 18-20). These creatures were intricately associated with the majestic glory of God. They are mentioned as guardians of the Garden of Eden and the Tree of Life (Gen. 3:24) and of the forces of nature in operation (Ps. 18:10). Cherubim were also woven into or embroidered upon the inward curtain of the tabernacle (Exod. 26:1 ff.) and the veil (Exod. 26:31). In the Temple two cherubim were placed in the holy of holies by Solomon (I Kings 6:23).

> The cherubim seem to be actual beings of the angelic order. They do not seem to be identical with the seraphim (Isa. 6:2). The cherubim apparently have to do with the holiness of God as violated by sin; the seraphim with uncleanness in the people of God.[29]

The word for mercy seat comes from a Hebrew root meaning "to cover" and thus depicts an important aspect of divine mercy. Above the mercy seat dwelt the Shekinah glory which was the symbol of God's presence (v. 22). The ark of the covenant with its mercy seat was quite clearly the most important object in the Tabernacle proper. It was the focal point of attention especially on the annual day of atonement when blood was sprinkled on that seat. What the mercy seat symbolized for Israel and typified for us Christ has fully accomplished for both (cf. Rom. 3:25 and Heb. 9:5 ff.).

## VI. The Table of Showbread (25:23-30; 37:10-16)

The table of showbread was to be constructed of acacia wood measuring two cubits in length, one cubit wide, and one cubit

---

[29]Merrill F. Unger, "Cherub, Cherubim," *ibid.*, p. 192.

high (v. 23). It was to be placed in the north side of the holy place (see diagram, p. 260). This, like the ark, was to be covered with pure gold with a rim of gold around the top (v. 24). The rim or border around the top probably prevented things from falling off. Rings were to be placed in the four corners at the bottom in order that the table might be carried by the use of staves (vv. 26, 28).[30] On it were placed twelve cakes, renewed each week, in two piles (cf. Lev. 24:5-9), together with dishes (for the bread), spoons (incense cups), and flagons and bowls (for drink offerings). All of these were made of pure gold (v. 29). The loaves could be eaten by the priests on the Sabbath but only in the holy place (Lev. 25:5-9).

The twelve loaves constituted a perpetual thank offering to God from the twelve tribes for the blessings that they received from Him day by day. More significant, however, was the fact that the twelve represented each of the tribes whether that tribe was small or great. In this we see an exhibition of the grace of God. The loaves furthermore point toward Jesus Christ who was the bread of life (John 6:32, 35). As the bread of the Tabernacle supplied the priests, so Jesus Christ meets the needs of His children in this dispensation (John 6:32-35). We now look to a new table however: that is, the Lord's table in which there is fellowship in His death and in His resurrection.

## VII. The Golden Lampstand (25:31-40; 37:17-24)

The golden lampstand was one of the most ornate objects in the holy place. It was made of pure gold and was situated on the south side of the Holy Place. Its dimensions are not given but the branches were decorated with almond-shaped bowls or cups (v. 33). It consisted of an upright shaft from each side of which three branches extended upward in pairs (v. 35). A good example of this type of lampstand (although 14 centuries later) is to be seen on the famous arch of Titus in Rome.[31] Josephus

---

[30]See Josephus, *Ant.* III:6:6. Similar representations also appear on some Maccabean coins.

[31]See R. E. Nixon, "Lamp, Lampstand," *The New Bible Dictionary*, p. 708.

The Library, Jewish Theological Seminary of America

The seven-branched candlestick.

confirms this description.[32] The lamps of the lampstand were to be trimmed every evening at sunset and again in the morning (Exod. 27:20-21; 30:7-8; Lev. 24:3-4). They were never to be extinguished all at one time. A special ordinance was established

[32]*Ant.* III:6:7.

to keep it supplied with pure olive oil (Exod. 27:20; Lec. 24:2). Some have estimated its value at $33,804.[33]

The practical function of the lampstand was, of course, to provide light for the priests who were serving in the holy place. From a symbolic point of view, however, it quite clearly typifies the Lord Jesus Christ who is the true Light (John 1:6-9; 8:12). It seems also to point to believers who in this age are "the light of the world" (Matt. 5:14). In the Book of Revelation the Church is symbolized by the golden candlestick or lampstand (Rev. 1:10-20). Many have found the oil to be a representation of the Holy Spirit.[34] Also gold has been regarded as a symbol of the deity of Christ.[35]

## VIII. The Linen Curtains (26:1-6; 36:8-13)

The third object of the holy place – the altar of incense – is not dealt with at this point but in Chapter 30. Because of this arrangement liberals have assumed that Exodus 30 was a late addition to the already late P writings. There is evidence, however, that the present order is deliberate and has value.[36]

The verses of this chapter deal with the tabernacle proper and its covering. From the information supplied, we know that the basic structure was a quadrangular enclosure which measured 30 cubits long by 30 cubits wide and 10 cubits high. The innermost curtains which covered this structure are described in verses 1 to 6 of this chapter. They consisted of ten curtains of fine linen dyed blue, purple and scarlet with cherubim embroidered in them. These curtains were two cubits shorter than the outer curtains (v. 7), making the inner covering one cubit shorter on each side than the outer covering. The beauty of these linen curtains therefore could only be seen from the inside. As has been noted earlier, the wooden framework for the building was probably not solid, but consisted of open frames thereby ex-

---

[33]Francis Nichol, *op. cit.*, p. 638.

[34]J. Vernon McGee, *The Tabernacle* (Wheaton: Van Kampen Press, n.d.), p. 78.

[35]*Ibid.*, p. 77.

[36]See A. H. Finn, "The Tabernacle Chapters," *Journal of Theological Studies*, XVI (1915), pp. 449-482.

posing this tapestry. One can only imagine the beauty of these curtains as framed by the gold-covered framework of the tabernacle itself. The curtains were held together by a series of fifty clasps made of gold (v. 6). The overall area covered by these tapestries would have been 45′ x 15′, the general dimensions of the tabernacle proper. The holy place measured 15′ square.

### IX. The Curtains of Goats' Hair (26:7-13; 36:14-18)

The curtains made of goats' hair were two cubits longer than the inner linen curtains. They laid over the flat top of the tabernacle reaching to the top of the silver "sockets" of bases on either side (v. 19). Goats' hair is still commonly used by Arabs in weaving their tents. It provides strength and gives protection from wet and stormy weather. There is widespread disagreement among interpreters as to the symbolism of the colors and materials in the various curtains. This very disagreement speaks to the fact that it is very dangerous to impose symbolic meaning on the text which the Scripture does not give to it.

### X: The Skin Coverings (26:14; 36:19)

Two additional coverings were required for the outer section of the tabernacle proper. One consisted of rams' skins dyed red and the other of "badgers'" skins. These were placed over the coverings of linen already described. The rams' skins with their distinctive red color seem to speak of atonement through the shedding of blood (cf. Isa. 1:18). The badgers' skins were probably the skins of the dugong or sea cow which has been discussed previously.[37] No size is given for the rams' skins or badgers' skins but they must have been sufficient to cover the goat hair curtains. From a purely aesthetic point of view the tabernacle could not be considered a thing of beauty, at least from the outside. We might note that through the eyes of sinful men, Jesus Christ was also not seen in His real beauty (Isa. 53:2). When He tabernacled among men in the flesh (John 1:14) He was rejected. The only ones who fully appreciated the beauty of

---

[37]See p. 252.

the tabernacle were those who fellowshipped inside by means of blood atonement. So it is today. The only ones who fully appreciate and love the Christ, who once tabernacled among us and who now lives in the heavenlies, are those who are of the royal priesthood of Christ and know Him as their personal Savior.

## XI. The Wooden Frames and Sockets (26:15-30; 36:20-34) 36:20-34)

The traditional interpretation of the word "boards" has led to the idea that the walls of the tabernacle were solid. If this were so, there is a problem concerning the visibility of the inner linen curtains. If they were draped over the outside of the boards they would not be visible either from the inside or the out. Some have suggested that they were draped inside the boards. If that were the case then the boards would have been largely covered by the linen curtains on the inside of the goats' hair, rams' skins, and badgers' skins on the outside. Thus, one wonders about the value of the gold covering of the wood since it would have been concealed. The solution to this problem comes with an improved understanding of the Hebrew word *qereš*. Rather than translating this as "board" it should be rendered "frame of wood." The idea of wooden frames has been very effectively proposed and defended by Kennedy.[38] If the wood mentioned in this section really were frames then the linen curtains would be exposed to the inside. This construction would also make the tabernacle considerably lighter and therefore more portable. An excellent example of a frame-constructed, portable pavilion comes from Gaza, dating about 2600 B.C. The pavilion of Hetep-heres is well preserved along with a chair, bed and headrest.[39]

The frames were to be made of acacia wood (v. 15) and were 10 cubits long and 1½ cubits wide (v. 16). The frames were fitted into sockets which were forty in number and laid side by side upon the ground, forming a continuous foundation for the frame walls (vv. 19-21). The frames were held in place by a series of five bars (v. 26). Four of these bars were to be passed

---

[38]*Op. cit.*, p. 660.

[39]For a drawing of this see Gooding, *op. cit.*, p. 1231, fig. 202.

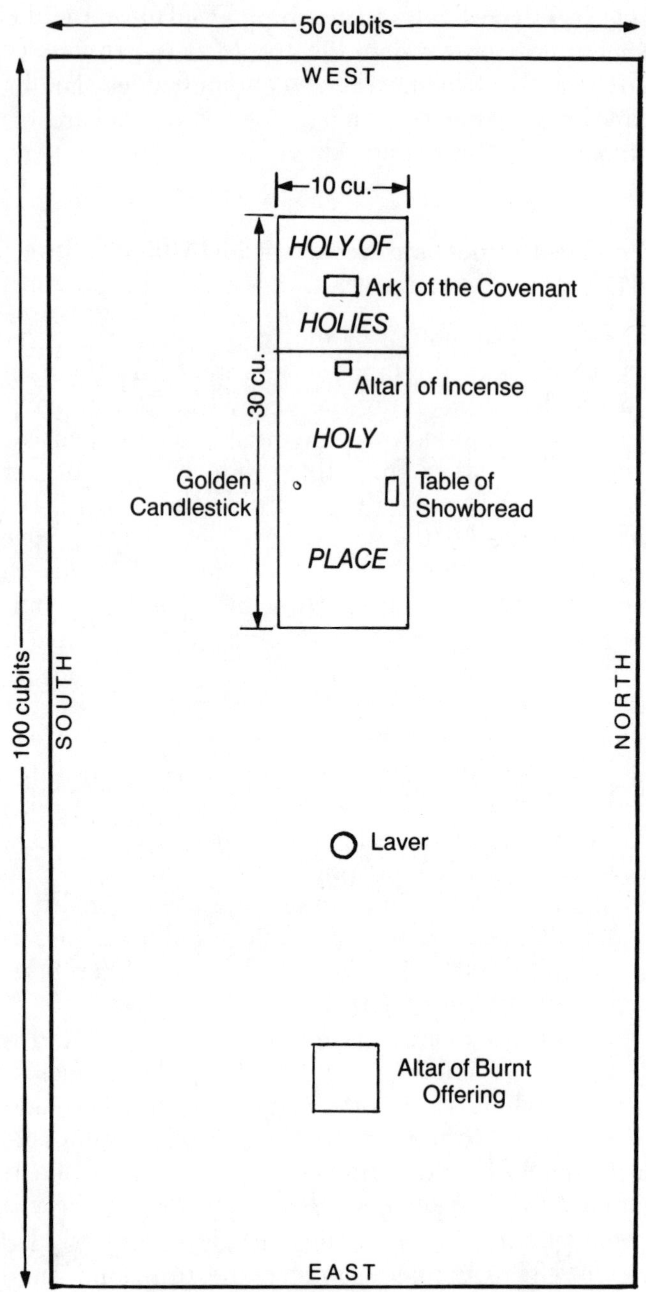


**The Plan of the Tabernacle Complex**

through "rings" fastened to the boards. The fifth or middle bar in each wall was to pass through the center of the frames (cf. v. 28). These bars were undoubtedly on the outside of the framework.

## XII. The Inner and Outer Veil (26:31-37; 36:35-58)

The inner veil of the tabernacle was made of finely spun linen in colors of blue, purple and scarlet and was richly ornamented with figures of cherubim (v. 31). This veil was to be of the same material and workmanship as the inner ten curtains (vv. 1-6). The veil was supported by four gold-covered acacia wood pillars and held together by hooks so that it might hang in the tabernacle to separate the holy of holies from the holy place. It might be noted here that there is no mention of variation in the size of these pillars. This coupled with the fact that no ridge pole is mentioned leads to the conclusion of a flat-roofed structure.

The outer veil of the tabernacle situated on the east end was also made of finely prepared linen. It also had the colors of blue, purple and scarlet (v. 36). The support for this veil consisted of five acacia wood pillars overlaid with gold. They were set in five sockets of bronze (v. 37).

The veils speak of the way in which the Old Testament saint had to approach his God. The necessity for a mediatorial priesthood is immediately apparent. What is most wonderful, however, is that with the death of Christ this inner veil was rent, thus giving the believer a permanent opening to the presence of God (cf. Heb. 10:19-22; Mark 15:38; Heb. 6:19; 9:3).

## XIII. The Altar (27:1-8; 38:1-7)

The altar of burnt offering stood just inside the door of the main court. It was to be built of acacia wood measuring 5 cubits long, 5 cubits wide, and 3 cubits high (v. 1). This altar is also given the name "the altar of burnt offering" (Lev. 4:7, 10, 18). The description of this altar is somewhat vague and has led to two basic viewpoints as to its appearance and function. The first maintains that the altar was basically a boxlike structure with a grate midway between the top and the bottom. The corners of the grate protruded through the sides so as to form rings through which the staves were inserted when the altar was carried. The altar is considered to have been covered by bronze thereby protecting it from the heat and fire.[40] Other interpreters, however, find difficulty with this viewpoint in the light of Exodus 20:24-25 where it is stated that the only altars to be made were to be of either earth or unhewn stones. Furthermore, it is argued, the tremendous heat of the fire would have a destructive effect on the inside of such an altar if a grate were placed that far down inside. The view traditionally held by Jewish commentators and by many modern scholars is that this was merely an altar box or altar case which was designed to be filled with earth when sacrifices were to be brought.[41]

One thing is clear and that is that a series of bronze rings was provided in the corners in order that acacia wood staves could be placed through them when the altar had to be moved (vv. 3-6). The horns of this altar were extentions of the corners and probably turned upward. They were used to bind certain sacrifices upon the altar for burning (Ps. 118:27). When a sin offering was made the priest would dip his finger in blood and touch these horns (Exod. 29:12; Lev. 8:15; 9:9; 16:18). Insomuch as an animal having horns generally uses them for attacking other animals, horns came to be symbolic of strength or power (I Sam. 2:1, 10; Ps. 75:10). Those charged of a crime who wanted sanctuary and mercy would often cling to them (cf. I Kings 1:50-51; 2:28). The very position of this altar near the entrance of the main court indicates very clearly the absolute necessity for blood atonement before real fellowship can be initiated with an infinitely holy God. The slaughter of animals on this altar was a very vivid reminder to Israel that sin indeed requires a high price. It was not a pleasant thing to see an innocent animal slaughtered and burned, but then sin is an ugly thing and the sacrifice here, as well as that on Calvary, should be a vivid reminder to everyone of the hideousness of sin and its price.

---

[40]See J. V. McGee, *op. cit.*, p. 34.

[41]Further discussion on this problem can be found in Kennedy, *op. cit.*, p. 658.

## XIV. The Court and the Gateway (27:9-19; 38:9-20)

From the information supplied in these verses we learn that the tabernacle was located in the western half of the courtyard which measured 100 x 50 cubits, the long sides running east and west. The door of the tabernacle faced eastward. The courtyard was bounded by a linen screen which was 5 cubits high and hung on acacia wood pillars which stood in copper sockets. They were stabilized by guy ropes and pegs, and had capitals overlaid with silver and silver bands called "fillets" round the neck. Twenty pillars stood on either of the long sides running north and south and ten or the shorter sides (east and west). It might be observed that the hangings around the outer court were exactly one half the height of the tabernacle itself which thus made the tabernacle plainly visible from outside the court.

The whole arrangement of the outer court and in particular the placement of the altar of sacrifice and the laver speak pointedly of man's approach to God. The tabernacle is a fitting example of how God provided for man's sin and guilt in the Old Testament economy. The gateway in the east to the main court consisted of a hanging of 20 cubits of blue, purple, scarlet and finely twined linen (v. 16). There are two different theories on the spacing of the pillars and the placement of the gate. One view is that each pillar was spaced exactly five cubits apart and no pillar was counted twice, thereby giving the total of sixty pillars. The outer court, therefore, with the enclosure was a rectangle. The second view abandons the assertion that pillars were necessarily spaced five cubits apart and admits that the corner pillars were counted twice as belonging, at least from the observers point of view, to both end and side. This would give a total of fifty-six pillars. This viewpoint maintains that the gate was actually recessed and consisted of four pillars covered with a permanent screen.[42]

## XV. The Oil for the Lamp (27:20-21)

Since the seven lamps were never to be extinguished at one time, but kept burning continuously day and night, there was a

[42]For additional discussion of this problem see Gooding, *op. cit.*, p. 1233.

great need for olive oil. Significantly this oil was to be supplied by the children of Israel (v. 20). It was to be prepared by using unripened fruit which would be beaten or pounded in a mortar rather than crushed in the mill. This process would result in a clear and colorless oil which would burn brightly with a minimal amount of smoke. It was the responsibility of Aaron and his sons to maintain the burning of the lamp morning and evening (v. 21). Josephus says that three lights were kept burning both day and night,[43] but there is nothing in Scripture to confirm this. Some have suggested that the lamps were lit every evening (30:8) and extinguished in the morning (I Sam. 3:3).[44] Others, however, feel that the seven lamps were never all extinguished at one time but burned continuously day and night except when the tabernacle was in transit from one campsite to another.[45]

The continuous need for oil and the importance of the provision of light symbolically speak of the believer's responsibility and need. Oil, as previously noted, is clearly a symbol of the Holy Spirit in Scripture. As such it fittingly points to the necessity for an effective, continuous ministry of the Holy Spirit in the life of the believer. Without this he can hardly expect to be a light to a generation wandering in complete darkness.

## XVI. The Altar of Incense (30:1-10; 37:25-28)

The description of the altar of incense in this part of the Book of Exodus has been somewhat problematic. Why the directions concerning this altar were delayed until this place is not indicated in the text. According to verse 1 it was to be made of acacia wood like the other objects in the holy place. Its dimensions were a cubit in length and breadth and 2 cubits in height and furnished with horns. The whole altar was to be covered with gold (vv. 1-3). It had the usual provision of rings for the staves (vv. 4-5). The position of the altar was to be in the holy place, in front of "the veil that is by the ark of the testimony" (v. 6). It will be noted that in Hebrews 9:3-4 the altar of incense

---

[43]*Ant.* III:7:7.
[44]Rawlinson, *op. cit.*, p. 290.
[45]Francis Nichol, *op. cit.*, p. 644.

was considered as belonging to the most holy place. This concept probably grew out of the fact that as the priests in their ministry approached the sacred presence of God above the mercy seat, the altar of incense was the place to which they first came. The priests were not permitted to go beyond that point except on the day of atonement. It was the responsibility of Aaron and his sons to offer "a perpetual incense" upon it in the morning and in the evening (vv. 7-8). The offering of "strange incense" was strictly forbidden. Strange incense was any that was composed differently from that which was prescribed in verses 34 and 35 of this chapter.

In Scripture, incense often symbolizes prayer and communion with the Father (Ps. 141:2; Luke 1:10; Rev. 5:8; 8:3-4). The "continual" burning is an example of the necessity for continuous and persistent prayer (cf. Ps. 16:8; 55:17; I Thess. 5:17-18).

### XVII. The Laver (30:18; 38:8)

The final object to be considered with respect to the tabernacle court and the tabernacle itself is the laver of cleansing. This laver was located between the altar of burnt offering and the door to the tabernacle. It was made of bronze and set aside for ceremonial washing of the priests prior to entrance into the holy place. The reading of verse 18 leads one to believe that this basin had a foot or pedestal upon which the main vessel stood. Others, however, have suggested that this foot was really a small basin into which water from the main vessel was poured. The majority of commentators seem to favor the idea of the basin having a foot or pedestal on which it was placed. Keil and Delitzsch however, argue for the other viewpoint as follows:

> . . . by this we are not to understand the pedestal of the caldron, but something separate from the basin, which was no doubt used for drawing off as much water as was required for washing the officiating priests.[46]

The symbolic meaning of this laver is indeed significant and precious. It provided for a type of cleansing which served to

---

[46] *Op. cit.*, II, p. 213.

maintain fitness for a spiritual ministry. The priests' guilt because of sin was dealt with at the altar of sacrifice, yet something else was required for effective fellowship and worship in the tabernacle. This had to do with the defilement of sin, that effect of sin which the blood did not remove. Before one could enter the presence of a holy God this had to be cared for. It followed the sacrifice at the altar and was based upon the merit of it but was a definite separate act. So it is with the believer in Christ today. He is freed from the guilt of sin and its penalty by the application of the blood (Rom. 5:9), yet there remains defilement of sin that comes through daily living. This is cared for by continuous washing of the water which is the Word of God (Eph. 5:25-26; John 15:3). The Holy Spirit also plays a significant role in the application of that Word of God thus producing a cleansing effect (I Cor. 6:11). There is a sanctification which is complete and final through the blood of Christ, but there is also a sanctification which is continuous and practical. It paves the way for continued effective fellowship with God. It helps a man to "purge himself" (II Tim. 2:21; cf. I Cor. 5:7).

## XVIII. The Craftsmen (31:1-11)

Not to be overlooked in the building of the tabernacle are the workmen whom God chose and prepared for that responsibility. The Lord personally selected the workmen He wanted to construct the building and work on the garments of the priests. Bezaleel was to have overall charge of the building with Aholiab as his assistant (vv. 2, 4). Without a doubt these men were selected because of their superior talent and previous experience. God promised that Bezaleel would be filled with the Holy Spirit thus giving him the necessary wisdom and knowledge to complete the task correctly.

Aholiab, the assistant to Bezaleel, was from the tribe of Dan (v. 6). It is interesting to note that Hiram, the chief artist Solomon employed to make the ornamental work of the Temple, was also from the tribe of Dan (II Chron. 2:13, 14). The construction of the tabernacle was no small task. It would take skill and imagination. For this responsibility God chose the best and gave them divine help.

## XIX. Completion of the Structure (40:1-38)

After the materials for the tabernacle were prepared for construction, Moses was instructed to erect the structure on the first day of the first month (v. 1). This would have been the month of Abib or Nisan. When final preparations were complete Moses along with the people of Israel erected the tabernacle at this appointed time which was about one year after they had left Egypt (v. 17). The furniture was put into proper place (vv. 22-30) and Moses, along with Aaron and his sons, washed themselves preparatory to entering the tent (vv. 31-33). The moment of real thrill and satisfaction, however, was when God put his approval on the place by exhibiting His personal presence in the form of a cloud (v. 34).[47] This was the same cloud that had accompanied the host and directed their journeys from Succoth (13:20-22). So great was this exhibition of God's glory that Moses was not able to enter the tent (v. 35). It is appropriate that the Book of Exodus should conclude with this sublime manifestation of God's glory.

Any study of the tabernacle, if sincerely pursued, ought to lead one to a deeper appreciation of the marvelous prophetic unity of the Word of God, but even more important, it should point him to the majestic greatness and infinite holiness of our Savior, Jesus Christ.[48]

---

[47]Compare the effect of the "glory" when it descended on Solomon's Temple, I Kings 8:11 and II Chron. 5:14; 7:2.

[48]For a recent study on the significance of the tabernacle see Martin H. Woudstra, "The Tabernacle in Biblical-Theological Perspective," *New Perspectives on the Old Testament,* J. Barton Payne, ed., (Waco, Texas: Word Books, 1970), pp. 88-103.

## Chapter 13

# *The Aaronic Priesthood*

(Exodus 28–29)

The idea of a priesthood naturally implies a consciousness of sin and the need for mediatorial representation. The building of the tabernacle was only the first step in the restitution of complete fellowship with God. While Moses was the mediator of the law and the covenant, Aaron and his sons were the mediators of the blood sacrifice. The concept of the priest, of course, was not new with Moses. In pre-Mosaic times the office of priest was occupied by the father of a family (cf. Job 1:5) or the head of a tribe for his own family or tribe. Abraham, Isaac and Jacob built altars, offered sacrifices, purified and consecrated themselves and their households (cf. Gen. 12:7; 13:18; 26:25; 33:20; 35:1, 2). Among the peoples that surrounded Israel, however, a professional priesthood had already been established and was functioning. Melchizedek combined kingship and priesthood in his own person (Gen. 14:18). Jethro is referred to as the priest of Midian (Exod. 2:16; 3:1). The Egyptians had a well-defined and well-organized priesthood long before the time of Moses as indicated in the Joseph story (cf. Gen. 47:22, 26). For Israel, however, the establishment of an official priesthood was something new and unique.

Exodus 28 and 29 deal only with the garments and the consecration of the Aaronic priesthood. This material will be treated and other matters will be discussed as they relate to the total function of the Israelite priesthood.

### I. The Origin of the Priesthood

The matter of the origin of the priesthood has been the subject of very lively debate among Old Testament scholars. With the development of the documentary hypothesis and its emphasis on the postexilic date for the completion of the "priestly code," the question of the origin of the priesthood no longer rested on the obvious history as presented in the Old Testament, but on the reconstructed form of the biblical text. Julius Wellhausen (1844-1918) devoted a great deal of space to the subject of the priests and the Levites in his *Prolegomena to the History of Israel.* Since the Aaronic priesthood is stressed only in the "priestly code," it was viewed by Wellhausen as fiction. This, of course, was his viewpoint on the tabernacle as well. According to this theory the priesthood was not separated from the Levites until very late in history. The only possible way of arriving at conclusions like this is to deny the fundamental historicity of the material in the Pentateuch and then to reorganize all biblical data to suit one's fancy. The theories of Julius Wellhausen have undergone considerable change largely due to recent archaeological discoveries.[1] Modern critics have generally traced the origin of the Hebrew priesthood back to the early days of Israel's social and religious revolution. Theophile Meek confidently asserts that

> the origin of priesthood is manifestly to be traced back to the earliest stage of social evolution and is doubtless to be found very close to the beginning of magical and religious practices. There was a time when each individual invoked the god for himself without the help of a mediator, but the idea early developed that certain individuals could get better, easier, and more intimate access to the spirit world than others. These were the first priests in religion.[2]

From this observation Meek proceeds to demonstrate that the Hebrew priesthood saw its origins in the tribe of Levi. This tribe was originally a purely secular tribe but in the course of time was invested with priestly functions.[3] The principal god of the tribe of Levi, according to this view, was the serpent god Nahash or Nehushtan. Their dedication to this god and subsequent renunciation of all earthly aspirations caused them to be welcomed as priests of Yahweh "and in this capacity, as priests, they must have been welcomed by the Judeans."[4] Meek then concludes:

---

[1]For an evaluation of Wellhausen's view of the priesthood see D. A. Hubbard, "Priests and Levites," *New Bible Dictionary*, pp. 1033-1034.

[2]Theophile J. Meek, *Hebrew Origins* (New York: Harper and Row, 1960), p. 119.

[3]*Ibid.*, p. 124.

[4]*Ibid.*, pp. 122-123, 128.

> Hence the early Levites were manifestly regarded as medicine men or shamans by the surrounding tribes, and now in a time of need that fame stood them in good stead and they became priests, because that is precisely what the Hebrew word for priest, *kohēn,* implies, identical with the Arabic *kahin,* "soothsayer, medium, shaman," one who acts as a medium between God and man and between man and God.[5]

It should be obvious to the reader that this viewpoint as well as others similar to it can be constructed only when the biblical text is manipulated at the whim of the interpreter. If the documentary hypothesis or the methods of form critical analysis are, in fact, not legitimate then the theory collapses under its own weight for lack of support. To the one who accepts the history of the Old Testament seriously the problem of the origin of the priesthood is not obscured by mystic expression. It is clear from Scripture that the priesthood was established by divine election. Whatever functions were made part of the responsibility of the priesthood came by special revelation and not by cultic discovery or experience. The original official priests were Aaron and his four sons. Aaron was the high priest (Exod. 28:2) and his sons were assistants or general priests. The entire tribe of Levi had semi-priestly functions and responsibilities.

The Hebrew word for priest, *kohēn,* has likewise been the subject of considerable speculation as to its origin and meaning. Gustave F. Oehler traces the root to the word *kûn.* His argument is as follows:

> The stem *kahan* appears to be connected with *kûn* . . . , and to mean either intransitively, "to present oneself," or transitively, *parare, aptare;* in the former case, *kohēn* would be one who stands to represent another, and in the latter case the priests would be named from preparing and presenting the sacrifice.[6]

The frequent occurrence of the word *khn* meaning "priest" in the Ras Shamra texts has led G. B. Gray to assume that the word

---

[5]*Ibid.*, p. 129.

[6]*Theology of the Old Testament*, p. 209.

is of Canaanite origin.[7] In Ugaritic the *khn* was the cultic official of the sanctuary in a very general sense. While the charismatic gift of prophecy or "seeing" was at times associated with the functions of a priest, it was not his main function. That it was one of his functions, however, is indeed significant. The priest of the Old Testament period not only brought sacrifices, but also with the aid of the Urim and Thummim also gave important information regarding God's will. In this very general sense the term *kohēn* of the Hebrew text is analogous to the Ugaritic *khn;* however, the analogy ends here. The theological premise upon which Israelite and Gentile priests operated and the message which was central to their function was entirely different and without real parallel. Note also that the priests of Dagon were called *kōh$^e$nîm* (I Sam. 5:5; 6:2) as were the priests of the "high places" (I Kings 12:32; II Kings 23:9).[8]

## II. The Nature and Purpose of the Priesthood

The priests were not self-appointed mystics or cultists that rose by their own power in Israel. They were selected by God and had to be descendants of Aaron. That selection even disqualified any who had a physical defect or infirmity (Lev. 21:16-24). Such individuals, however, were entitled to receive support as the other priests. The purpose of the priesthood as described in the Old Testament was clearly mediatorial in nature. The responsibilities of the priest were well defined in the law of Moses and remained substantially the same throughout their history. In short, they fell into four broad categories: (1) In the holy place they were to burn incense on the golden altar, morning and evening; clean and trim lamps and light them every evening as well as place showbread on the table every Sabbath (Exod. 30:7-8; 27:21; Lev. 24:5-8). (2) In the courtyard they were to keep a fire burning constantly on the altar of burnt offering (Lev. 6:9, 13), clear away the ashes from the altar (vv.

[7]*Sacrifice in the Old Testament* (Oxford: The Clarendon Press, 1925), p. 183.

[8]For the use of *khn* in Ugaritic Texts see C. H. Gordon, *Ugaritic Textbook: Glossary* (Rome: Pontifical Bible Institute, 1965) p. 418. See also Hans-Joachim Kraus, *op. cit.*, pp. 93 ff.

10-11), offer the morning and evening sacrifices (Exod. 29:38-44), and bless the people after the daily sacrifice (Lev. 9:22; Num. 6:23-27). Other duties are given to them that relate to the special feast days such as blowing silver trumpets, the jubilee horn, and so on. (3) Generally they were to inspect unclean persons, especially lepers, and when so warranted, to declare them clean (Num. 6:22 ff.). They had some judicial responsibilities as evidenced in Numbers 5 where they were to mediate in cases when the wife was accused of adultery. They were to appraise things that were dedicated to the sanctuary (Lev. 27: 2 ff.). (4) It was their sacred responsibility to instruct the people of Israel in the law and to act as a high court of appeals in any difficult case (Deut. 17:8 ff.; 19:17; 21:5). In times of war they had responsibilities to speak to the soldiers and even provide information for that battle (cf. Deut. 20:2 ff.).

## III. The Personnel of the Priesthood (28:1)

Israel's first official high priest was Aaron, the brother of Moses. His sons were to be priests after him. Their names are significantly grouped: Nadab and Abihu; Eliezar and Ithamar. The separation of the two pairs of brothers was probably due to the sin and early death of Nadab and Abihu (cf. Lev. 10:1-2). After the death of Aaron, Eleazar became the high priest (Num. 34: 17; Josh. 14:1). A slight hint of Aaron's responsibility is given in this verse in the expression "that he may minister unto me in the priest's office." That ministry included the offering of both gifts and sacrifices for sins as well as having compassion on the ignorant (cf. Heb. 5:1-2).

## IV. The Garments of the High Priest (28:2-43)

### A. *Introduction* (28:2-5)

The garments of the high priest are described in verse 2 as "holy garments." In the light of all that was included in the tabernacle and its spiritual symbolism it is appropriate that the garments of the priest should be described in this way. It reemphasizes the essential character of God and that which He requires for fellowship. According to this verse, they were to be for glory and for beauty. The priestly office was intentionally elevated in the eyes of the people. This apparel would serve to distinguish the priests as a class by themselves and in a certain sense above the rest of the nation. The distinctiveness of the garments along with their beauty would be a constant reminder to the priests themselves of their holy station and its demand for consecrated living. There was a "beauty of holiness" (I Chron. 16:29; Ps. 29:2; 96:9) that God wanted to emphasize. These sacred garments were always to be worn when the priests served in the sanctuary but never at other times (see Exod. 35:19; Lev. 16:4, 23, 24; Ezek. 42:14; 44:19).

Those who were to work in the making of the garments are described as "wise hearted" (v. 3 – Heb. *ḥaḵmê lēḇ*). This expression points to those who had the necessary skills and knowledge which would enable them to give effective aid in the production of such garments. These craftsmen were also "filled with the spirit of wisdom" (v. 3). It was not uncommon for God to enable certain individuals to perform tasks by filling them with His Holy Spirit. At a later period the judges were often described as having been filled with the Spirit in order to perform particular tasks. The fact that these workmen should be filled with the Spirit gives some indication of the high value God had placed on the making of the garments.

The garments of the high priest are considered first and described in great detail. The nature of the materials to be used gives some indication of the magnificent glory of the garments of the high priest (v. 5). It will be noted that the materials are the same as those employed for the veil and curtains of the sanctuary (cf. 26:1, 31, 36), but with the further addition of gold and precious stones. Many modern commentators consider the royal nature of Aaron's regalia as suggestive of the post-exilic period when, in the absence of a king, the high priests became a semi-royal figure.[9] Such viewpoints, however, are definitely out of harmony with the clear meaning of the biblical text as well as our knowledge of the regalia of priests in Egypt and elsewhere.

---

[9]Roy Honeycutt, Jr., *op. cit.*, p. 440.

B. *The Ephod* (28:6-14)

The ephod was considered one of the more sacred parts of the priestly vestments and later became the emblem of the priestly office (cf. I Sam. 2:18, 28; 14:3; 22:18). It was woven of blue, purple, scarlet and fine linen yarn, embroidered with figures of gold. It was designed to be a sleeveless outer garment probably going down to the waist. It consisted of two pieces, the one covering the back and the other the breast and upper part of the body. The two parts were fastened together on the top of each shoulder by a golden clasp or straps on the top of which were two onyx stones with the names of six tribes on each stone. There has been some difference of opinion as to what stones are meant by the word translated "onyx." According to the Septuagint they were "emeralds." Josephus calls them "sard-onyx" which is the best variety of onyx.[10] It was upon this ephod that the breastplate was fastened (vv. 6-12; 39:2-7). The purpose of having the names of the tribes on the stones was to demonstrate that whenever the priest ministered in the sanctuary he represented all the people. The ephod was held to the body by a girdle (Heb. *ḥēšeḇ* – "a belt") which was of the same material and manufacture as the ephod (v. 8).

C. *The Breastplate of Judgment* (28:15-29)

The breastplate was a square piece of cloth made of the same material and wrought in the same fashion as the ephod. It was folded in half and held firmly to the ephod over the priest's heart by means of rings and threads of gold and threads of blue. In all probability it was a sort of pouch, open at the top. Upon this breastplate were twelve precious stones set in gold and arranged in four rows. On the top of the stones were engraved the names of the twelve tribes of Israel (v. 21). Thus the nation was doubly represented before the Lord. The actual identity of the precious stones has long been a problem and still has not been completely solved. Recent studies, however, have aided a great deal in understanding the probable nature of most of these

---

[10]*Ant.* III:7:5.

stones.[11] The presence of such jewels reflected the great interest and love that God had for His people. They were His "jewels" (Mal. 3:17).

D. *The Urim and Thummim* (28:30)

These objects have been the subject of very lively debate and discussion. The terms themselves literally mean "lights" (Heb. *'ûrîm*) and "perfection" (Heb. *tummîm*). A complete identification and function of both the Urim and Thummim is difficult because of the limited number of references to them and their use (Exod. 28:30; Lev. 8:8; Num. 27:21; Deut. 33:8; I Sam. 28:6; Ezra 2:63; Neh. 7:65). The Urim and Thummim were often used by the high priest in times of crisis to determine the will of God (Num. 27:21). They were in common use during the Mosaic period as well as the days of the United Monarchy. The use of these objects seem to have declined or ceased until the postexilic period when they are not mentioned.[12]

There is a wide variety of views as to the particular form or identity of these objects. Early European commentators proved fertile in imagination and produced many theories which have found some favor with many commentators. These objects have been associated with (1) a necklace of gems (Clericus); (2) three antique stones which represented three possible answers: affirmative, negative and neutral (Michaelis); (3) polished and unpolished diamonds inscribed with the name of the Lord which the high priest could cast upon a table thereby deducing God's answer based on their final positions (Zullig); (4) revelation and truth, as interpreted by the Septuagint (Gesenius); (5) explanation and decision (Koster); (6) light and right (Luther); (7) light and salvation (Winer); (8) taking *tmm* as meaning "to be without fault" and *'rr* "to curse" as opposites and as the roots of Urim and Thummim. These stones, therefore, would indicate what God would or would not permit (Well-

---

[11]See A. Paul Davis, "The Re-Creation of an Exact Replica of Aaron's Breastplate," *Lapidary Journal* (Dec., 1968), pp. 1124-1128 and E. L. Gilmore, "Which Were the Original Twelve Gemstones of the First Biblical Breastplate?" *Lapidary Journal* (Dec. 1968), pp. 1130-1134.

[12]Hosea 3:4 may be a possible exception.

hausen, and Moore); (9) a message conveyed by inspiration to the high priest who was wearing the breastplate and the ephod (Schroder, Braun).[13] Josephus evidently identified them with the twelve stones in the breastplate of the high priest. He suggested that the stones were illuminated, thus giving divine information prior to the time of battle.[14] A Talmudic explanation suggests that certain letters appeared on the stones in the breastplate and were illuminated at the moment of revelation, thus giving the high priest an indication of God's will. Many scholars feel that there was nothing in the objects themselves that revealed the divine will, but they were merely symbols of God's revelation. When a problem was presented to the high priest, he merely laid the matter before God in prayer and by means of divine inspiration received the answer. More recent discussion on the subject attempts to identify the Urim and the Thummim as two flat objects (stones). On one side of each was the word Urim, derived from the Hebrew root *'ārar* – "to curse"; the other side was marked *tummîm* ("perfect – yes"). When both Urim sides appeared, the answer was negative, and when both the Thummim sides appeared the answer was positive.[15]

It appears that the high priest alone was permitted to use the Urim and the Thummim. Some have attempted identification of the Urim and the Thummim with the sacred lots. This suggestion has some merit but there are serious difficulties due to the fact that the answers ascribed to the Urim and Thummim are not always the equivalent to a yes or no answer (Judg. 1:2; 20:18; I Sam. 22:10; II Sam. 5:23; 21:1). It may well be that these objects only symbolized the special revelation to which the high priest had access. The handling of such objects may have been symbolic rather than necessary to achieving information. In other words, when information was needed and sought, the possession of these objects indicated that the high priest had special authority to approach God for an answer. Whatever was done with the objects would have been symbolic and comple-

---

[13]Edward Robertson, "The 'Urim and Tummim; What Were They?" *Vetus Testamentum,* XIV (Jan., 1964), p. 70.

[14]*Ant.* III:8:9.

[15]See Paul Haupt, "Babylonian Elements in the Levitic Ritual," *Journal of Biblical Literature,* XIX (1900), p. 58.

mentary to the whole process of inquiry. The problem of the function of these objects, therefore, remains unsolved until further archaeological data are forthcoming.[16]

E. *The Robe of the Ephod* (28:31-35)

The robe of the ephod was blue and woven without any seam. It was worn immediately under the ephod and was longer than it, reaching a little below the knees. It had no sleeves, but only slits in the sides for the arms to come through and a hole for the head to pass through. Along the hem were blue, purple, and scarlet pomegranates and golden bells which tinkled as the priest served in the tabernacle. The sound of the bells made the worshippers conscious that the priest was officiating in their behalf in God's presence. This aided them in following him in their thoughts and prayers as he went about the different aspects of the priestly ritual. The sound of the bells as the priest left the tabernacle called for great rejoicing for the atonement that had been completed.

F. *The Miter* (28:36-38)

The headdress of the high priest was to be of fine white linen. According to the description given by Josephus it appears to have been a kind of turban made of several thick swatches or folds in the usual manner.[17] The most conspicuous and significant feature of the miter was the plate made of pure gold with the expression "Holiness to the Lord" engraved on the outside. This plate was placed directly in front, and over the forehead. The fact that the plate is described first indicates something of its importance. The inscription indicated the very essence of Israel's worship. The blue lace mentioned in verse 37 was probably used to tie the golden plate to the miter itself (cf. 39: 31). Clearly this part of the attire focused attention upon the

---

[16]For additional information on this problem see Leon J. Wood, "Urim and Thummim," *The Theolog* (Winter, 1964), pp. 25-32; J. A. Motyer, "Urim and Thummim," *The New Bible Dictionary*, p. 1306; Nathan Isaacs, "Urim and Thummim," *The International Standard Bible Encyclopedia*, V, p. 3040.

[17]*Ant.* III:7:3.

essence of God's character and the requirements of true worship. It served to remind the priests and the people always of the character of God which is thrice-holy (Isa. 6:3).

### G. *The Inner Garments* (28:39)

All the garments described up to this point have been the outer garments. To these are now added the inner ones of which there is little description. Verse 39 gives the instructions for the long white linen coat or tunic which was worn over the linen breeches or drawers (cf. v. 42). According to Josephus "this vestment reaches down to the feet and sits close to the body; and has sleeves that are tied fast to the arms."[18]

The inner girdle (v. 39) was to be of "fine twined linen, blue, purple, and scarlet (39:29). In this respect it was like the ephod (cf. v. 6). It was not to be woven of these colors, but to have them worked into it with a needle. It was worn immediately above the tunic and underneath the robe of the ephod (Lev. 8:7). Little, if any of it, could have been seen.

## V. The Garments for Aaron's Sons (28:40-43)

The apparel described in the remaining verses of this chapter belongs to the common priests and has been called by some the ministerial attire of the priests. They are garments designated for Aaron's sons (v. 40). The official dress of all priests appears to have consisted of drawers, i.e., short breeches (v. 42) reaching only from the loins to the thighs and made of linen (39:38). Their attire also included girdles and bonnets (v. 40) for the purpose of providing "glory and beauty." They had nothing on their feet as they were not allowed to walk in the sanctuary without having their feet bare (cf. Exod. 3:5; Josh. 5:15).

## VI. Consecration of the Priests (29:1-46)

### A. *The Purpose of Consecration*

One of the most sacred events in connection with tabernacle service was the consecration of the priests. The investiture of the

---

[18]*Ant.* III:7:2.

high priest consisted of nine acts (Lev. 8:7-9), whereas that of the ordinary priests involved but three. The actual ceremony in the case of Aaron and his sons was performed by Moses (Lev. 8: 1-36). The candidate for consecration was taken to the door of the tabernacle and had his body washed with water (v. 4). Following this they were invested with the official dress and anointed with holy oil (vv. 5-7).

A sacrificial service followed these events with Moses officiating. The sacrifices consisted of one young bullock for a sin offering, one ram for the burnt offering, the ram of consecration, a basket of unleavened bread, unleavened cakes kneaded in oil, and thinner unleavened cakes sprinkled with oil (vv. 10 ff.). The first sacrifice was a bullock that was to be brought to the tabernacle (v. 10). Aaron and his sons then laid their hands on the head of the bullock which was then slaughtered and its blood sprinkled on the horns of the altar of burnt offering (vv. 10-12). The rest of the blood was poured beside the bottom of the altar (v. 12). The fat of the viscera, the liver and other entrails were to be burned upon the altar (v. 13). The remaining flesh of the bullock, his skin and dung were to be burned with fire outside the camp as a sin offering (v. 14).

The next sacrifice consisted of the ram for a burnt offering. After the hands of those being consecrated were placed upon the ram (v. 15) it was slain and the blood was sprinkled around the altar (v. 16). The ram was then cut in pieces and burned upon the altar (vv. 17-18). The other ram which was part of the ceremony was slain and the blood taken and put upon the tip of the right ear, the tip of the right hand and the great toe on the right foot (v. 20). This act implied the complete dedication of life and ability to the service of God. Symbolically the blood put on the right ear sanctified that organ to hear the word of God; that which was put on the right hand set the hands apart in their performance of mediatorial work. The right foot spoke of the sanctified walk of the life of the priest as an example to others. The remaining amounts of blood were to be taken and sprinkled upon Aaron along with the anointing oil. His garments were also to be sprinkled as part of the ceremony of sanctification (v. 21). Remaining parts of that ram including the fat, rump,[19] liver, and kidneys along with one loaf of bread, one cake of oil bread, and one wafer out of the basket of unleavened bread, were put in the hands of Aaron and his sons. These were then waved as a wave offering before the Lord (vv. 22-24). Following this the objects were taken and burnt upon the altar for a burnt offering to the Lord (v. 25). This concluded that portion of the ceremony. The remainder of the flesh was cooked by Aaron and his sons at the door of the tabernacle and eaten by them. Any portion remaining until the next day was to be burned. The consecration service lasted a total of seven days (Exod. 29:35). According to this verse the ritual consecration for Aaron and his sons was to be performed on each of the seven successive days.

After the consecration services the priests were to offer a special meat offering of one-tenth ephah of flour. This was kneaded with oil and baked in separate pieces – one half being offered in the morning and the other in the evening. This material was wholly burned upon the altar (cf. Lev. 6:19-23). On the eighth day of consecration, the exercise of the priestly function was begun by the newly consecrated ones in the offering of a calf for sin offering and a ram for burnt offering for themselves. This was immediately followed by the offering of sacrifices for the people (Lev. 9:1 ff.).

One cannot help but be impressed with the splendor and the significance of both the priest's garments and his mediatorial responsibilities. Aaron serves well as a type of the Lord Jesus. His duties and dress all seem to point to the person and work of Christ as our high priest. What the priesthood of Aaron could not do, Christ was able to do because He was a perfect high priest. He was a priest after the order of Melchizedek (Ps. 110:4; Heb. 5:6; 6:20; 7:21). Melchizedek very beautifully portrayed the Messianic type of king-priest (Heb. 7:23-24). Christ's priesthood was in no sense contrary to the Aaronic order. It fulfilled all the soteriological significance of it. But the priesthood of Christ furnished the substance of which the Aaronic priesthood was only the shadow and symbol (cf. Col. 2:17; Heb. 8:5).

[19]Literally "the fat tail," that is, of the Oriental broadtail sheep.

## Chapter 14

# *The Golden Calf*

(Exodus 32–34)

Effective leadership is characterized by two things: first, the knowledge of where one is going and second, the ability to encourage others to come along. Moses had already demonstrated his ability to lead the people of Israel. Their journey from the land of Egypt did not take them northeast into Canaan, but southward through the deserts of the Sinai Peninsula. The reason for this southern journey becomes more apparent as one studies the chapters of the Book of Exodus. The Israelites obviously were not ready to encounter the challenges and the temptations of the land of Canaan. They needed to be prepared both politically and spiritually for the difficulties they would face in possessing the promised land. Among the problems that they would have to face in the land of Canaan was the temptation of idolatry. In anticipation of this, God had provided Israel with a series of miracles to demonstrate the impotence and emptiness of heathen idolatry. These plagues also helped to bring about the deliverance of Israel. The lessons, however, were quickly forgotten.

Chapter 32 of Exodus records one of the dark moments in Israel's history up to this point. Rather than witnessing increased dedication and spiritual renewal as a result of God's revelation of the law and the tabernacle, we find the people of Israel thoroughly impatient with the activities of their leader Moses. This impatience, along with their spiritual immaturity led them to open idolatry and rebellion. The process by which they were caught up in this idolatry was subtle. It is a prime example of religious syncretism, that process by which ideas from one system are mingled with those of another. These chapters do not record total abandonment of the worship of Jehovah, however. On the contrary, they illustrate that subtle process by which idolatrous practices were used in the worship of the God of Israel.

## I. Idolatry in the Camp (32:1-6)

### A. *The Causes for Idolatry* (v. 1)

When Moses delayed in returning from the top of Mount Sinai, the people became anxious and impatient. Perhaps at the encouragement of the "mixed multitude" among them, they demanded that an object be made which would provide visible representation of the God (or gods) who was leading them. The people were without Moses for a mere forty days and forty nights (Deut. 9:11). In this short time their desires had shifted from the proper worship of God to a degraded form of idolatry. It is true that there had been a number of warnings against idolatry (cf. 20:4, 5, 23; 23:32-33), but the overwhelming desire for visible representation of their religious ideas led them into this sin. It is indeed amazing that a people would adopt that which was clearly condemned and shown to be useless in the ten plagues. This record, however, serves as a lesson and a warning to all who feel that miracles are the final answer to weak faith. Witnessing great and spectacular miracles may encourage one for the moment, but it does not guarantee a mature faith that will resist the temptations that lie ahead. No other people in the history of the earth received more encouragement through miracles than the people of Israel and yet their history is dotted with multiple periods of apostasy and failure.

In order to implement this desire for visible representations of their God, they came to Aaron and requested that "gods" be made (v. 1). The very language of the people is almost unbelievable. How could they possibly assume that a god could be "made" in the light of all that had been revealed in the exodus? In any event, Aaron listened and responded to their request. It is interesting that Hur (24:14) is not mentioned in this context. He and Aaron both were to aid the people when problems arose. Perhaps Aaron alone was consulted due to the fact that he had been a leader with Moses for a much longer period of time; whereas, Hur had only very recently been advanced to a position of authority (24:14; 27:10).

There is a question as to the interpretation of the Hebrew word *'ᵉlōhîm* ("gods"). The word which appears here is a masculine plural noun followed by a plural verb (Heb. *yēlᵉḵû* –

"they will go"). Normally when *'elōhîm* is used of the true God a singular verb form is employed (cf. Gen. 1:1). On the other hand, the pluralization of the verb form indicates that false gods are in view. It may be that they not only desired representation of Jehovah by the golden calf but perhaps other idols were desired as well. Some have suggested, however, that the noun should still be translated "God" in spite of the fact that the plural verb form occurs. They point out the fact that in the final analysis only one golden calf was made and worshipped. It is further argued (and correctly so) that the plural may have been used intentionally to emphasize the fact that the golden calf was a false god in contrast to the Lord who was the true God. In other words, the writer employed the plural verb form so as to emphasize the fact that the desires of the people were clearly idolatrous and in conflict with both the letter and the spirit of the law. What is perfectly clear, however, is that the people were weary of waiting for Moses any longer. They wanted to resume their journey to the promised land with a visible god at their head to inspire them with confidence and courage. Their disenchantment with the situation is reflected in the last words of verse 1, "We know not what is become of him." One gets the impression that the people had decided among themselves that Moses had forsaken them or that his behavior was incompatible with their needs and desires. In the light of this they decided to take matters into their own hands.

B. *The Participants in Idolatry*

According to 32:28 only 3,000 of the people were directly punished for this sin. This seems to imply that a relatively small number of the 2,000,000 residents of the Sinai area were directly involved in the events described. Most tragic, however, was the encouragement and help given the people by Aaron on this occasion. He should have known better and resisted with faith and courage the desires of the people at the outset. Presumably many Israelites did not directly participate in this event or perhaps merely gave passive assent to what was occurring. The very fact that such practices existed in the camp of Israel, however, caused the whole nation to bear the responsibility of that guilt. The covenant that God had made with Israel was with the whole nation and, therefore, as a nation and a community they bore collectively the guilt of a breached covenant (cf. Josh. 7).

C. *The Process of Idolatry* (vv. 2-6)

Had Aaron been strong in faith and in courage, this incident in Israel's history might have been avoided. There is no evidence that he took this occasion to speak out against the syncretistic trends which were evident among the people of Israel. They needed to learn to "walk by faith and not by sight" (II Cor. 5:7). They obviously lacked the faith of Moses and their fathers who "endured, as seeing him who is invisible" (Heb. 11:27). Perhaps Aaron felt that by requiring the giving up of golden earrings that the people could be discouraged in the pursuit of idolatry (v. 2). If this was his motive in making the requirement he sadly underestimated the heart and desire of the people. The golden earrings were obviously precious possessions, most likely having come from Egypt. The fact that the people broke off the golden earrings which were in their ears and brought them to Aaron (v. 3) was an indication of their deep desire to have a golden calf. That Aaron should bear the guilt of leadership on this occasion is supported by the words of verse 4. It was he who received these earrings from them and he fashioned them with an engraving tool (v. 4). The end product was a "melted calf" (Heb. *'ēgel massēḵāh*). This expression is used elsewhere in verse 8, Deuteronomy 9:16 and Nehemiah 9:18.[1] It has been suggested that the Hebrew word *'ēgel* may be a reference to a young bull, perhaps after the form of the Egyptian god Apis.[2] The image, however, was decidedly not dedicated to an Egyptian god, but was intended to be a representation of Jehovah. In all probability the statue was made of wood and covered with gold. Following its completion Aaron uttered the words, "These be thy gods, O Israel, which brought thee up out of the land of Egypt" (v. 4). That the golden calf was intended to

---

[1]Compare Exod. 34:17 and Lev. 19:4 where the expansion *'elōhê massēḵāh* ("molten gods") occurs.

[2]Keil and Delitzsch, *op. cit.*, II, p. 222.

represent Jehovah is made clear by these words. Surely Aaron would not attribute the exodus to any other deity; therefore, the term "gods" must be a reference to the God of Israel who was represented by this idol.

The process of idolatry was further enhanced by the building of an altar in front of the golden calf (v. 5). The institution of a "feast to the Lord" clearly demonstrated the syncretistic character of this event. Even though Moses destroyed the idol and punished those directly involved in leading this idolatry, the practice was reinstituted five hundred years later under the leadership of Jeroboam (I Kings 12:28-32). Not only did Jeroboam borrow the concept of the golden calf, but he stole Aaron's sermon outline for that occasion (cf. I Kings 12:28)!

The people were so enthusiastic about this new venture that they rose up early in the morning to offer burnt offerings and peace offerings to the Lord (v. 6). The expression "rose up to play" is a reference to all those practices common to idolatrous worship. The verb translated "to play" suggests illicit and immoral sexual activity which normally accompanied fertility rites found among the Canaanites who worshipped the god Baal. The word used is *ṣāḥaq* which normally means "to laugh." In the Pi'el stem it carries the sense of "to jest" (Gen. 19:14) or "make sport or play" (Gen. 21:9). It is the same verb which is used in Genesis 26:8 where it is said, "Abimelech . . . looked out of a window and saw Isaac caressing Rebekah his wife." The word "caressing" used here is the same Hebrew word employed in Exodus 32:6 and translated "play." It is the view of most that this involved conjugal caresses.[3] The nakedness of the people (v. 25) further substantiates the fact that the activity associated with the worship of the golden calf included sensuous fertility practices common to the peoples about Israel.

## II. God's Response (32:7-14)

The warm, intimate fellowship enjoyed by Moses was quickly broken by the cold statement by God that "thy people" have corrupted themselves (v. 7). The fact that the Lord spoke of

---

[3]Brown, Driver and Briggs, *op. cit.*, p. 850.

Israel as the people of Moses rather than "my people" (cf. Exod. 3:10) reflects the anger of God on this occasion. The people who had only a few weeks earlier entered into a solemn covenant with God and pledged themselves to obey Him (cf. 19:8; 24:3) had now chosen a course which was diametrically opposed to the principles and the practices of that covenant. The situation of the Israelites at this point is analogous to that which Peter described in II Peter 2:20-22. They had escaped "the pollutions of the world" through the deliverance that God had provided. According to Peter it would have been "better for them not to have known the way of righteousness than, after they have known it, to turn from the holy commandment delivered unto them" (v. 21). The wicked desires of their own hearts, coupled with the intense influence of the mixed multitude caused them to return to the mire of idolatry (cf. II Peter 2:22).

The word translated "corrupted" (v. 7) is the Hebrew word *šiḥēṯ* which has the idea of to "go to ruin."[4] It is the same word that is used in Genesis 6:12 to describe the corruption of the world of Noah's day. The apostasy of Israel was not only described as a process of corruption (v. 7), but a turning away from clearly revealed truth (v. 8). Their condition was also one of insensitivity and rebellion to God's leadership (v. 9). The phrase "stiffnecked people" is a common expression depicting the idea of perversity. It is likened to a horse that stiffens his neck when the driver pulls the reign right or left, thus refusing to go the way that it should. This expression was used frequently to describe the rebellions of Israel in her subsequent history (cf. Exod. 33:3, 5; 34:5; Deut. 9:6; 10:16; II Chron. 30:8; 36:13; Ps. 75:5; Jer. 17:23; Acts 7:51). The seriousness of God's charges is reflected in verse 10. It was proposed that Israel be set aside and even destroyed in order that a new people might be constituted. This, for Moses, was the severe test. It confronted him with an opportunity to choose between his own glory and honor and the well-being of the people whom God had put under his care. These words brought an immediate and decisive response from Moses. Verses 11 through 14 record the mediatorial prayer of this man for the people of God. He reasserted the

[4] *Ibid.*, p. 1007.

identification of the people as the people of God (v. 11, "thy people"). They were His not only by creation but by redemption. Moses also showed a deep concern for the name of Jehovah and His faithfulness to His people. What would the Egyptians say of a catastrophe such as the complete annihilation of the nation of Israel (v. 12)? They would undoubtedly rejoice and the result would be the complete dishonoring of the name of God. The accusations of the Egyptians would prove true, that instead of leading the people of Israel into the wilderness to sacrifice (5:1-3), He led them there to be sacrificed (10:10). Moses reminded the Lord of the covenant that he had to Abraham, Isaac and Jacob (v. 13). That covenant-promise Moses considered true and unchangeable. To destroy the people of Israel at this stage would be to end the possibility of covenant fulfillment.

The Lord was touched by the intercession of Moses, so much so that He "repented of the evil which he thought to do unto his people" (v. 14). The repentance of the Lord has long been a problem to commentators. Obviously it does not mean that God changed His mind as a result of a mistaken calculation or that God is unsure of His own desires. This word denotes a change in the actions of God as a result of a significant change among those with whom God is dealing. It is ". . . an anthropopathic description of the pain which is caused to the love of God by the destruction of His creatures."[5] The word "repent" is a translation of the Hebrew word *nāḥam* meaning "to be sorry, move to pity of have compassion." This word is used thirty times in reference to God and in each case He changes His mind or intention in accord with His righteous purposes and takes action commensurate with that purpose.[6]

## III. Condemnation and Judgment (32:15-29)

Following Moses' intercession for the people of Israel he turned and went down the mountain with the two tables of testimony in his hands (v. 15). The revelry and noise in the camp of Israel associated with the worship of the calf was heard by Joshua and initially considered by him to be the evidence

[5]Keil and Delitzsch, *op. cit.*, II, p. 225.
[6]Roy L. Honeycutt, Jr., *op. cit.*, p. 452.

of warfare (v. 17). Moses, however, knew that the noise was an evidence of the idolatry called to his attention by God (v. 18). When Moses came into the camp of Israel he saw not only the calf, but dancing (v. 19) and nakedness (v. 25). His anger found expression in the smashing of the tablets on which God had written the law. The act was appropriate and symbolic in the light of the broken covenant between God and Israel. Following this he came to the center of this idolatrous assembly and took the calf, burned it in the fire, and ground it to powder (v. 20). The remains of the idol were cast into the water and the children of Israel were made to drink it. The question has often been asked, "How could this idol be burned and scattered?" Two views have emerged on this problem. The one is that the golden calf had been placed on a wooden pedestal and it was this that was destroyed. The other is that the idol was made of wood and plated with gold.[7]

The destruction of this idol finds an interesting parallel in one of the Ugaritic texts. The goddess Anath is described as destroying the god Mot. This destruction included burning him, grinding him as grain in the handmill, and casting the remains out in the fields for birds to eat. The text as translated by H. L. Ginsberg reads as follows:

> She seizes the Godly Mot –
> With sword she doth cleave him.
> With fan she doth winnow him –
> With fire she doth burn him.
> With hand-mill she grinds him –
> In the field she doth sow him.
> Birds eat his remnants,
> Consuming his portions.[8]

It will be noted that the three actions regarding the destruction of this idol are similar to those performed by Moses. There was the burning, the crushing and the scattering. According to F. C. Fensham this may have been a ritual act in fixed form among

[7]See F. C. Fensham, "The Burning of the Golden Calf and Ugarit," *Israel Exploration Journal*, XVI, No. 1 (1966), p. 191.

[8]*ANET*, "Poems about Baal and Anat, h.IAB, ii, lines 30-38. See also C. H. Gordon, *Ugaritic Textbook*, text 49, pp. 137-139.

peoples of the ancient Near East.[9] There are not only analogies between this Ugaritic tablet and the biblical account, but obvious parallels exist between the golden calf made by Aaron and those made by Jeroboam. The destruction of the golden calf made by Aaron (Exod. 32:20; Deut. 9:21) and of Jeroboam's altars at Bethel (II Kings 23:15) were carried out in a similar manner. Both were burned and ground to fine dust.[10]

The requirement that Israel drink of the polluted waters has led to a number of views as to the nature and purpose of such an act. One observation is that this act of Moses resembled the ancient ordeal in which one was forced to drink a strange mixture with one's innocence or guilt determined by whether or not he reacted physically to the drink (Num. 5:5 ff.).

> Guilt was apparently easily established in the present case, however, and making the people drink the mixture probably reflected the belief that those guilty would suffer some type of plague, of which verse 35 may be reminiscent.[11]

On the other hand, Keil and Delitzsch suppose that "it was intended rather to set forth in a visible manner both the sin and its consequences."[12] According to this view, the sin was poured, as it were, into their bowels along with the water as a symbolism that they would have to bear it and atone for it just as a woman who was suspected of adultery was obligated to drink of the curse-water.[13] There is no doubt that the destruction of this idol and its scattering upon the waters that flowed from the mountain (Deut. 9:21) was a vivid illustration of the worthlessness of idolatry. If the calf could not save itself, it certainly could not save or even aid its worshipers (cf. Ps. 115:3-9; Isa. 46:5-7).

---

[9]*Op. cit.*, p. 192.

[10]For recent studies of these similarities see Moses Aberbach and Levy Smolar, "Aaron, Jeroboam and the Golden Calves," *Journal of Biblical Literature*, LXXXVI (June, 1967), pp. 129-140; S. E. Loewenstamm, "The Making and Destruction of the Golden Calf," *Biblica*, XLVIII (1967), pp. 481-490; I. Lewy, "The Story of the Golden Calf Reanalyzed," *Vetus Testamentum*, IX (1959), pp. 318-322.

[11]Roy L. Honeycutt, Jr., *op. cit.*, p. 453.

[12]*Op. cit.*, II, p. 226.

[13]*Ibid.*

Following the destruction of the idol and the polluting of the waters, Moses then turned to Aaron for an explanation of the events that had occurred. The explanation of Aaron is almost incredible. He began first of all by appealing to Moses not to become too angry because what had happened was something that could be anticipated in the light of the interest of the people to do mischief (v. 22). The words of Aaron clearly attempted to put the blame on the sinful tendencies of the people themselves rather than on himself. In this respect he illustrated the fact that he was indeed a true descendant of Adam and Eve (Gen. 3:12-13). He told of the demands of the people and indicated that he merely took the gold which had been given him and cast it into the fire and "there came out this calf" (v. 24). It is obvious that Aaron was trying to free himself from responsibility of having guided the people in the creation of this idol. Perhaps he was attempting to imply that a miracle had occurred and that by some means the gold cast into the fire had become a calf. The involvement of Aaron was no small matter as indicated by Deuteronomy 9:20. Had it not been for the earnest intercession of Moses in his behalf, Aaron would have been destroyed for this sin.

After speaking with Aaron, Moses turned again to the people whom he found "naked" and a shame among their enemies (v. 25). The word for "naked" in the Hebrew text is *pārua‘* which has the sense of loosening or uncovering. It is felt by some commentators that the term does not necessarily mean nakedness as much as giving free rein to their wild passions.[14] The enemies who are referred to in this verse may be Amalekites who still lingered in the area (cf. Exod. 17:8-16). The situation called not for mild platitudes or pithy sayings, but for a challenge to separation and godliness. Moses stood in the gate of the camp and said, "Who is on the Lord's side? Let him come to me" (v. 26). The response was immediately met by the sons of Levi whose hearts were undoubtedly pierced by the condemnation which Moses had pronounced upon this whole occasion. They perhaps felt the burden of guilt for not having done more, if anything, to restrain the people in this dark moment. The real

---

[14]Francis Nichol, *op. cit.*, p. 667.

test of their faith and consecration came when Moses commanded that they were to go out into the camp and "slay every man his brother, and every man his companion, and every man his neighbor" (v. 27). The command of Moses may seem harsh to some, but in the warfare between good and evil there is no such thing as neutrality. Either one is on God's side or on the side of evil (cf. Josh. 24:14-15; I Kings 18:21; Matt. 6:24). In the punishment of evil even family ties and friendships were to be ignored. This reminds us of the words of Jesus when He noted that family and earthly ties should not be allowed to stand between us and our duty to Him (cf. Matt. 8:21-22; 10:37). The result of this judgment was that about 3,000 men died by the hand of the Levites (v. 28). Following the burial of these men, Moses called for new consecration to the Lord in order that covenant blessings might be restored to the people of Israel (v. 29).

### IV. Prayer and Intercession (32:30-35)

The execution of judgment upon those most guilty in this affair was not the end of the matter. He reminded the people that their sin was a great sin and would require atonement (v. 30). Moses deeply loved his people in spite of their superficial spiritual attitudes. He was to make one of the most passionate pleas to God ever recorded in Scripture. So moved was Moses in his appeal to God that he did not complete the conditional sentence recorded in verse 32. The first part of this verse may have included the expression, "Then shall I be content," or "I will say no more." This would then be followed by the conditional suggestion, "If not, blot me, I pray, out of thy book which thou hast written." Moses was willing to give his own life rather than to see the people of God destroyed. The Apostle Paul manifested similar unselfishness toward his brethren as noted in Romans 9: 1-3.

The identity of the "book which thou hast written" has been the subject of considerable debate. Many argue that this is a reference to the Book of Life in which the names of believers are recorded.[15] Others take this book to be ". . . a register of living

[15]See Keil and Delitzsch, *op. cit.*, II, pp. 231-232. Also compare Matthew Poole, *Annotations Upon the Holy Bible* (New York: Robert Carter and Brothers, 1853), I, p. 190, and Francis Nichol, *op. cit.*, p. 668.

men — with reference to the earthly life of this world only and not of the next."[16] This view maintains that the book is a list of those living on earth and "to be blotted out" of this book means to meet an untimely or premature death. Another view is that of Adam Clarke who suggests that the book is a list of those who would enter the promised land.[17] The best interpretation of this phrase in the light of other occurrences in Scripture and its immediate context is that this is a book relating to temporal life and not eternal life. To be blotted out of this book because of sin indicated an untimely death. This should not be considered as the book of eternal life, or the Lamb's Book of Life as it is commonly called, but may have been a foreshadowing of such a book.

The Lord accepted the sincere plea of Moses. Complete destruction of the nation was prevented, but God warned Moses that He would visit the people with judgment because of their sin (v. 34). As a result, the people were plagued because of the idolatry permitted by Aaron (v. 35). This plague served as a warning to all who would entertain ideas of idolatry in the future.

## V. Repentance and Humiliation (33:1-11)

The intercession of Moses recorded in the previous chapter not only led to a softening of the wrath of God, but also to the reaffirmation of the covenant promise of a land (v. 1). This verse is actually an expansion of the assurance of the promise given in 32:34. An angel was to lead them into the land of Canaan (v. 2; cf. 23:20). Because of the apostasy of the people, Jehovah himself would not go up with them in their midst (v. 3) lest He consume them along the way (cf. Heb. 12:29 — "God is a consuming fire."). Even though the promise of the land was renewed, the people considered the news to be "evil" (v. 4).

---

[16]Henry Cowles, *The Pentateuch* (New York: D. Appleton and Co., 1873), p. 346. See also Roy Honeycutt, Jr., *op. cit.*, p. 454; Paul Heinisch, *Theology of the Old Testament*, trans. by William Heidt (Collegeville, Minn.: The Liturgical Press, 1950), p. 260; S. R. Driver, *The Book of Exodus* (Cambridge: University Press, 1911), p. 356.

[17]*The Holy Bible* (New York: Carlton & Phillips, 1854), I, p. 465.

They expressed their disappointment and sorrow by putting away their ornaments (vv. 4-6). The removal of ornaments implies mourning and reformation (Gen. 35:4; Ezek. 26:16). From the tomb paintings in Egypt it is known that both men and women wore various types of ornaments.

The mediatorial responsibility of Moses not only included personal intercession for the people, but the establishment of a temporary tent in which the people could worship their God. This tent was pitched outside the camp and was called "the tabernacle of the congregation" (v. 7). The structure of the Hebrew text at the beginning of verse 7 indicates that what Moses did here was not a single event but one repeated many times. The verse might well be translated, "And Moses used to take the tent and pitch it without the camp."[18] The tent was a temporary structure until the completion of the more permanent "tent of meeting." The fact that the tent was moved "far off from the camp" symbolized the removal of God's presence from the people because of their iniquity. The presence of this tent was definitely the focal point of interest as evidenced by the words of verse 8. Whenever Moses went into the tent, the people stood and watched to see what would happen. The evidence of the fact that Moses was communicating with God is seen in the descent of the cloudy pillar (vv. 9-10). The fact that the Lord spoke to Moses "face to face, as a man speaketh to a friend" (v. 11) indicated the warm communication that Moses had with his God. The expression denotes familiar conversation. The meetings and conversations between God and Moses were common and the sensitive heart of Moses made it easy for God to speak to him (cf. Num. 12:8 and Deut. 34:10). The position that Moses had was indeed a favored one enjoyed by very few men in Old Testament history.[19]

---

[18]The Hebrew reads *ûmōšeh yiqqaḥ 'eṯ hā'ōhel wᵉnāṭāh lô miḥûṣ lammaḥᵃneh.* It will be noted that the normal waw consecutive with the imperfect does not begin the sentence. The use of the imperfect aspect here is repetitive or reiterative. See E. Kautzsch and A. E. Cowley, *Gesenius' Hebrew Grammar* (Oxford: The Clarendon Press, second English edition, 1957), p. 315.

[19]Only Isaiah (Isa. 6:1-5) and Ezekiel (Ezek. 1:28) seemed to have approximated this experience.

## VI. Prayer and Petition (33:12-23)

Verses 12 and 13 are an example of the intimate way in which Moses was able to talk with God. The words of Moses do not reflect arrogant boldness or a lack of godly reverence. On the contrary, they represent a confidence in prayer which is only achieved when one is honestly searching the heart of God. The confidence of Moses in prayer attests to the fact that he sustained a unique and vital relationship with his Lord. This is expressed in the words, "I know thee by name" (v. 12). To be known of God is to be one of His children. Those whom He does not know will be judged (cf. Ps. 1:6). Moses is also described as having "found grace" in the eyes of the Lord (cf. Gen. 6:8). His petitions found in the verses to follow are basically three in number. First, he requested that the Lord would show him the way. Moses wanted further revelation about God's intentions for his people in the immediate future. The Lord's reply was simple and meaningful. He stated that "my presence shall go with you and I will give you rest" (v. 14). The Hebrew is very vivid here. It literally states, "My face will go with thee" (Heb. *pānay yēlēḵû*). The presence of the Lord spoken of here relates back to the angel mentioned in 32:34 and 33:2 (cf. Isa. 63:9 – Heb. *malʾaḵ pānāyw*). The idea of receiving rest is not to cease from activity, but to enjoy God's protection and blessing in the land (cf. Deut. 3:20; 12:10).

Moses presented a *second* request that related to confirmation of God's presence (v. 15). These words do not express doubt as to the assurances given him in verse 14, but a certain feeling of the insufficiency or perhaps incompleteness of that assurance. The warnings of God's wrath continued to concern Moses so he asked for further clarification of God's intentions. The persistent, fervent prayer of this godly man did avail much (cf. James 5: 16). The Lord responded with a strong affirmation that He would do that which He had promised, again reminding Moses that he had found grace in His sight and that He knew him by name (v. 17).

The *third* request of Moses was that he should see the glory of God (v. 18). This request is almost without parallel in human history up to this point. He had been speaking in behalf of the people up to now, but at this point he asked for personal confirmation of God's presence in his life. This request must have been something surpassing all former revelations of the glory of Jehovah (16:7, 10; 24:16-17). What he wanted was a revelation or an experience that even exceeded Jehovah's talking with him face to face, on which occasions he merely saw "a similitude of Jehovah" (Num. 12:8). What this visible representation of God was we are not told. Moses wanted a more unveiled view of the God with whom he was speaking. The request of Moses was answered by God in a unique way. It was, of course, impossible for Moses to get a glimpse of His glory which no other man had seen (vv. 21-23). So great was this vision that precautions had to be made to protect Moses. Scripture states that no man has ever seen the Lord's face (John 1:18; 6:46; I Tim. 1:17; I John 4:12). There is no discrepancy between this passage and New Testament statements. What really occurred on Mount Sinai between Moses and God on this occasion will never be fully known. Undoubtedly Moses saw things which the human tongue would be incapable of uttering. Perhaps his experience was somewhat like that of the Apostle Paul's when he was caught up to the third heaven and heard unspeakable words which were not lawful for man to utter (II Cor. 12:4).

## VII. Covenant Renewal (34:1-35)

### A. *The Second Tables of the Law* (34:1-4)

Before the covenant could be renewed and fellowship reestablished, new tables of stone had to be made and the people had to recommit themselves to the commandments of God. It was appropriate that Moses should hew for himself the new stones (v. 1). It was he who broke the former tablets (32:19) which "were the work of God" (32:16). The writing on the tablets, of course, was that of the Ten Commandments (34:28; Deut. 4:13; 10:4). This meeting of Moses was so sacred that not even Joshua was to accompany him (v. 3; cf. 24:13; 32:15-17).

### B. *Covenant Warnings* (34:5-17)

The return of Moses to the top of Mount Sinai was not only to restore the broken tables but also that he might again witness the glory of God and experience His mercy. A new vision of God's glory encouraged Moses that the Lord would indeed exercise mercy with His people.

Moses took this occasion to worship his God and again to plea for pardon on behalf of the people (vv. 6-9). The covenant renewal included the promise that the Lord would again work miraculously in behalf of His people (v. 10). The exercise of such power, however, was contingent on the obedience of the people. If they obeyed the covenant stipulations, they would enjoy full victory over the inhabitants of Canaan (v. 11). Warning was given also that no covenant should be made with inhabitants of the land, for they would indeed turn Israel aside from the worship of the true God (v. 12). The command was clearly given to destroy completely their altars and their images and to cut down their idols (v. 13). The reason for this, among other things, was to prevent the infiltration of idolatry into the covenant community of Israel (cf. Deut. 7:1-11). Earlier in the Book of Exodus (23:24) the command had been simply to "break down their images" but after the Israelites had displayed an interest in idolatrous practices, they were now commanded to destroy the altars and the groves: in other words, all forms of idolatry were to be destroyed completely. Another reason for destruction of such forms of idolatry was the fact that there was only one true God and He was a jealous God (v. 14; cf. Deut. 4:24; Josh. 24:19). Strong prohibition was given with regard to intermarriage with the Canaanites (v. 16). Any such international marriages would require the recognition of the deities of that land. This in turn would ultimately lead to the establishment of sanctuaries and the official recognition of such gods; therefore, all intermarriage was banned. The lesson that God was teaching His people was that with covenant blessing there is covenant responsibility.

### C. *The Law of the Feasts and the Sabbaths* (34:18-26)

The preceding verses emphasize the negative aspects of covenant responsibility: that is, that which should be avoided. Verses 18 through 28 highlight the positive aspects of worship: namely, what is to be done to please a holy God. The importance of the feast of unleavened bread is underscored by the many commands given to commemorate that feast (cf. 12:15-20; 13:3-10; 23:15). Intricately connected with the celebration of the feast of unleavened bread was the dedication of all firstborn (vv. 19-20). This practice was most appropriate in light of the fact that, spiritually, Israel was the firstborn of Jehovah and free from His wrath in the final plague. Important also to continued fellowship with God was the keeping of the Sabbath (v. 21) and the observance of the feast of weeks (v. 22; cf. Lev. 23:15-17).

In order to maintain unity within the covenant community of Israel, all males were to appear three times each year before the Lord (v. 23; cf. 23:14-17). If the children of Israel were obedient to the covenant responsibilities given to them, they could be assured not only of possession of the land, but the enlargement of their borders as well (v. 24). The first promise of the land was made to Abraham and his descendants (Gen. 12:5-7). Later this promise was widened to include the whole area between the "river of Egypt and the Euphrates" (Gen. 15:18; I Kings 4:21; II Chron. 9:26). Faithfulness and obedience would lead to national unity and strength. This strength would guarantee not only possession of the land but control of it. So impressive would Israel's power be that other nations would not desire that land (v. 24).

The Lord commanded that all these words should be written (v. 27). The existence of a written covenant at this period is not unusual. The fact that Moses was commanded to do the writing is in agreement with all that Scripture says about the origin of the books of the Pentateuch. According to verse 28 Moses spent forty days and forty nights in Mount Sinai which was a duplication of the length of time he formerly stayed in the mountain (cf. 24:18). On the previous occasion the people indulged in idolatry and syncretistic forms of worship. On this occasion, however, the people apparently remained true and met the test occasioned by the absence of Moses. During the forty days and forty nights Scripture records that Moses did not eat bread or drink water. A similar fast had been kept on the previous occasion (Deut. 9:9) though it is not mentioned in the Exodus account. Fasts of this extraordinary duration are recorded only of Moses, Elijah (I Kings 19:8) and the Lord Jesus (Matt. 4:2).

The means by which these individuals were sustained must be regarded as miraculous in nature.

D. *The Descent of Moses* (34:29-35)

At the end of forty days Moses, having completed the writing of the tablets, came down from Mount Sinai. His skin evidently had a radiant, divine glow about it as a result of his coversation with the Lord. The English translation, "while he talked with him," is better understood as "on account of or because of his talking with God" (Heb. *b^e^d̲abb^e^rô 'ittô*). The radiance of Moses' face was a reflection of divine glory (II Cor. 3:7). A changed countenance, however, was not attributed to Moses' first experience on Mount Sinai (cf. Exod. 24:12-18). Perhaps Moses, in a unique sense, had seen the glory of God and reflected that glory in his face. When the children of Israel saw Moses they were afraid to come near him (v. 30). Such fear is easily understood in the light of their previous sinfulness and idolatry. The wounds of covenant rebellion were not completely healed and there was still reticence to stand in the glory of God.

Finally, after Moses talked with them they drew near to hear the commandment of the Lord (v. 32). Moses spoke to them with the full glow of God's presence. When he finished speaking with them he put a veil on his face (v. 33). From this time onward the veil became part of his ordinary dress. It was worn by Moses on all occasions with two exceptions: (1) When he was alone with God either in the temporary tent of meeting or in the tabernacle, and (2) when he had a message for the people from God. Speaking as God's representative he authenticated that message by uncovering his face, allowing the glory of God to be seen. According to the interpretation of the Apostle Paul the reason for this veil was so that the Israelites could not see "the end of the fading splendor" (II Cor. 3:13 – RSV). The Apostle Paul used the veil of Moses to teach three important truths. The first is that the veiling of Moses' face typified the veiled glory of the old covenant in contrast of the unveiled and abiding glory of the new covenant. The full and majestic revelation of God's glory was to be witnessed in the New Testament period (II Cor. 3:13). The veil, in the second place, represented the veil which was upon the heart of the Jews of his day. It was a way of symbolizing their spiritual blindness in not discerning the identity of Jesus the Messiah (II Cor. 3:14-16). The third reference to the veil is found in II Corinthians 3:18 and is a reference to the unveiled vision given to the believer by the ministry of the Holy Spirit. Every believer is in the process of being changed into the image of our Lord as a result of the new life which is within him. The culmination of this process will be when the Lord returns and we will behold Him face to face.

# *Bibliography*

Aharoni, Yohanan. *The Land of the Bible: A Historical Geography*. Translated by A. F. Rainey. Philadelphia: The Westminster Press, 1962.

Aharoni, Yohanan, and Avi-Yonah, Michael. *The Macmillan Bible Atlas*. New York: The Macmillan Co., 1968.

Albright, W. F. *From the Stone Age to Christianity*. 2nd ed. Garden City, N.Y.: Doubleday and Co., 1957.

Allen, Clifton, J., ed. *The Broadman Bible Commentary*. Nashville: Broadman Press, 1969.

Allis, Oswald T. *The Five Books of Moses*. Philadelphia: The Presbyterian and Reformed Publishing Co., 1949.

Archer, Gleason. *A Survey of Old Testament Introduction*. Chicago: Moody Press, 1964.

Baly, Denis. *The Geography of the Bible*. London: Lutterworth Press, 1957.

Beer, George. *Exodus Handbuch zum Alten Testament*. Tubingen: Verlag von J. C. B. Mohr, 1939.

Blaiklock, E. M., ed. *The Zondervan Pictorial Bible Atlas*. Grand Rapids: Zondervan Publishing House, 1969.

Bright, John. *A History of Israel*. Philadelphia: The Westminster Press, n.d.

Brown, Francis; Driver, S. R.; and Briggs, Charles. *A Hebrew and English Lexicon of the Old Testament*. Oxford: The Clarendon Press, Corrected Impression, 1952.

Budde, Karl. *Religion of Israel to the Exile*. New York: G. P. Putnam's Sons, 1899.

Buttrick, George, ed. *The Interpreter's Bible*. New York: Abingdon Press, 1952.

Cassuto, U. *A Commentary on the Book of Exodus*. Translated from the Hebrew by Israel Abrams. Jerusalem: The Magnes Press, The Hebrew University, 1967.

Cerny, Jaroslav. *Ancient Egyptian Religion*. London: Hutchinson's University Library, 1952.

Clarke, Adam. *The Holy Bible with a Commentary and Critical Notes*. New York: Eaton and Mains, n.d.

Cundall, A. E. and Morris, L. *Judges and Ruth*. Chicago: Inter-Varsity Press, 1968.

Davis, John J. *Biblical Numerology*. Grand Rapids: Baker Book House, 1968.

———. *Conquest and Crisis*. Grand Rapids: Baker Book House, 1969.

Dillmann, August. *Exodus and Leviticus*. Leipzig: Verlag vons Hivzel, 1897.

Douglas, J. D., ed. *The New Bible Dictionary*. Grand Rapids: Eerdmans Publishing Co., 1962.

Driver, S. R. *The Book of Exodus*. Cambridge: University Press, 1911.

Ellicott, Charles J., ed. *Ellicott's Commentary on the Whole Bible*. Grand Rapids: Zondervan Publishing House, n.d.

Engnell, I. *The Wilderness Wandering*. Nashville: Vanderbilt University Press, 1969.

Erman, Adolf, ed. *The Ancient Egyptians*. New York: Harper and Row, 1966.

Erman, Adolf Von. *Die Religion der Agypter*. Berlin and Leipzig: Walter De Gruyter and Co., 1934.

Falk, Ze ev W. *Hebrew Law in Biblical Times*. Jerusalem: Wahrmann Books, 1964.

Finegan, Jack. *Let My People Go*. New York: Harper and Row, 1963.

———. *Light from the Ancient Past*. London: Oxford University Press, 1946.

Frankfort, Henri. *Kingship and the Gods*. Chicago: The University of Chicago Press, 1948.

———. *Ancient Egyptian Religion*. New York: Harper and Brothers, 1948.

Free, Joseph P. *Archaeology and Bible History*. Wheaton: Van Kampen Press, 1950.

Garstang, John. *Joshua-Judges: The Foundations of Bible History*. New York: Richard R. Smith, Inc., 1931.

Garstang, John, and Garstang J. B. E. *The Story of Jericho*. London: Marshall, Morgan and Scott, Ltd., 1948.

Ghalioungui, Paul. *Magic and Medical Science in Ancient Egypt*. London: Hodder and Stoughton, 1963.

Glueck, Nelson. *The Other Side of the Jordan*. New Haven: American Schools of Oriental Research, 1940.

Gordon, C. H. *Ugaritic Textbook*. Rome: Pontifical Bible Institute, 1965.

Grimmelsman, Henry J. *The Book of Exodus*. Cincinnati: The Seminary Book Store, 1927.

Grollenberg, L. H. *Atlas of the Bible*. Translated and edited by Joyce Reid and H. H. Rowley. New York: Thomas Nelson and Sons, 1956.

Harrison, R. K. *Introduction to the Old Testament*. Grand Rapids: Eerdmans Publishing Co., 1969.

Heinisch, Paul. *Theology of the Old Testament*. Translated by William Heidt. Collegeville, Minn.: The Liturgical Press, 1950.

Hilprecht, H. V. *Explorations in Bible Lands During the Nineteenth Century*. Philadelphia: A. J. Holman and Co., 1903.

Hoskins, Franklin E. *From the Nile to Nebo*. Philadelphia: The Sunday School Times Co., 1912.

Jack, J. W. *The Date of the Exodus in the Light of External Evidence*. Edinburgh: T. & T. Clark, 1925.

James, Fleming. *Personalities of the Old Testament*. New York: Charles Scribner's Sons, 1939.

Jamieson, Robert. *Critical and Experimental Commentary*. Grand Rapids: Eerdmans, 1945.

Keil, C. F., and Delitzsch, F. *The Pentateuch, Biblical Commentary on the Old Testament*. Grand Rapids: Eerdmans Publishing Co., 1949.

Keller, Werner. *The Bible as History*. New York: William Morrow and Co., 1956.

Kenyon, Kathleen. *Archaeology in the Holy Land*. 3rd ed., rev. New York: Praeger, 1970.

———. *Digging Up Jericho*. London: Ernest Benn Limited, 1957.

Kitchen, K. A. *Ancient Orient and Old Testament*. Chicago: Inter-Varsity Press, 1966.

Knopf, Carl A. *The Old Testament Speaks*. New York: Thomas Nelson and Sons, 1933.

Kraus, Hans-Joachim. *Worship in Israel*. Translated by Geoffrey Buswell. Richmond, Va.: John Knox Press, 1962.

Loewenstamm, S. E. *The Tradition of the Exodus in its Development*. Jerusalem: Magnes Press, Hebrew University, 1965.

Manley, G. T. *The Book of the Law*. Grand Rapids: Eerdmans Publishing Co., 1957.

McFayden, John E. *Introduction to the Old Testament*. London: Hodder and Stoughton, 1909.

McGee, J. Vernon. *The Tabernacle*. Wheaton: Van Kampen Press, n.d.

McNeile, A. H. *The Book of Exodus*. London: Methuen and Co., Ltd., n.d.

Meek, Theophile J. *Hebrew Origins*. New York: Harper and Row, 1960.

Mendenhall, George E. *Law and Covenant in Israel and the Near East*. Pittsburgh: The Biblical Colloquium, 1955.

Mertz, Barbara. *Red Land, Black Land*. New York: Dell Publishing Co., 1966.

———. *Temples, Tombs and Hieroglyphs, The Story of Egyptology*. New York: Dell Publishing Co., 1965.

Meyer, F. B. *Exodus*. Grand Rapids: Zondervan Publishing House, 1952.

Meyer, Lester. *The Message of Exodus*. Minneapolis: Augsburg House, 1983.

Montet, Pierre. *Eternal Egypt*. New York: The New American Library, 1964.

———. *Egypt and the Bible*. Philadelphia: Fortress Press, 1968.

Murphy, James C. *Commentary on the Book of Exodus*. Andover: Warren F. Draper, 1868.

Nahmani, Hayim S. *Human Rights in the Old Testament*. Tel Aviv: Joshua Chacik Publishing House, Ltd., 1964.

Nichol, Francis D., ed. *The Seventh-Day Adventist Bible Commentary*. Washington, D.C.: Review and Herald Publishing Association, 1953.

Noth, Martin. *Exodus*. Trans. by J. S. Bowden, Philadelphia: The Westminster Press, 1962.

Oehler, Gustave F. *Theology of the Old Testament*. Grand Rapids: Zondervan Publishing House, n.d.

Payne, J. Barton, Ed. *New Perspectives on the Old Testament*. Waco, Texas: Word Books, 1970.

Petrie, W. M. Flinders. *Researches in Sinai*. London: Hazell, Watson and Viney, Ltd., 1906.

Pfeiffer, Charles F. and Harrison, Everett F., eds. *The Wycliffe Bible Commentary*. Chicago: Moody Press, 1962.

Plastaras, James. *The God of Exodus*. Milwaukee: The Bruce Publishing Co., 1966.

Pritchard, James B., ed. *Ancient Near Eastern Texts*. 3rd edition with Supplement. Princeton, N.J.: Princeton University Press, 1969.

Rand, Howard B. *Primogenesis*. Haverhill, Mass.: Destiny Publishers, 1953.

Redford, Donald B. *History and Chronology of the Eighteenth Dynasty of Egypt: Seven Studies*. The University of Toronto Press, 1967.

Ridout, S. *Lectures on the Tabernacle*. New York: Loizeaux Brothers, 1945.

Rimmer, Harry. *Dead Men Tell Tales*. Berne, Ind.: The Berne Witness Co., 1939.

Rowley, H. H. *The Rediscovery of the Old Testament*. Philadelphia: The Westminster Press, 1946.

———. *From Joseph to Joshua*. London: Oxford University Press, 1950.

Scott, Thomas. *The Holy Bible Containing the Old and New Testaments*. Boston: Samuel T. Armstrong, 1830.

Shorter, Alan W. *The Egyptian Gods*. London: Kegan Paul, Trench, Trubner and Co., Ltd., 1937.

Smith, William, ed. *Dictionary of the Bible*. New York: Hurd and Houghton, 1870.

Steindorff, G., and Seele, Keith C. *When Egypt Ruled the East*. 2nd ed. Chicago: The University Press, 1957.

Thompson, J. A. *The Ancient Near Eastern Treaties and the Old Testament*. London: Tyndale Press, 1964.

Toffteen, Olaf A. *The Historic Exodus*. Chicago: The University of Chicago Press, 1909.

Unger, Merrill F. *Archaeology and the Old Testament*. Grand Rapids: Zondervan Publishing Co., 1954.

———. *Biblical Demonology*. Wheaton: Scripture Press, 1965.

———. *Introductory Guide to the Old Testament*. Grand Rapids: Zondervan Publishing Co., 1951.

———. *Unger's Bible Dictionary*. Chicago: Moody Press, 1957.

Van Seters, John. *The Hyksos*. New Haven: Yale University Press, 1966.

Wallace, Ronald S. *The Ten Commandments*. Grand Rapids: Eerdmans Publishing Co., 1965.

Ward, William. *The Spirit of Ancient Egypt*. Beirut: Khayats, 1965.

Wood, Leon T. *A Survey of Israel's History*. Grand Rapids: Zondervan Publishing House, 1970.

Wright, G. Ernest. *Biblical Archaeology*. Philadelphia: Westminster Press, 1957.

Young, E. J. *An Introduction to the Old Testament*. Grand Rapids: Eerdmans Publishing Co., 1960.

Youngblood, Ronald F. *Exodus*. Chicago: Moody Press, 1983.

## Articles and Periodicals

Aberbach, Moses and Simolar, Leivy. "Aaron, Jeroboam and the Golden Calves." *Journal of Biblical Literature*, LXXXVI (June, 1967).

Aharoni, Yohanan. "Nothing Early and Nothing Late: Rewriting Israel's Conquest." *Biblical Archaeologist*, XXXIX (1976).

Albright, W. F. "The Early Alphabetic Inscriptions from Sinai and Their Decipherment." *Bulletin of the American Schools of Oriental Research*, No. 110 (1948).

———. "Exploring in Sinai with the University of California African Expedition." *Bulletin of the American Schools of Oriental Research*, No. 109 (Feb. 1948).

———. "The Name of Yahweh." *Journal of Biblical Literature*, XLIII, No. 2 (1924).

———. "Northwest Semitic Names in a List of Egyptian Slaves from the Eighteenth Century B.C." *Journal of the American Oriental Society*, LXXIV (1954).

Aling, Charles F. "The Biblical City of Ramses." *The Journal of the Evangelical Theological Society*, XXV, No. 2 (June 1982).

———. "The Sphinx Stele of Thutmose IV and the Date of the Exodus." *Journal of the Evangelical Theological Society*, XXII, No. 2 (1979).

Anati, Emmanual. "Has Mt. Sinai Been Found." *Biblical Archaeology Review*, XI, No. 4 (1985).

Archer, Gleason. "Old Testament History and Recent Archaeology—From Moses to David." *Bibliotheca Sacra*, CXXVII, No. 506 (1970).

Armerding, C. "Moses the Man of God." *Bibliotheca Sacra*, 116 (1959).

Arnold, William R. "The Divine Name in Exodus 3:14." *Journal of Biblical Literature*, XXIV (1905).

Auffret, Pierre. "The Literary Structure of Exodus 6:2-8." *Journal for the Study of the Old Testament*, XXVII (1983).

Batto, Bernard F. "Red Sea or Reed Sea?" *Biblical Archaeology Review*, X, No. 4 (1984).

———. "The Reed Sea: Requiescat in Pace." *Journal of Biblical Literature*, CII, No. 1 (1983).

Beitzel, Barry J. "Exodus 3:14 and the Divine Names: A Case of Biblical Paranomasia." *Trinity Journal*, I (1980).

Bleiber, Edward L. "The Location of Pithom and Succoth." *The Ancient World*, VI (1983).

Bodenheimer, F. S. "The Manna of Sinai." *The Biblical Archaeologist*, X, No. 1 (Feb. 1947).

Bretscher, P. G. "Exodus 4:22-23 and the Voice from Heaven." *Journal of Biblical Literature*, LXXXVII (1968).

Calloway, Joseph. "New Evidence on the Conquest of Ai." *Journal of Biblical Literature*, LXXXVII (Sept. 1968).

Childs, B. S. "Deuteronomic Formulae of the Exodus Traditions." *Hebraische Wortforschung—Baumgartner*, Supplement to *Vetus Testamentum*, XVI. Leiden: Brill, 1967.

Clark, R. E. D. "The Large Numbers of the Old Testament." *Journal of the Transactions of the Victoria Institute*, LXXXVII.

Coates, George W. "Despoiling the Egyptians." *Vetus Testamentum*, XVIII (1968).

_______. "The Traditio-Historical Character of the Reed Sea Motif." *Vetus Testamentum*, XVII (1967).

Cody, A. "Exodus 18:12; Jethro Accepts a Covenant with the Israelites." *Biblica*, XLIX (1968).

Copisarow, Maurice. "The Ancient Egyptian, Greek and Hebrew Concept of the Red Sea." *Vetus Testamentum*, XII, No. 1 (1962).

Cross, Frank M. "The Tabernacle." *Biblical Archaeologist*, X, No. 3 (Sept. 1947).

Cross, F. M. and Freedman, D. N. "The Song of Miriam." *Journal of Near East Studies*, 14 (1955).

David, M. "The Codes Hammurabi and Its Relation to Provisions of Law in Exodus." *Oudtestamentische Studien*, VII. Leiden: E. J. Brill, 1950.

David, A. Paul. "The Re-Creation of an Exact Replica of Aaron's Breastplate." *Lapidary Journal* (Dec. 1968).

Davis, John J. "The Patriarchs' Knowledge of Jehovah." *Grace Journal*, IV, No. 1 (1963).

De Guglielmo, A. "What Was the Manna?" *Catholic Biblical Quarterly* II (1940).

Dennison, James T. "The Exodus: Historical Narrative, Prophetic Hope, Gospel Fulfillment." πρεσβυτέριον: *Covenant Seminary Review*, VIII, No. 2 (1982).

Dothan, Moshe. "The Exodus in the Light of an Archaeological Survey in Lake Sirbonis." *Fifth World Congress of Jewish Studies*, (1969).

Dyer, Charles H. "The Date of the Exodus Reexamined." *Bibliotheca Sacra*, CXL, No. 559 (1983).

Edelman, R. "Exodus 32:18." *Journal of Theological Studies*, LVI (1950).

Enz, J. J. "The Book of Exodus as a Literary Type for the Gospel of John." *Journal of Biblical Literature*. LXXVI (1957).

Exum, J. Cheryl. "You Shall Let Every Daughter Live: A Study of Exodus 1:8–2:10." *Semeia*, XXVIII (1983).

Fensham, F. C. "Exodus 21:18-19 in the Light of Hittite "10." *Vetus Testamentum*, X (1960).

———. "'D' in Exodus 22:12." *Vetus Testamentum*, XII (1962).

———. "The Burning of the Golden Calf and Ugarit." *Israel Exploration Journal*, XVI, No. 1 (1966).

———. "The Possibility of the Presence of Casuistic Legal Material of the Covenant at Sinai." *Palestine Exploration Quarterly*, XCIII (1961).

Finn, A. H. "The Tabernacle Chapters." *Journal of Theological Studies*, (1915).

Fortheringham, D. R. "The Date of the Exodus." *Expositor*, (1908).

Francisco, Clyde T. "The Exodus in Its Historical Setting." *Southwest Journal of Theology*, XX, No. 1 (1977).

Franken, H. J. and Power, W. J. A. "Glueck's *Explorations in Eastern Palestine* in the Light of Recent Evidence." *Vetus Testamentum*, XXI (1971).

Free, J. P. "Abraham's Camels." *Journal of Near Eastern Studies*, (July, 1944).

Freedman, D. N. "The Burning Bush." *Biblica*, L (1969).

———. "The Name of the God of Moses." *Journal of Biblical Literature*, LXXIX (June, 1960).

Gese, Hartmut. "The Structure of the Decalogue." *Fourth World Congress of Jewish Studies*, Jerusalem: World Union of Jewish Studies, (1967).

Gilmore, E. L. "Which Were the Original Twelve Gemstones of the First Biblical Breastplate?" *Lapidary Journal*, (Dec. 1968).

Goldberg, Michael. "Exodus 1:13-14" *Interpretation*, XXXVII, No. 4 (1983).

Gordon, Cyrus H. "The Ten Commandments." *Christianity Today*, (April 10, 1964).

Greenberg, M. "*Nish* in Exodus 20:20 and the Purpose of the Sinaitic Theophany." *Journal of Biblical Literature*, LXXIX (1960).

Harding, G. L. and Reed, W. L. "Archaeological News from Jordan." *The Biblical Archaeologist*, XVI, No. 1 (Feb. 1953).

Harner, P. B. "Exodus, Sinai and Hittite Prologues." *Journal of Biblical Literature*, LXXXV (1966).

Harris, R. Laird. "Problem Periods in Old Testament History." *Seminary Review*, XVI, No. 1 (Fall, 1969).

Haupt, Paul. "Babylonian Elements in the Levitic Ritual." *Journal of Biblical Literature*, XIX (1900).

Hauser, C. "From Hazeroth to Mt. Hor. Notes of the Topography of the Wilderness." *Palestine Exploration Fund Quarterly*, (1908).

Helck, Von W. "Tkw und die Ramses-Stadt." *Vetus Testamentum*, XV (1965).

Hoehner, Harold W. "The Duration of the Egyptian Bondage." *Bibliotheca Sacra*, CXXV. No. 501 (1969).

______. "The Duration of the Egyptian Bondage." *Bibliotheca Sacra*, CXXVI, No. 504 (1969).

Hoftijzer, J. "Exodus 21:8." *Vetus Testamentum*, VII (1957).

Horn, S. "What We Don't Know About Moses and the Exodus." *Biblical Archaeology Review*, III, No. 2 (1977).

Hort, Greta, "The Plagues of Egypt." *Zeitschrift fur die alttestamentliche*, LXIX (1957), LXX (1958).

Hosch, Harold. "Exodus 12:41: A Translational Problem." *Hebrew Studies*, XXIV (1933).

Hoffmon, Herbert B. "The Exodus, Sinai and the Credo." *The Catholic Biblical Quarterly*, XXVII (April, 1965).

Hull, E. and Greene, J. B. "The Route of the Exodus." *Palestine Exploration Fund Quarterly*, (1885).

Isbell, Charles. "The Structure of Exodus 1:1-14." *Art and Meaning: Rhetoric in Biblical Literature*, ed. D. J. A. Clines, *et al*. Sheffield: *Journal of the Study of the Old Testament*, XIX (1982).

Jarvis, C. S. "The Israelites in Sinai." *Antiquity*, (1932).

Kosmala, Hans. "The 'Bloody Husband!'" *Vetus Testamentum*, XII (1962).

Krahmalkov, Charles. "A Critique of Professor Goedicke's Exodus Theories." *Biblical Archaeology Review*, VII, No. 5 (1981).

Liebovitch, J. "Le Probleme des Hyksos et celui de l'exode." *Israel Exploration Journal*, (1953).

Lewy, Immanuel. "Dating of Covenant Code Sections on Humaneness and Righteousness." *Vetus Testamentum*, VII (1957).

______. "The Story of the Golden Calf Reanalyzed." *Vetus Testamentum*, IX (1959).

Livingston, David. "Location of Biblical Bethel and Ai Reconsidered." *The Westminster Theological Journal*, XXXIII, No. 1 (Nov. 1970).

Loewenstamm, S. E. "The Bearing of Psalm 81 upon the Problem of Exodus." *Eretz-Israel*, V (1958).

———. "The Making and Destruction of the Golden Calf." *Biblica*, XLVIII (1967).

Loretz, von O. "Ex. 21:6, 22:8 und angebliche Nuzi—Parallelen." *Biblica*, (1960).

Lucus, A. "The Date of the Exodus." *Palestine Exploration Quarterly*, LXXIII (1941).

———. "The Number of Israelites at the Exodus." *Palestine Exploration Journal*, LXXVI (1945).

Mallon, A. "La Mer Rouge et L'exode." *Biblica* (1924).

May, Herbert G. "Moses and the Sinai Inscriptions." *The Biblical Archaeologist*, VIII, No. 4 (Dec. 1945).

McCarthy, Denis. "Israel My First-Born Son." *The Way*, V (1965).

McCarthy, D. J. "Moses' Dealing with Pharaoh: Ex. 7:8–10:27." *The Catholic Bible Quarterly*, XXVII, No. 4 (Oct. 1915).

———. "Plagues and Sea of Reeds (Ex. 5-14)." *Journal of Biblical Literature*, LXXXV (1966).

Mendelsohn, I. "The Conditional Sale into Slavery of Freeborn Daughters of Nuzi and the Law of Ex. 21:7-11." *Journal of the American Oriental Society*, LV (1935).

Mendenhall, George E. "Ancient Oriental and Biblical Law." *The Biblical Archaeologist*, XVII (May, 1954).

Meshel, Zeev. "An Explanation of the Journeys of the Israelites in the Wilderness." *Biblical Archaeologist*, XLV, No. 1 (1982).

Morgenstern, Julian. "The 'Bloody Husband' (?) (Ex. 4:24-26) Once Again." *Hebrew Union College Annual*, XXXIV (1963).

———. "The Book of the Covenant." *Hebrew Union College Annual*, V (1928), VII (1930), VIII-IX (1931-1932), XXXIII (1962).

———. "The Despoiling of the Egyptians." *Journal of Biblical Literature*, XLVIII (1949).

Mowinckel, S. "The Name of the God of Moses." *Hebrew Union College Annual*, XXXII (1961).

Muilenburg, J. "The Form and Structure of the Covenantal Formulations." *Vetus Testamentum*, IX (1959).

Neumann, J. "Evaporation from the Red Sea." *Israel Exploration Journal*, II, No. 3 (1952).

Nims, Charles F. "Bricks Without Straw." *The Biblical Archaeologist*, XIII, No. 2 (May 1950).

North, Robert. "Flesh, Covering and Response, Ex. 21:10." *Vetus Testamentum*, V (1955).

Oren, Eliezer. "How Not to Create a History of the Exodus—A Critique of Professor Goedicke's Theories." *Biblical Archaeology Review*, VII, No. 6 (1981).

Paul, S. M. "Ex. 21:10, A Threefold Maintenance Clause." *Journal of Near Eastern Studies*, XXVIII (1969).

Petrie, W. Flinders. "The Date of the Exodus." *Palestine Exploration Fund Quarterly* (1896).

Perevolotsky, Aviram and Finkelstein, Israel. "The Southern Sinai Exodus Route in Ecological Perspective." *Biblical Archaeology Review*, XI, No. 4 (1985).

Pfeiffer, R. H. "The Transmission of the Book of the Covenant." *Harvard Theological Review*, (1931).

Phillips, Anthony. "The Decalogue—Ancient Israel's Criminal Law." *Journal of Jewish Studies*, XXXIV:1 (1983).

———. "The Laws of Slavery: Exodus 21:2-11." *Journal of the Study of the Old Testament*, XXX (1984).

Phythian-Adams, W. J. "The Volcanic Phenomena of the Exodus." *Journal of the Palestinian Oriental Society*, XII (1932).

Plaut, W. Gunther. "The Israelites in Pharaoh's Egypt—A Historical Reconstruction." *Judaism*, XXVII, No. 1 (1978).

Porter, J. R. "The Role of Kadesh-Barnea in the Narrative of the Exodus." *Journal of Theological Studies* (1943).

Proffitt, T. D. III. "Moses and Anthropology: A New View of the Exodus." *Journal of the Evangelical Theological Society*, XXVII, No. 1 (1984).

Rabinowitz, J. J. "Exodus 22:4 and the Septuagint Version Thereof." *Vetus Testamentum*, IX (1959).

Raddy, Yehuda. "A Bible Scholar Looks at BAR's Coverage of the Exodus." *Biblical Archaeology Review*, VIII, No. 6 (1982).

Ramm, Bernard. "The Theology of the Book of Exodus." *Southwestern Journal*, XX (1977).

Rea, John. "New Light on the Wilderness Journey and the Conquest." *Grace Journal*, II, No. 2 (Spring, 1961).

_______. "The Time of the Oppression and the Exodus." *Grace Journal*, II, No. 1 (Winter, 1961).

Redford, Donald B. "Exodus 1:11." *Vetus Testamentum*, XIII, No. 4 (Oct. 1963).

_______. "The Hyksos Invasion in History and Tradition." *Orientalia*, XXXVIII, No. 1 (1970).

Rees, L. W. "The Route of the Exodus; the First Stage, Ramses to Etham." *Palestine Exploration Quarterly* (Jan.-Apr. 1948).

Reist, Irwin W. "The Theological Significance of the Exodus." *Journal of the Evangelical Society*, XII, No. 4 (Fall, 1969).

Riggs, Jack R. "The Length of Israel's Sojourn in Egypt." *Grace Journal*, XII No. 1 (Winter, 1971).

Robertson, Edward. "The Urim and Tummim; What Were They?" *Vetus Testamentum*, XIV (Jan. 1964).

Rowe, Alan. "The Famous Solar-City of On." *Palestine Exploration Quarterly* (July-Dec. 1962).

Rowley, H. H. "The Date of the Exodus." *Palestine Exploration Quarterly*, LXXIII (1941).

_______. "Early Levite History and the Question of the Exodus." *Journal of Near Eastern Studies* (1944).

_______. "The Exodus and the Settlement in Canaan." *Bulletin of the American Schools of Oriental Research*, No. 85. (Feb. 1942).

Rowton, M. B. "The Problem of the Exodus." *Palestine Exploration Quarterly*, (1953).

Schild, E. "On Exodus 3:14—'I am that I am.'" *Vetus Testamentum*, IV (1954).

Schrieber, Paul L. "Mishkan—Mitswah: Toward a More Unified View of Exodus." *Concordia Journal*, III, No. 2 (1977).

Shulze, Von Dr. "'Ehejeh ascher ehejeh' (Ex. 3:14)." *Judaica*, II (1955).

Shalit, Leon. "How Moses Turned a Staff into a Snake and Back Again." *Biblical Archaeology Review*, IX, No. 3 (1983).

Shanks, Hershel. "The Exodus and the Crossing of the Red Sea, According to Hans Goedicke." *Biblical Archaeology Review*, VII, No. 5 (1981).

Smith, H. P. "Ethnological Parallels to Exodus 4:24-26." *Journal of Biblical Literature* (1906).

Smith, Ralph L. "Covenant and Law in Exodus." *Southwestern Journal of Theology*, XX (1977).

Smith, R. H. "Exodus Typology in the Fourth Gospel." *Journal of Biblical Literature*, LXXXI (1962).

Sparks, D. F. D. "Lachish and the Date of the Exodus." *Journal of Theological Studies* (1941).

Stiebling, Jr., William. "Should the Exodus and the Israelite Settlement be Redated?" *Biblical Archaeology Review*, XI, No. 4 (1985).

Tunyogi, A. C. "The Rebellions of Israel." *Journal of Biblical Literature*, LXXXI (1962).

Uphill, E. P. "Pithom and Raamses: Their Location and Significance." *Journal of Near Eastern Studies*, XXVII, No. 4 (Oct. 1968), XXCIII, No. 1 (Jan. 1969).

Vriezen, von T. C. "Exodusstudien: Exodus 1." *Vetus Testamentum*, XVII (1967).

Waltke, Bruce. "Palestinian Artifactual Evidence Supporting the Early Date of the Exodus." *Bibliotheca Sacra*, 513 (1972).

Wenthe, Dean. "The Theological Significance of the Passing Through the Sea at the Exodus for Old Testament Theology." *Springfielder*, XXXVI (1972).

Wicke, Donald W. "The Literary Structure of Exodus 1:2–2:10." *Journal for the Study of the Old Testament*, XXIV (1982).

Williams, J. G. "Concerning One of the Apodictic Formulas." *Vetus Testamentum*, XIV (1964); XV (1965).

Winter, W. "Biblical and Archaeological Data on Ai Reappraised." *The Seminary Review*, XVI, No. 3 (Summer, 1970).

Wood, Leon T. "Date of the Exodus." *New Perspectives on the Old Testament*, Ed. J. Barton Payne. Waco: Word Books, 1970.

———. "Urim and Thummin." *The Theolog* (Winter, 1964).

Youngblood, Ronald. "A New Occurrence of the Divine Name 'I Am.'" *Journal of the Evangelical Theological Society*, XV, No. 3 (1972).

# Name Index

# *Scripture Index*

**Leviticus**



**Numbers**

**Deuteronomy**